Derrida: Ethics Under Erasure

Continuum Studies in Continental Philosophy

Series Editor: James Fieser, University of Tennessee at Martin, USA

Continuum Studies in Continental Philosophy is a major monograph series from Continuum. The series features first-class scholarly research monographs across the field of Continental philosophy. Each work makes a major contribution to the field of philosophical research.

Derrida: Ethics Under Erasure

Nicole Anderson

Continuum Studies in Continental Philosophy

continuum

Continuum International Publishing Group

The Tower Building
11 York Road
London SE1 7NX

80 Maiden Lane
Suite 704
New York NY 10038

www.continuumbooks.com

British Library Cataloguing-in-Publication Data
A catalogue record for this book is available from the British Library.

ISBN: HB: 978-1-4411-5942-7

Library of Congress Cataloging-in-Publication Data
A catalog record for this book is available from the Library of Congress.

Typeset by Deanta Global Publishing Services, Chennai, India
Printed and bound in Great Britain

Contents

Acknowledgements

An earlier version of the first two sections of Chapter 2 was published as a paper, 'The Ethical Possibilities of the Subject as Play: in Nietzsche and Derrida', in the *Journal of Nietzsche Studies* 26 (2003): 79–90. I am grateful to The Pennsylvania State University Press for permission to reproduce this material in this book.

A substantially different version of Chapter 4 is forthcoming in a book entitled *Chiasmatic Encounters*, published by Lexington Books.

I would like to thank those who have commented on various draft chapters, or who have read an entire draft version of the book, or have shown encouragement and support more generally. Among them are Steven Barker, Lennard J. Davis, Mark Evans, Joanna Hodge, Elaine Kelly, Nick Mansfield, Martin McQuillan, Katrina Schlunke, Linnell Secomb, Robert Sinnerbrink, and Peter Steeves. A very special thanks to Claire Colebrook and Michael Naas. Also to my family, and to my partner Peter Evans for 'being there'. Last but *not* least, to Simon Morgan Wortham for his wonderful generosity and support my heartfelt thanks and gratitude that no words can adequately convey.

Introduction

'In both general and abstract terms, the absoluteness of duty, of responsibility, and of obligation certainly demands that one transgress ethical duty.'

– *Derrida,* The Gift of Death, 66

Ethics Under Erasure

Derrida's work continues to be misunderstood, misinterpreted, accused, critiqued and defended, reviled and revered. It is appropriated to topics as diverse as law, architecture, painting, language, literature and philosophy. It is also frequently invoked to support and legitimate, or to subvert, the political and ideological agendas of both the left and right. Debate is endemic: is Derrida's deconstruction indeterminate or determinate, incommensurable or commensurable, nihilistic or ethical? Is it poststructuralist or postmodernist, philosophical or literary? Is it a serious enterprise or a private joke? Is Derrida's deconstruction Heideggerian, Nietzschean or Levinasian or something else altogether? So controversial is Derrida's work that John Caputo has commented, with some amusement:

> Derrida and 'deconstruction' . . . have been blamed for almost everything. For ruining American departments of philosophy, English, French, and comparative literature . . . for dimming the lights of the Enlightenment, for undermining the law of gravity, for destroying all standards of reading, writing, reason – (and 'rithemtic, too) – and also for Mormon polygamy. (Caputo 1997b, 41)

There is seriousness to Caputo's levity: that is, serious issues of academic probity are involved. More often than not the most scathing critiques and false accusations levelled at Derrida have been made by those who have not actually read his texts (Derrida and Norris 1989, 74). The famous 'Cambridge and Heidegger affairs' and the disparaging *ad hominem* attack of Derrida in an obituary by Jonathan Kandell published two days after

Derrida's death in the *New York Times* on 10 October 2004 are pertinent examples.[1] In cases like these, what is evident is that little account had been taken of either the rigorous argumentation that characterizes Derrida's writing, or his notion of deconstruction as that which is *not* negative and destructive. And yet, critics of Derrida's work continue to misinterpret and promote it as unethical, nihilistic and irresponsible, or have appropriated deconstruction as a form of textual freeplay.[2] These misinterpretations and appropriations, along with the important critiques of these positions by scholars such as Christopher Norris (1987, 1989, 1989a) and Rodolphe Gasché (1981, 1988, 1997), are very familiar,[3] yet despite this, the Introduction begins in this way so as to set the ethical scene and lay the groundwork, before opening into a rigorous re-reading of the complex question of the ethical in Derrida later in this Introduction, and in the chapters that follow. But for the moment let us return to the ethical scene.

Given the epigraph above, taken from Derrida's book *The Gift of Death*, it might seem that the critics are right, and that they have a point. Is not this epigraph evidence enough for Derrida's detractors to accuse him of an outright rejection of ethics? It might be if an important clause in the sentence wasn't missing, which it deliberately is in order to reveal how easy it is to quote out of context (both grammatically and thematically). The full sentence reads: 'In both general and abstract terms, the absoluteness of duty, of responsibility, and of obligation certainly demands that one transgress ethical duty, *although in betraying it one belongs to it and at the same time recognizes it*' (Derrida 1995b, 66; italics mine). If one started to think that Derrida was abandoning ethics for some kind of moral or ethical freeplay (which reading only the first part of the sentence might possibly convey to those unfamiliar with Derrida's work), by the end of this sentence one should realize that what Derrida is arguing is that one can't abandon, even if one transgresses, ethics.

Quoting Derrida out of context, then, is something some of Derrida's critics and appropriators have a tendency to do either accidentally or wilfully in order to promote their own ideological, political or philosophical agendas, and as we can see from the partly quoted epigraph, this can cause 'so many misunderstandings' (Derrida 1992b, 9) and contribute to various misinterpretations and (mis)appropriations of deconstruction. We are familiar with Richard Rorty's form of appropriation that aligns Derrida's work with Rorty's brand of 'anything goes' postmodernism, characterized by a rejection of metaphysics, ethics and the subject. Yet Rorty believes Derrida's work can justifiably be aligned in this way because he understands Derrida's work to be deliberately promoting an 'undifferentiated textuality', nicknamed 'freeplay' (that is, the belief that there are endless substitutions of one sign for another so that any sign can mean anything at any time, no matter what the context). However, Rorty only achieves this alignment by often quoting Derrida out of context.

For example, quoting a passage from Derrida's essay '*Ousia and Gramme*. Note on a Note from *Being and Time*', Rorty suggests that 'Derrida wants to make us conscious of that text by letting us "think a writing without presence and without absence, without history, without cause, without *archia* [sic], without *telos*, a writing that absolutely upsets all dialectics, all theology, all teleology, all ontology"' (Derrida qtd in Rorty 1984, 8). Significantly, Rorty leaves out an important clause in the first part of this passage he quotes. The full sentence reads: 'Such a *différance* would at once, again, give us to think a writing without presence and without absence', and so on (Derrida 1986, 67).[4] Quoting selectively here, Rorty redescribes the original meaning of Derrida's passage in a number of ways. First, Rorty uses the verb 'wants' which implies a volition on Derrida's part that has no parallel in the original: in the French, what leads us to think 'a writing without presence' is 'différance' (not Derrida). Second, Rorty has ignored the force of the conditional *donnerait* ('could give or cause us to') and represents Derrida's heavily modalized hypothesis as assertion. Derrida does not claim that this is how writing is (or how *he wants* it to be), but merely that différance leads us to think of writing in this way. Reinterpreting Derrida's original in this way, Rorty is then free to argue that writing should be read as an 'infinite undifferentiated textuality' because it refers to nothing, no history, no cause, no archia, no telos, and so on. Examples of this kind of quoting out of context riddle the works of both Derrida's appropriators and detractors alike.

*

This book does not endorse the interpretation of Derrida's work as promoting an 'undifferentiated textuality', or as a rejection of metaphysics and ethics, hence a celebration of nihilism, if we mean by that a complete denial and destruction of authority, institutions or meaning for its own sake. Rather, the first aim of this book is to present the development of Derrida's thinking on, and deconstruction of, ethics. The book reveals that the ethical is a focus of Derrida's work from his earliest writings on language, to his work on hospitality, justice, responsibility, politics, and beyond. The book begins tracing this development of the ethical, justice and responsibility by presenting in Chapter 1 the critical reception of, and debates around, scholars' interpretations and defences of Derrida's thinking on ethics, with the main focus being on Simon Critchley's influential book *The Ethics of Deconstruction*. If the ethical is a focus in Derrida's work, this is not to say that either deconstruction per se is ethical, or that deconstruction opposes itself, or can be opposed, to metaphysical ethics. To convey this, my coined phrase *ethics under erasure* is key to unlocking not only what I argue to be the paradoxical structure of ethics but, in turn, how Derrida's deconstruction enables us to rethink or move away from the binary choice-making and decision-taking characteristic of metaphysical and normative ethics, but without rejecting metaphysical ethics.

The other aim of this book, the main one, is to explain the *positive* (not the negative, the nihilistic or the destructive) nature of this paradox. The phrase *ethics under erasure* conveys this positive paradox. That is, by bringing together Derrida's 'under erasure'[5] with 'ethics', the single phrase attempts to capture the profound paradox and complexity of this tension and relationship between the ethically singular and the general. For Derrida, placing a word or concept under erasure means to 'rub it out' or change it, while simultaneously retaining its original meaning or concept. By erasing *without* erasing, the original meaning *haunts* a new meaning, a new context. What is conveyed in the process is a demonstration of a word or concept's inaccuracy or inadequacy of meaning. But this does not deny the possibility of meaning or intention; rather it is more a means by which to reveal the metaphysical assumptions underlying a word or concept's meaning so as to expose the contextuality and alterity of language (more of this below). Thus the phrase 'ethics under erasure' attempts to convey how our singular ethical responses to an 'Other'[6] entails both a transgression of ethical duty (the general or universal) and negotiation with, and retention and acknowledgement of, those ethical systems (and hence social values and norms built on those systems) that carry universal status. Singular responses can neither transcend nor dispense with the general. Likewise, universal ethical laws require negotiation with the singular.

The phrase ethics under erasure is the book's theoretical fulcrum, with Chapter 3 dedicated to unfolding its operation and implications. Ethics under erasure can perhaps help us rethink metaphysical ethical systems, and the paradox by which they are simultaneously perpetuated and undermined in the inter-subjective dialectic of everyday human experience (the theme of Chapter 4). Meanwhile let's now turn to an example of how Derrida's work is considered to be nihilistic by both Rorty and Habermas because of what they see to be Derrida's affirmation of Nietzschean demolition. This will set the foundation for the issues of language and subjectivity raised throughout the book, and particularly in Chapter 2.

Redescribing Derrida: The Problems of 'Indeterminacy' and 'Freeplay'

Rorty's appropriation of deconstruction to his brand of postmodernism not only takes Derrida out of context, but in doing so, has contributed to the dissemination of the interpretation that Derrida's work is unethical and nihilistic and not only in Anglo-academic departments, but throughout the wider community. As Niall Lucy argues, the conflation of deconstruction, and hence poststructuralism, with postmodernism has been a result of the 'misinterpretation' of Derrida's word 'play' in his essay 'Structure, Sign and Play' (Lucy 1997, 97), where 'Derrida's sense of "play" as "give" was transformed ecstatically to mean "play" as "playfulness" or ("unruliness")' (Lucy 1997, 102). The following passage from 'Structure, Sign and Play' confirms Lucy's observation, but it is also significant for revealing how and why Rorty (and, as we will see shortly, Habermas) believes that Derrida promotes freeplay by adopting Nietzschean affirmation and demolition. Derrida argues:

> There are thus two interpretations of interpretation, of structure, of sign, of play. The one seeks to decipher, dreams of deciphering a truth or an origin which escapes play . . . The other, which is no longer turned towards the origin, affirms play and tries to pass beyond man and human-ism, the name of man being the name of that being who . . . has dreamed of full presence, the reassuring foundation, the origin and the end of play. The second interpretation . . . to which Nietzsche pointed the way, does not seek . . . 'the inspiration of a new humanism'. . . [Rather], the Nietzschean *affirmation*, that is the joyous affirmation of the play of the world and the innocence of becoming, the affirmation of a world of signs without fault, without truth, and without origin . . . *This affirmation then determines the noncenter otherwise than as loss of center.* (Derrida 1995a, 292)

Rorty chooses to focus on the second interpretation of play (as Nietzschean affirmation) in his reading of Derrida (without acknowledging either the first interpretation or the context of the larger point Derrida makes in this essay). This then allows him to associate Derrida's notion of play with 'the affirmation of a world of signs without fault, without truth, and without origin' (Derrida 1995a, 292), with frivolity, non-seriousness, game-playing, and thereby, in turn, implying that Derrida's work avoids intellectual rigour and seriousness associated with philosophical writing. Thus for Rorty, this is the 'good side' of Derrida's work (what Rorty labels 'private irony'): that which forms a fantasizing style and word play (puns, neologisms, palaeonymy's, and so on) (Rorty 1982, 93; 1989a, 126).

However, shortly after the passage from 'Structure, Sign and Play' quoted above, Derrida goes on to argue that 'although these two interpretations must acknowledge and accentuate their difference and define their irreducibility, I do not believe that today there is any question of choosing . . . because we must first try to conceive of the common ground, and the différance of this irreducible difference' (Derrida 1995a, 293). And again, some years later in *Positions*, Derrida argues that 'by means of this double play . . . I try to respect as rigorously as possible the internal, regulated play of philosophemes or epistimemes by making them slide – without mistreating them – to the point of their nonpertinence, their exhaustion, their closure' (Derrida 1982a, 6). Yet for all of Derrida's qualifications, Rorty continues to focus on the second interpretation of play, and reinterpreting it as 'free-play'. In contradistinction to this postmodern appropriation of play, Derrida insists: 'I never spoke of "complete freeplay or undecidability" . . . Greatly overestimated in my texts in the United States, this notion of "freeplay" is an inadequate translation of the lexical network connected to the word *jeu*, which I used in my first texts, but sparingly and in a highly defined manner' (Derrida 1997a, 115–16).

'Undifferentiated textuality' (or 'freeplay') became not only a widely adopted notion to define Derrida's work, but as a result made Derrida's work vulnerable to misdirected critique. Generically the critique goes something like this: Derrida's adoption of 'Nietzschean demolition' and affirmation, along with his radicalization of Saussurian linguistics as a differential play of signs (différance) and the contamination of binary oppositions in language, is an assault on metaphysics, ethics and subjectivity. It is an assault because Derrida's differential play of signs is an abandonment of absolute meaning and intention in favour of contextual indeterminacy and transcendental solipsism. Consequently, Derrida's deconstruction is nihilistic and therefore unethical.

Two famous and influential examples of this critique in a sustained form are found, first, in Jürgen Habermas' *The Philosophical Discourse of Modernity* (1987), where Derrida argues that it is a profound irony that Habermas has not read his work and yet accuses him of being unethical (Derrida 1997a, 156, fn. 9).[7] And second, in John Searle's paper, 'Reiterating the Differences' (1977), which is a response to Derrida's paper 'Signature Event Context' (1986, first English translation in *Glyph* 1977), and to which Derrida, in turn, responds in book-length form in *Limited Inc* (1997a). More specifically, interpreting Derrida's notion of context as indeterminable, and as an all-embracing context of texts, leads both Searle and Habermas to argue that for Derrida there is no authentic 'intention of meaning'

(Searle 1977, 207), thus Derrida relativizes meaning and communication (Habermas 1987, 197).

Overall, while Rorty thinks aligning Derrida with what he argues to be Nietzsche's rejection of metaphysics is a positive move, the same assumption leads Habermas and Searle to argue that deconstruction endorses an indeterminacy of meaning and thus demolishes in nihilistic fashion all values, truth and reason (Habermas 1987, 96–7, 181). However, Derrida's neologism 'deconstruction' is an attempt to avoid the negative connotations associated, whether rightly and wrongly, with 'Nietzschean demolition' (Derrida 1988b, 1). Either way, by aligning Derrida solely with what they consider to be Nietzschean demolition, appropriators such as Rorty and critics such as Habermas and Searle perpetuate, in different ways, not only an unbalanced view of Nietzsche's notion of nihilism and his project in general, but also a misunderstanding of Derrida's engagement with Nietzsche.

Derrida's 'context'

The purpose of this section is to elaborate on Derrida's notion of context as preparation for the discussion in the next section (and throughout the book) of how metaphysical ethics is inevitably transformed as a result of context. Needless to say that for Derrida context is extremely important, not something one can abandon even if one wanted to, and therefore the accusation of Derrida perpetuating *absolute* contextual indeterminacy is simply inaccurate. For example, when Derrida's famously states '[t]here is nothing outside of the text [*il n'y a pas de hors-texte*]' (Derrida 1976, 158), he means 'there is nothing outside context' (Derrida 1997a, 136), rather there are only contexts that open the possibility of recontextualization, or 'contextual transformation' (Derrida 1997a, 79). Thus, there is no mark or sign that is 'valid outside of context'. However, it does not follow, as Habermas or Searle assume, that because context is not absolutely determinable, communication ceases to be meaningful or valid. Rather, Derrida argues that while the sign or utterance can be limited by context – for example, limited by environment; experience; 'the presence of the writer to what he has written'; 'semiotic context'; by the semantic stratum of language, and so on – nevertheless 'by virtue of its essential iterability, a written syntagma can always be detached from the chain in which it is inserted or given without causing it to lose all possibility of functioning, if not all possibility of "communicating" precisely' (Derrida 1997a, 9).

All Derrida is arguing here is that depending on context, a mark or a sign (due to its *iterability*) can be grafted, or inscribed onto other semantic chains. He gives an example, demonstrating that the sequence of words 'the green is either' is unacceptable in the context of 'an epistemic intention', or an intention to know, and yet, 'the green is either' is not prevented from 'functioning in another context as signifying marks' (Derrida 1997a, 12). And which is why one can quote out of context. To put it another way, every sign or utterance is structured by 'iteration' (which is what makes every sign quotable). Iteration is not simply repeatability, which entails a traditional concept of representation. Rather, '[i]terability requires the origin to repeat itself originarily, to alter itself so as to have the value of origin, that is, to conserve itself' (Derrida 1992b, 43).Therefore, iterability as 'a differential structure' escapes the dialectical opposition of presence and absence, and instead 'implies both identity and difference' (Derrida 1997a, 53). For Derrida, then, this is why the sign or utterance 'can never be entirely certain or saturated' (Derrida 1997a, 3).

While Derrida argues that no context is entirely determinable (Derrida 1997a, 9), this does not mean that context is absolutely indeterminable and thus destroys intentionality:

> *Sec* ['Signature Event Context'] has not simply effaced or denied intentionality, as Sarl [Searle] claims. On the contrary, *Sec* insists on the fact that 'the category of intention will not disappear, it will have its place . . .' (Let it be said in passing that this differential-deferring (*différantielle*) structure of intentionality alone can enable us to account for the differentiation between 'locutionary', 'illocutionary' and 'perlocutionary' values of the 'same' marks or utterances). (Derrida 1997a, 58)[8]

Both iterability and context enable normal felicitous speech acts and utterances to take place. Thus Derrida insists that '[b]y no means do I draw the conclusion that there is no relative specificity of effects of consciousness, or of effects of speech' (Derrida 1997a, 19). Despite Derrida's insistence, and his demonstrations, Habermas still persists in misreading Derrida as positing an all-embracing context that dispenses with unified meaning and communication. Yet what is instructive about Derrida's understanding of context is that even though deconstruction cannot be permanently fixed within a particular context (precisely because it is not a method, analysis, critique, act or operation (Derrida 1988b, 3)), and thus 'is different from one context to another', at the same time, deconstruction is 'absolutely responsible' because it 'takes the singularity of every context into account' (Derrida and Norris 1989, 73), and therefore it does not abandon meaning. There could not be responsibility or singularity without meaning, even though this meaning might not fulfil Habermas's requirements of universal consensus in communication and language (Habermas 1987, 296–7, 315, 322).

Deconstruction, then, is not only constantly transformed as it becomes different in and through multiple and heterogeneous contexts, but it is also transformed in and by the same context. Derrida's neologisms and paleonyms testify to how deconstruction moves across, and becomes different in, multiple contexts:

> The word 'deconstruction', like all other words, acquires its value only from its inscription in a chain of possible substitutions, in what is too blithely called a 'context' . . . the word has interest only within a certain context, where it replaces and lets itself be determined by such other words as 'écriture', 'trace', 'différance', 'supplement', 'hymen', 'pharmakon', 'marge', 'entame', 'parergon', etc. By definition, the list can never be closed, and I have cited only names, which is inadequate and done only for reasons of economy. (Derrida 1988b, 4–5)

The endless possible substitutions that (in)form deconstruction are also called 'quasi-transcendentals',[9] such as différance, arche-writing, under erasure, supplement, auto-immunity, khora, pharmakon, parergon, and so on. In turn, these quasi-transcendentals are also constituted by a certain context (circumscribed by grammar, semantics, topic, discourse and discursive function, etc.). Thus, deconstruction is determined by each context albeit differently each and every time, and is not simply indeterminate as critics like Habermas have argued (Habermas 1987, 181).

The Irreducible Plurality of Ethics

It is because of both 'singular' and multiple contexts that Derrida argues there can only be 'deconstructions in the plural' (Derrida and Norris 1989, 73), or what he calls the disseminating 'irreducible plurality' of deconstruction (Derrida 1992b, 56). What Derrida's irreducible plurality makes clear is that deconstruction 'cannot be homogenised' (Derrida and Norris 1989, 73). Consequently, as Andrew Benjamin argues, Derrida 'is refusing . . . the possibility that Deconstruction has an essential nature', and in so doing offers 'a fundamental challenge to the dominance of a certain theory of naming within philosophy' (Benjamin 1989, 76; see also 2008, 1–2).

For Derrida, deconstruction, in its irreducible plurality, exposes the unde-cidability[10] constitutive of the metaphysics of presence in all its formula-tions, from ethics to the proper name. In other words, because all naming is inhabited by différance, the proper name (and the act of naming proper or otherwise) is 'always already under erasure' (Derrida 1976, lxxxiii). In this way deconstruction enables an interruption to reidentification which naming produces (Benjamin 1989, 76). What this interruption means for the common assignation of a metaphysical foundation to ethics and to sub-jectivity is a question that is explored in various ways throughout the book. For instance, if metaphysics constructs an ethically autonomous subject, one that has ethical self-determination and autonomy, and thus can make 'free' and independent ethical decisions as well as pose ethical questions, then what happens to ethics and the subject once they are put under erasure? This question is addressed in Chapter 3.

Metaphysics cannot be exceeded, therefore deconstruction disrupts, intervenes, displaces and thus opens a system (writing or language or ethics, for instance) to its 'other' within itself. In other words, under erasure is an iteration of a metaphysical tradition or inheritance: iterative because it does not and cannot entirely erase a concept or metaphysical system, such as ethics; nor does it perpetuate a binary between that which is erased and that which erasure points to: otherness. Instead, in its iterative process, under erasure contaminates the potential opposition (without dismantling them altogether) so that what is produced is transformation rather than 'binary and hierarchized oppositions' (Derrida 1998, 31), by which a 'metaphysical ethics' constructs behaviour and decisions along yes/no, right/wrong, good/bad choices. An answer to the above question, then, is that by putting ethics under erasure, the subject as autonomous is transformed or recontextualized as heteronymous, while ethics itself is revealed to be constituted by what Derrida calls the 'non-ethical' (in *Of Grammatology*) or 'irresponsibilization' (in *The Gift of Death*). This point will be discussed in more detail shortly.

There is not 'one' form of metaphysical ethics; indeed there are varying accounts: from contract, Christian, deontological, utilitarian to feminist ethics, as well as varying critiques (some of which will be discussed in detail in Chapter 3). However, what they all have in common, as Rosalyn Diprose succinctly puts it, is a focus on 'the logical status of our moral judgements or as setting down a set of universal principles for regulating behaviour' (Diprose 1994, 18). To be able to have a common focus relies on the common assumption 'that individuals are present as self-transparent, isolated, rational minds and that embodied differences between individuals are inconsequential' (Diprose 1994, 18), and 'that the individual comes prior to relations with others' (Diprose 1994, 102). Derrida's work challenges these assumptions.

For example, Derrida's notion of decision as haunted by undecidability, producing dilemmas in our ethical choice-making and decision-taking (and thus contaminating the dichotomy between right/wrong and good/bad), is a challenge to, and we could even say following the epigraph, a 'transgression', but not rejection of, ethics as a metaphysical-philosophical discourse. This is why deconstruction is neither ethical nor unethical (in the metaphysical sense). In fact, given deconstruction's 'irreducible plurality', to oppose the ethical to the unethical would be to perpetuate the binary opposition on which metaphysics has been founded. For Derrida,

> there is in fact no philosophy and no philosophy of philosophy that could be called deconstruction and that would deduce from itself a 'moral component'. But that does not mean that deconstructive experience is not a responsibility, even an ethico-political responsibility, or does not exercise or deploy any responsibility in itself. By questioning philosophy about its treatment of ethics, politics, the concept of responsibility, deconstruction orders itself I will not say on a still *higher* concept of responsibility . . . but on an exigency, which I believe is more *inflexible* [intraitable], of response and responsibility. Without this exigency, in my view no ethico-political question has any chance of being opened up or awakened today. (Derrida 1995d, 364)

Therefore, to put metaphysical ethics, 'under erasure' is to deconstruct a conception of ethics as that which provides directions for behaviours along prescriptive lines. But this is not to reject ethics as a metaphysical-philosophical discourse. Instead, it is a means of bringing to the fore the instability of such a discourse by signalling that ethics contains its own transformation. And this transformation occurs precisely because ethical 'presence' (the coalescing into a homogenous unity of universalization in and through ethical systems) contains the trace of absence, or *another* presence (alterity) *within* presence (within closure).[11] Thus, not only is ethics *itself* as a universal metaphysical discourse always already under erasure, but as will be explored in Chapter 4, our singular responses in our everyday experiences in negotiation with social, cultural and moral norms, also places ethics, under erasure.

Given the 'irreducible plurality' of deconstruction, it is understandable, and somewhat inevitable, that it is appropriated in negative ways. Its heterogeneity may also explain why many critics view deconstruction as destructive of metaphysical foundations. But to label Derrida and deconstruction this way is to presume that metaphysical ethics (where the subject is prioritized over the Other) is, or should be, the only grounds for behaviour. This metaphysical determination of ethics is useful when thinking about why Derrida hesitates in characterizing deconstruction 'in ethical or political terms' (Derrida 1997a, 153), even when it would save him from accusations of nihilism or irresponsibility.

One of the arguments of this book then is that rather than being nihilistic or unethical, the complex nuances of deconstruction's 'irreducible plurality' are absolutely affirmative in that they not only open the way for the other – as alterity; as an irreducible difference to come – but consequently allow for a nuanced ethical, or rather responsible, *relationship* with difference; with the other/Other, itself. In Derrida's words, deconstruction is 'the *yes* of the other, no less than the *yes* to the other' (Derrida 1999a, 35). It is in *The Gift of Death* that we can begin to understand how Derrida, in the quote above, associates exigency with deconstruction and responsibility, and how deconstruction provides a challenge to, without constructing alternative, metaphysical ethical systems. To this purpose the discussion of the book's chapters, and in particular Chapter 3, that begin the following section is prefaced by a brief exposition on *The Gift of Death* in order to outline the differing modes of enquiry into the ethical as well as the congruencies and differences between 'ethics under erasure' and what Derrida in his book calls 'absolute responsibility' and 'irresponsibilization'.

Singular Trajectories

In *The Gift of Death* Derrida retells a well-known biblical story: Abraham is commanded by God to sacrifice, as a burnt offering on Mount Moriah, his beloved son Isaac (Genesis 22: 1–19). There is much to say about Derrida's interpretation of this story, but for the purposes of setting the scene for the congruencies between ethics under erasure and irresponsibilization, the following brief exposition will focus on what Derrida considers to be the moral of the Abraham story. The moral is in fact about 'morality itself' and how morality and ethics are paradoxically constituted by what Derrida argues is the 'irresponsible'. The irresponsible is not in opposition or antithesis to ethics and responsibility. Rather, the latter are constituted by irresponsibility, or what Derrida calls 'absolute responsibility', which entails an inevitable and unjustifiable sacrifice.[12]

Derrida describes 'absolute responsibility' as that which is extraordinary, as something that remains 'inconceivable' and 'unthinkable', precisely because it involves the other in its 'uniqueness, absolute singularity, hence nonsubstitution, nonrepetition, silence and secrecy' (Derrida 1995b, 61). And when Derrida talks of 'singularity', by this he means the uniqueness of the Other (or event, or subject). This does not mean a simple difference to the Other, or between Others, and it does not simply mean something secret or private, which can be known but is hidden; rather, by singularity Derrida is referring to that which is irreducible, unrepeatable, heterogeneous and idiosyncratic. Absolute responsibility is thus in itself unique and singular, while general responsibility (or the universality of ethics and the law) is so precisely because it requires substitution, repetition, and thus applicability and commensurability to all Others. Hence absolute responsibility 'is not a responsibility, at least it is not general responsibility or responsibility in general', 'it must therefore be irresponsible in order to be absolutely responsible' (Derrida 1995b, 61). Derrida captures this *aporia*[13] and paradox through the story of Abraham.

The aporia for Abraham is that he has *either* to fulfil his responsibility towards the singular, in this case God, by obeying God's command, *or* to obey the general ethical laws of his society, and fulfil his responsibility towards all Others (Isaac, Sarah, his friends, family and community). Thus in paradox upon paradox Abraham has to sacrifice the singularity of each and every Other: all Others, and thereby betraying and disobeying the universal general laws of his society and culture, and in turn sacrificing himself and his duty to all Others known (family) and unknown (larger community), in order to keep his responsibility to God (the absolute singular and unique Other). There is more than one sacrifice going on here. To labour the point a little further, Abraham has to break the law, has to act unethically, irresponsibly, in order to be responsible to the *one* Other over *all* Others (Derrida 1995b, 68–9).

Not *all* of us today would sacrifice a general ethics and murder another that we love in order to be responsible to the One (God), but the aporetic structure is analogous: at times we sacrifice a general ethics for the singularity of the Other, or vice versa (whatever this Other may be: another person, event or situation). As J. Hillis Miller so eloquently puts it in a sustained discussion of Derrida's *The Gift of Death*, this aporia is 'a universal feature of the human condition anywhere at any time' (Miller 2007, 218).[14] Derrida formulates this aporia as a universal human condition in the following way:

There are also others, an infinite number of them, the innumerable generality of others to whom I should be bound by the same responsibility, a general and universal responsibility (what Kierkegaard calls the ethical order). I cannot respond to the call, the request, the obligation, or even the love of another without sacrificing the other other, the other others. *Every other (one) is every (bit) other* [*tout autre est tout autre*], every one else is completely or wholly other. The simple concepts of alterity and of singularity constitute the concept of duty as much as that of responsibility. As a result, the concepts of responsibility, of decision, or of duty, are condemned a priori to paradox, scandal, and aporia. Paradox, scandal, and aporia are themselves nothing other than sacrifice, the revelation of conceptual thinking at its limit, at its death and finitude. As soon as I enter into a relation with the other, with the gaze, look, request, love, command, or call of the other, I know that I can respond only by sacrificing ethics, that is, by sacrificing whatever obliges me to also respond, in the same way, in the same instant, to all the others. I offer a gift of death, I betray, I don't need to raise my knife over my son on Mount Moriah for that. (Derrida 1995b, 68)

Not only do we *not* need to raise our knives over our sons on Mount Moriah to betray a universal ethics in order to be responsible to the Other, but this Other does not need to be 'God' (that is, a transcendental signified). This Other can also be another human and/or non-human animal. Derrida gives examples of his everyday betrayal or sacrifice, from the sacrifice of his family, his sons, his friends and himself in and for his public duty as a philosopher, to the sacrificing of 'all the cats in the world to the cat that you feed at home every morning' (Derrida 1995b, 71). Examples are endless: every day we sacrifice through betrayal, disloyalty, injustice, either the ones we love (our friends, lovers, families, spouses), or we sacrifice those we don't know: all Others, in order to save or privilege our friends, families, lovers, ourselves. Every day, in some way or another, no matter how small, we either sacrifice a general universal ethics for what Derrida calls 'absolute responsibility', or we sacrifice an absolute responsibility for a general ethics. But the choice of course is not so black and white,[15] because as J. Hillis Miller points out: '[w]hat is irresponsible in general ethics is responsible in absolute ethics and vice versa' (Miller 2009, 214). In the case of Abraham, this means that he is 'at the same time the most moral and the most immoral, the most responsible and the most irresponsible of men, absolutely irresponsible because he is absolutely responsible, absolutely irresponsible in the face of men and his family, and in the face of the ethical, because he responds absolutely to absolute duty . . . answering to God and before God' (Derrida 1995b, 72).

At this point some disturbing questions arise: does absolute responsibility mean that we can simply do what we like: rape, steal, lie, murder, in the name of some personal notion of our responsibility to some singular Other: cause, event, person, God or Idea? Is this absolute responsibility a form of ethical indeterminancy (in the Habermasian sense)? Is there a difference between murdering someone in the name of religion, or as a result of religious belief, and obeying a direct command from God? What is the difference? And if absolute responsibility is calculated, rather than exigency, could this be defined as evil? These questions highlight not only the aporia of the question of ethics per se, but the aporia of ethical experience. The aporia itself precludes any definite answers, and yet oblique answers may offer themselves in and through an understanding of the inextricable relation between responsibility (ethical duty) and irresponsibility. As the missing sentence from the epigraph suggests 'in betraying [responsibility or ethical duty] one belongs to it and at the same time recognizes it' (Derrida 1995b, 66), and therefore without responsibility (ethical duty) there would be no irresponsibility and 'absolute responsibility', and vice versa. Again the story of Abraham conveys this inextricability and aporia: 'Abraham must assume absolute responsibility for sacrificing his son by sacrificing ethics, but in order for there to be a sacrifice, *the ethical must retain all its value; the love for his son must remain intact,* and the order of human duty must continue to insist on its rights' (Derrida 1995b, 66; italics mine). It is this aporia that Derrida calls 'ethics as "irresponsibilization"', because it is 'an insoluble and paradoxical contradiction between responsibility in general and absolute responsibility' (Derrida 1995b, 61). This suggests that the difference between 'doing anything one wants' in the name of some 'Other' (be it God, religion, another person or event), and 'absolute responsibility'(in the case of Abraham, being absolutely responsible to God), is that in the moment of absolute responsibility to the Other, the 'ethical must retain all its value'. That is, one must know that one is doing the wrong thing by not obeying ones ethical duty, and care about it, and thus continue to respect and love all Others that one acts irresponsibly towards, just as Abraham retained the love for his son as he raised his knife.

This inextricability of irresponsibility with responsibility is inevitable. After all, how would we know or recognize absolute responsibility without reference to the common, to the universal, to general responsibility or ethics? And as absolute responsibility is marked by singularity it cannot be reduced to a realm (such as the public), that is, formalized and structured by universal laws. In other words, how do we in fact know the singularity of someone or some situation without the common, the share-able, without what Derrida calls an understanding of genercity (Derrida 2006, 1)? Here we have a further paradox: an absolute responsibility has to be both singular, outside and beyond the common (an alterity), and yet common or generic enough to be understood as 'irresponsible'; and also common or generic enough to be practised as an absolute responsibility. Without this practice, absolute responsibility would be unrecognizable.

Meanwhile, despite what seems to be Abraham's awareness of having to make a choice, no matter how harrowing, between absolute responsibility and ethics, what the phrase ethics under erasure attempts to convey is the inextricability of this relationship of absolute responsibility with ethics, singularity with generality, respectively. Therefore 'sacrifice' is not an uncomplicated or unambiguous decision or choice between the (singular) 'one' and 'all Others' (general). 'Sacrifice' here is not equivalent to 'choice'; if by choice we mean we have agency and autonomy to choose between options. Rather, sacrifice *is the condition* of every decision or choice. This means that in our day-to-day lives, here and now, we always already, inevitably, sacrifice one (either the singular or the general) and both (the singular and general) at the same time, but unlike Abraham, without always necessarily knowing we are doing so. In other words, there are two equal, because absolutely imperative, duties: one to the singularity of any 'one', and one to the duty of being responsible to 'every Other' (the general, and thus the law). This produces a tension between the two ('irresponsibilization'); a paradox; aporia and tension not resolved by a simple decision or choice between the two, but rather an aporia that exposes the undecidability within, and the inherent violence of, every choice or decision; an undecid-ability that constitutes responsibility as exigency.

Undecidability, then, reveals that our choice-making and decision-taking cannot be entirely or absolutely governed by calculation, and thereby free of ambiguity and uncertainty, but instead ensures that our responsibility towards and for otherness and Other(s) happens urgently in the here and now. As Chapter 3 elucidates further, the 'here' (this singular context) and 'now' (in the singularity of this particular time) does not necessarily mean that response requires no thought at all. It means, rather, that response cannot be ultimately calculated in advance and thus prefabricated (and thus prescriptive and universal and applicable over time and across all contexts).

Ethics under erasure not only reveals this aporia or paradox ('irresponsibilization') between absolute responsibility and ethical duty (general), or the inextricable relation between the two, but the phrase also attempts to capture the debt to, and acknowledgement of, ethics at the moment it is betrayed by our absolute responsibility to the singular Other/event. While Chapter 3 does not discuss *The Gift of Death*, this debt, or inheritance, is instead conveyed in and through Derrida's term hauntology as he outlines it in *Specters of Marx* (1994). Hauntology is important for understanding 'under erasure', and consequently, Chapter 3 forges a connection between hauntology (and spectrality) and under erasure, in order to attempt to elucidate the link made between under erasure and ethics. Hauntology thus brings to the fore the idea of negotiation. In other words, ethics is *haunted* by that which it inherits (other ethical principles or systems, laws and rules), and by the singular call of the Other/other.

Furthermore, ethics under erasure extends the condition of paradox or aporia articulated in *The Gift of Death*, by revealing not only the sacrifice constitutive of every ethical decision, but the *negotiation* inherent in every sacrifice. There is a negotiation between not only the singular and the general, between absolute responsibility and ethics, respectively, but also between one singularity and another; one general principle of duty (ethical theory) and another. It is a question of not only *who* we sacrifice, but *what* we sacrifice. Bringing under erasure together with ethics, then, encapsulates how our singular ethical responses to 'others' entails *negotiation* with and within ethical systems (and hence social values and norms built on those systems) that carry universal status. It entails a negotiation with our ethical inheritance.

The coinage ethics under erasure is an interpretation of, an interposition on, Derrida's notion of responsibility and irresponsibilization. But it also offers, in Chapter 4, a means of understanding the contemporary lived experience of the ethical through an analysis of Todd Haynes' film *Far From Heaven* (2003). While in the *Gift of Death* Derrida presents us with a popular and yet old biblical story, revealing its relevance for modern times, contemporary film fiction and narrative also has the potential to construct alternative or possible ontologies, raising questions about some of the most profound problems of human experience not only in the past, but for our culture and society today.

Given this, the film has been chosen for analysis for the following reasons. First, by presenting us with a series of fictional or cultural (re)presentations of ethical relations and (im)possibilities (such as inter-racial and homosexual relationships), *Far From Heaven* opens a space for critical reflection: for rethinking such relations, and for recognizing the simultaneous universality and singularity of any ethical moment. In short, the film iterates[16] previous theoretical discussion of ethics under erasure, in and through visual and narrative representation, thus enabling identification with how ethics under erasure is lived or can be experienced in our contemporary everyday lives. Second, the film makes thematically central the problem of reconciling universal ethical systems and social and moral norms, and singular ethical moments or events, thus raising political questions about the conventional understanding of ethical acts and the norms on which they are based. Ethics under erasure, then, is a means by which to think how we negotiate, what in Chapter 4 is referred to as the 'ethically singular', and the social and institutional politics inevitably entangled with ethics. In this way, the film questions and undermines Simon Critchley's construction of an opposition between ethics and politics in Derrida's work, and his argument that deconstruction reaches a political impasse (a focus of Chapter 1).

However, a question still remains: why not an analysis of several films?[17] Of the many debates in the area of film-philosophy one of them revolves around film's ability to potentially generate 'socially critical attitudes'. To foster this attitude this particular debate presents a choice of either following 'film theory's tendency to make broad generalizations . . . which are not grounded in careful analysis of individual films', or to focus instead on giving detailed interpretation of films that demonstrate 'how their narratives present critical takes on various social practices and institutions' (Wartenberg 2008, online; see also Carroll and Choi 2006). What the debate doesn't focus on is the way in which context might also determine this choice. Thus the choice between a detailed analysis of one film and a broad generalization of ethics under erasure in several films is partly determined by context. In the context of this book, analysing a single film allows the singularity of that film (as an event in itself) to come to the fore, through a concentration on the various aspects of the film (such as character development and relationships, narrative and plot structures, and cinematic devices). These aspects, in turn, contribute to, and enhance, the interpretation of the film in relation to ethics under erasure, and vice versa. That is, the detailed analysis of the manifestation of ethics under erasure in and through the film's cinematic devices, and also at the level of character relations, challenges more broadly the socially dominant attitudes in contemporary society regarding race, class, gender and sexuality. By examining the interactions and relationships of some of the characters in the film, and comparing the film genre to other similar genres of which *Far From Heaven* pays homage, Chapter 4 demonstrates how ethical norms governing race, class and identity are transgressed and undermined, while simultaneously kept intact or maintained. Through this analysis this chapter attempts to demonstrate why ethical norms are experienced in this paradoxical way in our cultural (re)presentations and everyday intersubjective relations.

Chapters 3 and 4 are built on Chapters 1 and 2. Chapter 1 begins with a discussion of the place of the ethical defences and interpretations of Derrida that developed since the 1980s, in response to the criticisms of nihilism made by Habermas and others, and thus sketches the ethical landscape in which Derrida's work has been received and located. But the main focus is on Simon Critchley's ethical interpretation of Derrida set out in his book *The Ethics of Deconstruction* (1992, reprinted 1999). He is one of the first to mount a full-scale book-length account of the importance of Levinas for understanding Derrida. Among others, Bernasconi's articles (1988, 1999) on Levinas and Derrida are also extremely significant. The focus, however, is on Critchley's book because he constructs an opposition between ethics and politics in Derrida's work. First, Critchley claims that deconstruction can be read ethically but that this can only be done via Levinas (Critchley 1999, xiii). Second, he claims that deconstruction reaches a political impasse that Levinasian politics alone can overcome (Critchley 1999, xiv–xv). The argument of Chapter 1 is that there is no such impasse in Derrida's work. Critchley's arguments are important and ground breaking, nevertheless this aspect of his reading of Derrida is questioned because it inadvertently lends support to the Habermasian position that Derrida's deconstruction produces contextual indeterminacy that leads to political ineffectuality. Consequently, in arguing that deconstruction reaches a political impasse, Critchley's book arguably led the way for the proliferation of writings around Derrida and the political, which continues to this day. Richard Beardsworth's influential book *Derrida and the Political* was one of the first to challenge 'Critchley's general claim that Levinasian ethics serves the "political" supplement to Derrida's negotiation with aporia' (Beardsworth 1996, 163 n.8).

Chapter 2 simultaneously challenges and accepts Levinas' importance to Derrida's thinking on ethics, by not only arguing that Derrida radically complicates Levinas' ethics, but by stressing that other philosophers are just as influential to Derrida's thinking. Nietzsche is one of these influences. In this chapter there is a detailed discussion of the congruencies and differences between Derrida and Nietzsche, as well as a suggestion for another, or alternative, way (certainly not the only one) of thinking the ethical. In this chapter Derrida's formulation of différance via Nietzsche is elaborated because Rorty's postmodern and Habermas' nihilistic interpretations of Derrida's deconstruction are based on an inappropriate and reductive view of Derrida's inheritance of Nietzsche.

For instance, in Nietzsche's works nihilism comes in many forms and is not simply destructive but also affirmative or active. As Michael Haar argues, for Nietzsche nihilism passes through '*incomplete nihilism*': the rejection of life, and where our highest values devalue themselves; to '*complete nihilism*': where the will to nothingness manifests itself as an abolition of oppositions and leads to the indefinite play of interpretations and appearances; to '*active nihilism*': one that overcomes the destructive tendencies of incomplete and complete nihilism (Haar 1995, 14–15). Furthermore, Haar argues that for Nietzsche, '[i]n order to transform "complete" nihilism . . . it is necessary that we pass from a recognition of the dissolution to an active, an affirmative dissolution', which Nietzsche associates with the Dionysian: 'the perspective of the joyous, pure affirmation of the unity of contraries' (Haar 1995, 15–16). In fact, it is over the Dionysian that Habermas makes one of his most vehement objections to Nietzsche's project, arguing that Nietzsche sets the aesthetic experience of Dionysian rapture 'outside the horizon of reason' (Habermas 1987, 96), and thus dispenses with reason and subjectivity altogether.[18] It is also on this level that Habermas likens Derrida's project to Nietzsche's and thus the accusations Habermas levels at Nietzsche are also, similarly, directed towards Derrida. One of the aims of Chapter 2, then, is to argue (pace Habermas) that Derrida's negotiation or engagement with Nietzsche *does not* prove that Derrida's work is 'nihilistic' in the destructive sense or necessarily entails a theory of 'undifferentiated textuality', but rather argues that Nietzsche, as well as Levinas, influences Derrida's concept of justice: that is, deconstruction in the form of différance, open ethical possibilities, but only in and through what Derrida calls 'impossibility'. The chapter concludes that there is a contamination between Nietzsche and Levinas in Derrida's elaboration of justice. Bringing Nietzsche and Levinas together to explore (im)possibility and justice is what allows for the development of 'ethics under erasure'.

In summary, the argumentative trajectory of this book moves from a demonstration of misinterpretations and defences in the critical reception of Derrida's thinking on responsibility (and thereby providing an intimate connection between Derrida's work on language and his work on justice and responsibility), through an extension of Derrida's deconstruction to ethics under erasure, and then to an iteration of this new critical paradigm in film analysis, thus reflecting the relevance of ethics under erasure to everyday ethical experience.

Chapter 1

The 'Ethics of Deconstruction'?

The border between the ethical and the political here loses for good the indivisible simplicity of a limit . . . the determinability of this limit was never pure, and it never will be.

— *Derrida,* Adieu: To Emmanuel Levinas, 99

Ethical–Political Turns: Setting the Scene

Key to this chapter is the relation between ethics and politics. Not only are both extremely important to Derrida, but deconstruction is important to an understanding of 'ethics' and 'politics' and the way they operate in our cultural and social institutions, (re)presentations and everyday intersubjective relations. Yet Derrida does not offer a political or ethical treatise or philosophy; to do so would be to perpetuate what ethics and politics already are – metaphysical concepts – and thus also the opposition between them which sustains their metaphysical determinations. This does not mean that there is no difference between the two terms. While Derrida has argued that he does not dissociate them because '[e]thical problems are already taken up in the so-called space of the political' (Derrida 2002, 302) and 'it is necessary to deduce a politics and a law from ethics' (Derrida 1999a, 115), nevertheless he insists that the difference between ethics and politics is in the way they are structured in relation to action and response.

It is precisely Derrida's deconstruction of these terms that has led to his work being dismissed as ethically useless or nihilistic, even though the ethical has been a concern of his from the very beginning in books such as *Of Grammatology* through to, and more obviously, 'The Force of Law: The "Mystical Foundation of Authority"', *Of Hospitality, Adieu: To Emmanuel Levinas* and *The Gift of Death.* Moreover, many scholars (such as Simon Critchley) argue that deconstruction is politically neutral, or reaches a political impasse, because, as the general argument goes, deconstruction is not a method or form of analysis and therefore can't produce concrete formulas for action. And yet many of Derrida's books – if not providing a prescriptive political treatise – address the political as such; for instance, *Negotiations, The Politics of Friendship, Specters of Marx* and *Rogues: Two Essays on Reason*; not to forget also Derrida's involvement in what can only be described as his political action, from his attempted reform of the University (see Derrida 1983) through his intervention in various political injustices, which can be seen in his letters to the American President Bill Clinton asking him to intervene in the case of Mumia Abu-Jamal (see Derrida 2002, 125–32). In all these works and issues, the ethical is taken up in the political and vice versa.

If the ethical–political is the key theme of this chapter, then the theme is rigorously unravelled through Simon Critchley's book *The Ethics of Deconstruction*. This book was first published in 1992 (and again in 1999), and the reader may ask why address the ethical and political via Critchley, especially because in the time between 1999 and the present there has been a proliferation of writings on deconstruction and the political, not least by Critchley whose position on this issue in relation to Derrida has shifted over the years.[1] In answer, it is by unpacking and challenging Critchley's ethical-political interpretation of Derrida that this chapter aims to not only expose the weakness of Critchley's argument, but in doing so, more generally address the various positions (for example, Badiou's, Spivak's and Žižek's among others) that have since developed the Critchley line that deconstruction reaches a political impasse, albeit for different reasons: because too utopian; too formless; too much focused on the 'other', to produce political 'action'. In preparation for this unravelling, however, let us briefly situate Critchley's book within the historical scene of the reception of Derrida's work in the Anglo-American community, before ending this section with an outline of the argumentative trajectory of this chapter.

Writing in 1999, Critchley argued that there were three waves or trends in the Anglo-American reception of Derrida's work. The 'first wave' occurred in the 1970s and was characterized by the literary emphasis on, and appropriation of, deconstruction represented by the 'Yale School' (Geoffrey Hartman, Paul de Man, Harold Bloom and J. Hillis Miller) (Critchley 1999, 1). Christopher Norris, Rodolphe Gasché, John Llewellyn and Irene Harvey represent the 'second wave': the philosophical reception of Derrida (Critchley 1999, 1; see also Bennington 1988, 76).[2] Finally, Critchley argues that his book *The Ethics of Deconstruction* (originally in 1992), along with J. Hillis Miller's *The Ethics of Reading* (1987), moves 'beyond its literary and philosophical appropriation' by focusing on the 'ethical', which marks the 'third wave' (Critchley 1999, 2–3).

This is undoubtedly a convenient and useful way to understand the 'history' of the reception of Derrida's work in the Anglo-American community. It is also a legitimate way of recalling the context out of which

Derrida's works, and Critchley's response to them, arise. Nevertheless, at the same time, it is also worth keeping in mind that any 'periodizing' account, no matter how useful, potentially risks missing, at least in regards to Derrida, the way his individual works also speak to each other 'connect[ing] forward and back' (Hobson 1998, 3) across eras from Derrida's earliest to latest works and vice versa. These periodizing accounts also risk homogenizing the differences between various scholars' arguments on the ethical in Derrida's work. We at least have to take into account that there is more than one ethical reception of deconstruction, with different emphasis on what constitutes the 'ethical', even *within* the 'third wave'.

Furthermore, the idea of 'waves' or trends proposed by Critchley, while useful, inevitably raises several questions: exactly what characterizes this ethical turn? Is it characterized, for instance, by a Levinasian emphasis on understanding the ethical in Derrida, or by a concern with how, if at all, deconstruction poses ethical questions, especially given that deconstruction is not a 'method, critique, analysis, act or operation' (Derrida 1988b, 3)? Or does this 'third wave' have to necessarily follow a linear trajectory? At what point in time, in history, does this ethical turn occur, especially given, as we will see, that there seems to be various writings on Derrida and ethics that fall outside the 'ethical turn'? For instance, in regards to this last question, by situating Miller's *The Ethics of Reading* (1987) as well as his own book at the vanguard of this ethical turn, Critchley marks the trend as beginning in the very late 1980s and early 1990s. Certainly during this time a proliferation of writings came to the fore focusing on the Levinasian connection when thinking about the ethical in relation to Derrida's work, such as Robert Bernasconi (1987, 1988) and David Wood (1987). But also a number of other scholars at this time were making the connection between deconstruction and ethics, justice or law, and applying this connection to topics as diverse as feminism, literature, economics and religion: John Caputo (1987), Drucilla Cornell (1992), Henry Louis Gates (1992), Christina Howells (1999), J. Hillis Miller (1992), Samuel Weber (1992), and so on. (While in the first decade of the twenty-first century this has continued with writings on the ethical by prominent scholars such as Geoffrey Bennington (2000), Hent de Vries (2001), Martin Hägglund (2008), John Llewellyn (2002), J. Hillis Miller (2009) and Michael Naas (2008)).

Critchley situates this ethical turn in the context of the prevailing prejudice of the times, which believed deconstruction to be 'a species of nihilistic textual freeplay' and thus unethical (Critchley 1999, 3). One of the ways of challenging this prejudice, then, was to reveal Derrida's concern for the question of the ethical by turning to his engagement with Levinasian ethics in his essay 'Violence and Metaphysics'. It is this Levinasian emphasis that Critchley implies *dominates* this third wave or ethical turn, although it is not until Critchley's publication that a full-scale book-length account of the importance for understanding Derrida's relation to ethics via Levinas was undertaken. (The importance of Levinas for Derrida's thinking on ethics was also later confirmed by the first publications in French, in 1997, of Derrida's books *Of Hospitality* and *Adieu*.)

The significance and importance of Critchley's book for this chapter, however, *is not* primarily the connection it established between Levinas' ethics and Derrida's deconstruction. Its significance lies, first, in the relation Critchley constructs between ethics and politics in Derrida's work, and second in Critchley's notion of 'clôtural reading', both of which, he argues, moves his book beyond the philosophical into the ethical reception of Derrida. Critchley uses the term 'clôtural' to extend Derrida's notion of closure as he uses it in relation to metaphysics. Critchley interprets closure as 'the double refusal both of remaining within the limits of the tradition [metaphysics] and of the possibility of transgressing that limit' (Critchley 1999, 20). While what he coins 'clôtural reading' is defined as 'the production of a dislocation within a text' (Critchley 1999, 88), which reveals how this 'double refusal' and thus the possibility of transgressing the metaphysical tradition (by opening the text to a moment of alterity) can occur. More on this later.

Clôtural reading is also what Critchley believes sets his project apart from other writings on ethics and deconstruction (but which do not necessarily focus on the Levinasian influence). Marking the 'ethical turn' as developing in the late 1980s and early 1990s and characterizing it as dominated by a Levinasian perspective, Critchley inadvertently precludes these other writings. For example, the works of Richard Kearney, initially in 1981, and Christopher Norris (in 1987) made the correlation between 'the other' and ethics in Derrida's early work, specifically emphasizing the ethical importance of deconstruction in its connection with the 'other' of writing, language and the text, and in the process demonstrating that Derrida has always been concerned with the ethical right from his earliest works, such as *Of Grammatology*. In this book Derrida argues that 'there is no ethics without the presence of the *other* but also, and consequently, without absence, dissimulation, detour, writing' (Derrida 1976, 139–40). Here Derrida suggests that a metaphysical determination of ethics is made possible by what makes it impossible: archewriting, différance, trace, and so on. That is, these quasi-transcendental palaeonymies and neologisms make possible the ethics of speech as presence, but which means, at the same time, that presence is never absolute.[3] In this sense metaphysical ethics, or the 'ethic of speech', 'is the *delusion* of presence mastered' (Derrida 1976,

139). And in the next sentence Derrida defines archewriting as 'the origin of morality as of immorality. *The non-ethical opening of ethics.* A violent opening' (Derrida 1976, 140). How the 'other' is connected to the non-ethical, and ethics to violence, will be investigated in more detail throughout this chapter. Suffice to say that because non-ethics haunts ethics as presence, ethics *exceeds* its metaphysical determination.

This now brings us to the central arguments of this chapter. Critchley claims, first, that the opening of ethics in Derrida can only be understood through Levinas' notion of ethics and 'the other'. That is, deconstruction can be read 'ethically', but only in the Levinasian sense (Critchley 1999, xiv–xv). He further claims, second, that deconstruction reaches a political impasse that only a 'Levinasian politics of ethical difference' can overcome (Critchley 1999, xiv–xv). This chapter questions the opposition Critchley sets up between the first and second claims: that is, between ethics and politics respectively. While Critchley's work in general, and his notion of 'clôtural reading' in particular, is extremely important in revealing the ethical dimension of Derrida's notion of 'double reading', his claims lead him to constitute further oppositions within Derrida's work more generally. The second section of this chapter, entitled 'Conversing with Critchley' attempts to demonstrate how and why he does this, so as to be able to answer questions that arise from his claims: is there, in fact, a political impasse in Derrida's deconstruction? And is Critchley's reading of the 'ethics of deconstruction', perhaps, too Levinasian? These questions will be addressed in both the third section, 'Derrida's reading of Levinas', and the final section, 'Dancing with Derrida', through a detailed reading of Derrida's 'Violence and Metaphysics' and *Adieu.*

Referring to Critchley and raising these familiar questions is relevant to understanding Derrida's thinking on ethics and politics, because first, as mentioned earlier, unpacking in detail what Critchley argues in regards to Levinas' ethics and politics places this chapter in the context of the continuing debate around these questions.[4] Specifically, this chapter argues that Critchley constructs an unfortunate opposition between ethics and politics by not placing enough emphasis on the congruencies between Derrida and Levinas regarding the political. As a result, Critchley does not take sufficient account of the way Derrida, to use Bennington's term, 'radicalises', or as Bob Plant suggests, 're-articulates', refines and develops Levinas' notion of the ethical (Bennington 2000, 44; Plant, 2003, 443). This is most evident when Critchley argues that there is a 'political impasse' in deconstruction that can *only* be overcome by a 'Levinasian politics of ethical difference' (Critchley 1999, xiv). In Critchley's view, then, the 'ethical demand' of deconstruction should be read and understood through Levinas' ethics (Critchley 1999, xiii). I agree with Critchley, and with Plant, that Derrida's 'ethical writings' are situated 'within their Levinasian heritage' (Plant 2003, 443), and with Bennington that Levinas is important for Derrida's 'ethical reflection' (Bennington 2000, 39). Further, I have no quarrel with Critchley revealing the 'ethics of deconstruction' via Levinas. But it is concerning when Critchley, arguing that deconstruction needs to be supplemented by Levinas, subsumes deconstruction into a Levinasian ethics, and thereby takes insufficient account of Derrida's radicalization of Levinas. In doing so, Critchley downplays Derrida's radicalization and deconstruction of ideas latent in Levinas (Plant 2003, 443). On this basis, Critchley establishes and sustains a hierarchic opposition between the political thinking of Derrida and Levinas, where Levinas' views are privileged. And much later this chapter argues that there is a dance of separation and contamination between Derrida and Levinas that challenges Critchley's opposition. Second, in addressing these questions, this chapter also sets the groundwork and thus paves the way for another, different, ethical interpretation of deconstruction in the following chapters. Specifically, Chapter 2 argues that we can rethink, through Nietzsche, as well as Levinas, the positive ethical possibilities evident in, and enabled by, Derrida's deconstruction. While Chapter 3 resituates the relation between ethics and politics in the context of 'ethics under erasure', which in turn is elucidated by Derrida's notion of hauntology as he discusses it in *Specters of Marx*.

Conversing with Critchley

In the second edition of *The Ethics of Deconstruction*, Critchley includes appendices and footnotes clarifying and/or modifying his original argument. In one of these footnotes, Critchley acknowledges that '[i]n personal correspondence, Dominique Janicaud has rightly criticized my book for speaking of deconstruction in the singular, "as if there were only one", and thereby presupposing some unity to Deconstruction (with a capital "D") and identifying the latter solely with the work of Derrida' (Critchley 1999, 265, fn. 4). Critchley's decision to speak of deconstruction in the singular was, perhaps, in part, a result of his concept of ethics. In other words, despite Critchley's claim that 'an ethics [cannot] be derived from deconstruction, like an effect from a cause' (Critchley 1999, 2), deconstruction is unified because connected with only one type of ethics: a Levinasian ethics.

There are good reasons why Critchley ties Derrida's deconstruction so closely to Levinas' ethics: in the 'Appendix' to the second edition, and with the benefit of hindsight, Critchley explains his growing awareness of the problems that the words 'ethics', 'morality', 'responsibility', and so on, have for Derrida (Critchley 1999, 250). Nonetheless, his intentions are admirable because he explains his use as strategic: to defend Derrida against the accusations of nihilism or 'immoralism' levelled by some of his critics. Critchley suggests that he used the word 'ethics' in his book 'to reclaim quasi-polemically the language of morality from those proponents of the anti-deconstructionist *doxa*' (Critchley 1999, 251). Furthermore, in response to Derrida's article 'Passions: An Oblique Offering' (published just after the first edition of Critchley's book), Critchley argues that his use of the word 'ethics' was not a repetition and restoration of the traditional sense of morality, but a displacement of its meaning in order 'not to fall prey to the fatal . . . *doxa* outlined by Derrida, that of the "remoralisation of deconstruction"' (Critchley 1999, 252).

Thus, in order not to fall into either 'moralism' (the deconstructionist or anti-deconstructionist *doxa*), Critchley delineates the 'ethical demand' he sees in deconstruction's relation to Levinas' ethics (Critchley 1999, xiii). Levinas defines his ethics as a 'calling into question of my spontaneity by the presence of the Other . . . The strangeness of the Other, his irreducibility to the I, to my thoughts and my possessions, is precisely accomplished as a calling into question of my spontaneity, as ethics' (Levinas 1996, 43). This ethics precedes ontology; it precedes and displaces traditional under-standing of metaphysical ethics. Critchley's defence of Derrida is compelling, and his use of Levinas understandable, given Derrida's engagement with Levinas. However, if deconstruction is an aporetic (non)structure (that is, not unified and formalized: a structure without being a structure), then it is hard to understand why Critchley should 'privilege' Levinas' ethics, and that alone, in his attempt to explain the 'ethical demand' of deconstruction (Critchley 1999, xiii). We will return to this discussion later.

The more immediate concern in this section is Critchley's claim that deconstruction can move neither from ethics to politics, nor from the transcendental to the empirical. And Critchley claims this despite acknowl-edging that deconstruction is quasi-transcendental. Consequently, he tends to foster an opposition between the transcendental and the empirical *within* Derrida's work, but in doing so posits, in and through a discursive logic/structure, an inadvertent opposition between a Levinasian and metaphysical ethics.[5] Finally, having done this, Critchley is in a position to oppose Levinas' 'politics of ethical difference' (Critchley 1999, xiv) and Derrida's deconstruction. The irony here, as Bennington notes, is that Critchley constructs these oppositions 'in a context (the quasi-transcendental) which de-limits' oppositions (Bennington 2000, 200, fn. 20). Why does Critchley do this? One answer might be that Critchley's oppositions are a consequence of his view that Derrida's deconstructive, and hence quasi-transcendental, notion of 'undecidability' is politically ineffective, and the aim of the next two subsections is to attempt to demonstrate this.

Opposition 1: Critchley's opposing of traditional and Levinasian ethics

Critchley creates an opposition between a traditional, metaphysical ethics (by which he means 'ethics *qua* region or branch of philosophy') and a Levinasian ethics (Critchley 1999, 2). It is from this initial, seemingly innocuous, dichotomy that his other oppositions derive. The result is a troubling array of oppositions in Critchley's arguments. However, let us begin by examining this initial opposition in detail. It first arises when Critchley juxtaposes Levinas to J. Hillis Miller's 'ethics of reading'.

For Critchley, deconstruction takes place as the disruption and interruption of the limit of the metaphysical tradition (the *logos*) (Critchley 1999, 20). These interruptions he argues are alterities, 'moments of *ethical transcendence*, in which a necessity other than that of ontology announces itself within the reading' (Critchley 1999, 30). When Critchley says here that ethics is 'other' (meaning an absolute otherness or alterity) than ontology, this is a direct reference to Levinas' argument in *Totality and Infinity* that ontology has been, in the traditional conception of metaphysics, a relation between knowledge and theory, and being, a relation that 'reduces the other to the same'[6] (Levinas 1996, 42). Similarly, when Critchley argues that deconstructive ethics 'announces itself in reading' this is an appropriation of Miller's notion of the 'ethics of reading'. This methodological combination of Miller and Levinas is confirmed later in Critchley's 'Introduction' when he expresses his hope that 'my book will take up Miller's fascinating, but finally aporetic, formulation of the ethics of reading and deepen it philosophically with specific reference to Levinas, in order to show that this necessity is ethical in a sense not so far discussed by him' (Critchley 1999, 47).

In his book *The Ethics of Reading* (1987), Miller argues that the act of reading is not just about how stories reveal ethical judgement, choices or situations in their thematic dramatization or narrative (Miller 1987, 1). Rather, there is an 'ethical moment in that act of reading as such, a moment neither cognitive, nor political, nor social, nor interpersonal, but properly and independently ethical' (Miller 1987, 1). Critchley rightly interprets Miller to be arguing that the 'ethical moment' arises in and through the *act* of reading a book, which 'demands a response from and responsibility on the part of the reader' (Critchley 1999, 44). And indeed, following

Henry James, Miller argues that these ethical moments are part of the 'conduct of life'. Miller explains: 'Let me look closely at James' own words, taking them as the things I, for the moment, most respect. "The whole conduct of life", says James, "consists of things done, which do other things in their turn" (Miller 1987, 102). Miller confirms in his article 'Is There an Ethics of Reading?' (1989) that by '"ethical" I mean more or less what Henry James means': the conduct of life as things done (Miller 1989, 85). Thus, the 'conduct of life' consists in *doing things*, in other words, in *action*. Despite Miller's confirmation here that ethics is action (and hence also political), Critchley posits – perhaps understandably given Miller's argument, quoted earlier, that there is an 'ethical moment in the act of reading . . . a moment neither cognitive, nor political' (Miller 1987, 1) – that Miller's ethical moment in reading is not necessarily reducible to the political realm. As a result, he wonders how Miller's ethics can be 'derived from a text and then somehow translated into political action' (Critchley 1999, 48). Perhaps it is because there is a difference in Miller's and in Critchley's understanding of politics and action (or political action) that Critchley finds a paradox here. This difference in understanding certainly suggests itself if we examine the relation between Miller's 'act of reading', taken from James, and Kant's 'moral law'.

Despite reservations he expresses about Kant's ethics in his book, Miller's notion of the political seems to be closely linked with the ethical in the Kantian sense. Miller's reading of Kant informs his notion of the political, which in turn shapes his understanding of action. This reading takes the following form: Miller argues that '[t]he ethical moment in the act of reading . . . is a response to something, responsible to it, responsive to it, respectful of it. In any ethical moment there is an imperative, some "I must" or *Ich Kann nicht anders*. I *must* do this. I cannot do otherwise' (Miller 1987, 4). The 'I must' in this quote is evidence of Kant's influence. That is to say, what is appropriated to the act of reading is Kant's concept of 'free will' (autonomy) as determined and constituted by the moral law. Moreover, the moral law (as universal legislation) is what gives free will its objectivity and rationality (practical reason) (Kant 1959, 29; Deleuze 1984, 29). Miller explains that 'the effect on the reader of the text would be like the effect on him of the moral law, that is, a categorical imperative, necessarily binding his will or leading him willingly to bind his own will. The act of reading would lead the reader voluntarily to impose the necessary ethical law embodied in that text on himself' (Miller 1987, 18–19). Thus, Miller's 'action', or act of reading, resembles Kant's categorical imperative that states that action is moral if one is able to act 'according to that maxim by

which you can at the same time will that it should become a universal law'
(Kant 1959, 39). Hence, reading leads to action.

Critchley objects to Miller's ethics because it is based on Kant, and thus
leads 'to an empty, formal universalism' (Critchley 1999, 48). In contrast to
Miller, then, and following Levinas, the ethical for Critchley is 'that of being
pre-reflectively addressed by the other person in a way that calls me into
question and obliges me to be responsible'. It 'is first and foremost a respect
for the concrete particularity of the other person in his or her singularity, a
person who is not merely an example of the law, in the way that Miller
claims that a text, analogous to a person, can be an example of the law . . . but
rather the condition of possibility for an experience of the law' (Critchley
1999, 48). In other words, Critchley argues that, for Levinas, '[p]olitics
begins as ethics'. This is because ethics does not arise from a 'consciousness
of respect for the universal law'. Rather, it begins with the subject being
called into question by a unique Other, which only then 'calls me to the
universal discourse of reason and justice' (Critchley 1999, 48). And it is
here that an opposition starts to form between a traditional ethics (that of
Kant and represented by Miller) and Levinas' ethics. The latter is based on
a pre-reflective responsibility to the Other, and thus critiques ontology and
a metaphysical ethics on which it is based.

There is, however, another reason why Critchley objects to Miller's ethics:
because it is too 'narrowly' textual. That is, ethics arises only as a response to
reading a book (a text in the narrow sense) (Critchley 1999, 47). Moreover,
because Miller suggests that the text (the book) is an example of law, Critchley
fails to see how Miller's passage from ethics (as an act of reading) to politics
(as action in the empirical world) can occur: 'I would want to ask . . . in what
direction – the *doxai* of left, right, or centre – one's political action might be
transformed after one has put down a book that has been read ethically?'
(Critchley 1999, 48). That Critchley can ask this question suggests a tendency
to reduce the 'political' to 'political action' that I am uncertain Miller shares.
(And note that Critchley's question here anticipates his criticism that
Derrida's deconstruction does not move from ethics to politics.)

For instance, based on his appropriation of the categorical imperative
described above, Miller argues, '[i]f the [ethical] response is not one of
necessity, grounded in some "must", if it is a freedom to do what one likes,
for example to make a literary text mean what one likes, then it is not
ethical' (Miller 1987, 4). That is, we are not free to read how we like, or
interpret what we read as we wish. Instead, in the act of reading we *must* be
responsible (Miller 1987, 4). Why must we be responsible?[7] Because, as
Derrida argues, if literature is tied closely to the public realm and institution,
to the point where it is part of the history and genealogy of democracy, then

'literature' is a 'political, democratic and *philosophical'* operation, one that takes place under the 'guise of a poem, a fiction or a novel', which lawfully authorizes 'literature' to say 'anything publicly'. Because literature can say 'anything publicly' it encapsulates responsibility and also the possibility of irresponsibility. 'I can say anything,' argues Derrida, 'and thus, not only do I not simply say what I please, but I also pose the question concerning to whom I am responsible' (Derrida 1996a, 80). Like Derrida, what Miller, rightly, seems to be suggesting more broadly is that thought, as well as action, is not just political in the narrow sense but also social and institutional, and always entails responsibility (and the final chapter of this book highlights this). Miller argues that 'the ethical moment in reading leads to an act. It enters into the social, institutional, political realms, for example in what the teacher says to the class or in what the critic writes' (Miller, 1987, 4). Furthermore, an ethical act cannot be 'fully determined by political considerations or responsibilities', otherwise it is no longer ethical. Nevertheless, 'the political and the ethical are always intimately intertwined' (Miller 1987, 4).

Miller's position vis-à-vis Critchley has been outlined not only to highlight the opposition Critchley constructs between Levinas' ethics and a traditional (metaphysical) ethics (exemplified in Miller's appropriation of Kant), but also because the conclusions reached here will inform the discussion of Critchley on politics later in this chapter.

While Critchley generally rejects Miller's ethics, he *does* appropriate aspects of Miller's 'ethics of reading', bringing it together with Levinas' ethics and Derrida's deconstruction. If Critchley attempts to go further than Miller by supplementing the 'ethics of reading' with a Levinasian ethics, then what Critchley terms 'clôtural reading' is also an attempt to move beyond Miller's understanding of deconstructive reading because, as Critchley claims, 'Miller's understanding of the concept of text is limited – namely to books – and thus quite distinct from the Derridean notion of the general text *qua* context and archiwriting' (Critchley 1999, 47). Therefore, according to Critchley, Miller's reading of deconstruction as a 'rhetorical' textual practice (Critchley 1999, 44) does not take into account 'archewriting', which opens alterities, and produces the ethical moment within the text. In other words, like Kearney and Norris, Critchley argues that archewriting can be equated with the 'opening of another ethics'. He explains that archewriting, which inhabits writing (in the narrow sense), does not issue from the *logos* but provides 'the "rationale" for the *dé-construction* . . . of the *logos*' (Critchley 1999, 38). Thus, in agreement with Kearney, Critchley argues that deconstruction is the search for the other of language through the critique of logocentrism (Kearney 1993, 33; Critchley 1999, 20–1).

Furthermore, Critchley links archewriting to Derrida's notion of the 'general text' or 'context' (for Critchley these terms are equivalent), which he understands to mean 'a limitless network of differentially ordered signs which is not preceded by any meaning, structure, or *eidos*, but itself constitutes each of these. It is here, upon the surface of the general text, that there "is" deconstruction (*"Il y a de la déconstruction"*), that deconstruction takes place (*a lieu*)' (Critchley 1999, 38). For Critchley, following Derrida, archewriting is the general text, or context, that constitutes writing (and hence reading) in the narrow sense. We thus return, by a different route, to the point made about archewriting at the beginning of this and the previous section: by disrupting or interrupting the dominant interpretation or meaning, it opens something other, not only within the text, but in the act of reading itself. In taking account of Derrida's archewriting, Critchley believes that his reading of 'texts' goes much further than Miller's.

Yet how exactly is archewriting manifested in textual practice? As Critchley formulates it, archewriting takes place in and through deconstructive 'double reading': on the one hand, deconstruction repeats (or more aptly, iterates, because there is no pure repetition for Derrida) and reconstructs through commentary the dominant interpretation of a text, which is a necessary moment for deconstructive reading (Critchley 1999, 24). On the other hand, deconstruction simultaneously 'traverses' a text so that a reading cannot, as Critchley explains by quoting Derrida, '"simply be that of commentary nor that of interpretation"' (Derrida, quoted in Critchley 1999, 26). This is so because commentary only *protects* and perpetuates the dominant interpretation. This second, but simultaneous, moment of reading works to open a text by revealing its blind spots and ellipses (Critchley 1999, 23). Thus, the second moment 'brings the text into contradiction with itself, opening its intended meaning, its *vouloir-dire*, onto an alterity which goes against what the text wants to say or mean' (Critchley 1999, 27). Critchley emphasizes that this second moment arises from, and exists because of, the first moment of commentary that conveys the dominant meaning. Deconstructive double reading displaces, disrupts or interrupts the limits of the logocentric tradition – to which the dominant meaning of a text is aligned – while at the same time remaining within the limits of this tradition, and keeping the dominant meaning in place.

It is this disruption effected in and through double reading that also enables Derrida to respond more broadly to the 'problem of metaphysics'. The problem of metaphysics can be defined as the attempt to determine the absolute structure or principle through 'thought' alone. Specifically, the problem, as Theodore Adorno argues, is 'that thought, which in its conditionality is supposed to be sufficient to have knowledge only of the conditional, presumes to be a mouthpiece, or even the origin, of the unconditional' (Adorno 2000, 7). However, for E. J. Lowe this problem obtains only for those critiquing metaphysics, since any critique of metaphysics 'associated "universalist" conceptions of reason and ration-ality' is self-defeating. This is because critique is metaphysical in that it requires an engagement with rationalist thinking, which in turn is a 'claim about the fundamental nature of reality' (Lowe 2002, 4). Thus the question,'if we are closed or caught within (*inside*), then how are we to think, can we think, *outside* metaphysics?'captures what Derrida calls the problem of metaphysical 'closure' (Derrida 1995a, 110). As articulated in the quote from *Of Grammatology* below, deconstruction is Derrida's response to this problem:

> The movements of deconstruction do not destroy structures from the outside. They are not possible and effective, nor can they take accurate aim, except by inhabiting those structures. Inhabiting them *in a certain way*, because one always inhabits, and all the more when one does not suspect it. Operating necessarily from the inside, borrowing all the strategic and economic resources of subversion from the old structure, borrowing structurally, that is to say without being able to isolate their elements and atoms, the enterprise of deconstruction always in a certain way falls prey to its own work. (Derrida 1976, 24)

Thus deconstruction exposes the metaphysical presumption to universality and rationality in order to reveal the ethical and political implications of metaphysics, and *how* transgressing metaphysical concepts and determinations are both *impossible* and *possible*. Critchley puts it this way: '[c]losure is the double refusal both of remaining within the limits of the tradition and of the possibility of transgressing that limit. At the moment of historical and philosophical closure, deconstructive thinking occurs as the disruption and interruption of the limit that divides the inside from the outside of the tradition' (Critchley 1999, 20).[8] And as Chapter 3 argues, 'under erasure' is a phrase (one among many) Derrida employs to convey the movements of deconstruction that do not destroy structures from the outside, but by 'inhabiting' those structures erases *without* erasing; transforms *without* transforming; dismantles *without* destroying metaphysical structures from *within*.

Defining how deconstructive double reading is situated in relation to metaphysical closure, Critchley explains that, traditionally, reading involves making a decision or choice between 'two lines of thought' or even between two readings. But to make this choice involves circumscribing a reading into a unitary notion. A deconstructive double reading doesn't do this, but rather provokes an '"infinite and infinitely surprising reading"' (Derrida, quoted in Critchley 1999, 76) that does not close down but opens the text to alterity. And in doing so, a deconstructive double reading 'shows the shortcomings of any unitary, finite notion of the tradition or totality and the absence of any *end* to the historico-metaphysical epoch within which reading is undertaken'. Applying Derrida's deconstruction to reading, Critchley calls 'such reading *clôtural*' (Critchley 1999, 76). Thus, clôtural reading can be understood as an extension of deconstructive double reading 'to include the analysis of closure'. Clôtural reading is the 'production of a dislocation within a text' (Critchley 1999, 88), which as we have seen occurs in and through iteration of reading, which opens the text to ellipsis and then alterity. Moreover, the disruption and interruption produced by clôtural reading that opens alterity within the text is, for Critchley, the ethical moment or the 'ethical dimension of deconstruction' (Critchley 1999, 88). It is an ethical moment, argues Critchley, again following Levinas, that puts the subject into question when faced with the irreducible alterity of the Other. Thus, 'clôtural reading allows the question of ethics [in the Levinasian sense] to be raised within deconstruction' (Critchley 1999, 30), which is why Critchley claims that there is, indeed, an 'ethics of deconstruction' (Critchley 1999, 2).

But is Critchley's reading of deconstruction through a Levinasian ethics justified? He gives two justifications. First, Critchley quotes Derrida as claiming, in an interview with Andre Jacob, that not only does he not object to Levinas' thinking, but rather 'subscribes to everything Levinas says'. This despite the fact that 'Derrida does not think the same thing in the same way as Levinas' (Critchley 1999, 10). Second, the privileging of Levinasian ethics for understanding the 'ethics of deconstruction' is justified for Critchley by the fact that Derrida enters into dialogue with Levinas' ethics in two articles, 'Violence and Metaphysics' and 'At this very moment in this work here I am'. (Remember that *Of Hospitality* and *Adieu* were published after the first edition of Critchley's book.) For Critchley, this proves the relevance of Levinas for understanding Derrida's work (Critchley 1999, 11). We will return to Critchley's justifications in the concluding section, 'Dancing with Derrida'.

To summarize, while Critchley sees Levinas' ethical relation as a critique of ethics and ontology based on traditional metaphysics, it seems that by privileging Levinasian ethics and rejecting Miller's account in *The Ethics of Reading*, Critchley, arguably, implicitly constitutes an opposition between Levinas' ethics and a traditional, metaphysical notion of ethics. And 'opposition' here is not meant as something 'outside' of traditional ethics or politics, but rather as something that is *opposed to* and *distinct from* something else. Then through the connections he establishes, and the alignment forged, between Levinasian ethics and deconstruction, Critchley also opposes deconstruction to the ethics of the metaphysical tradition. In other words, this opposition fixes Levinasian ethics (and therefore deconstruction) as *the* alternative to traditional ethics (represented in and through Miller's Kantian approach). Consequently, Critchley appears to gloss over the 'otherness' within traditional, or metaphysical, determinations of ethics, which deconstructive double reading reveals. The irony is that having constructed this opposition, Critchley undermines it through his constitution of yet another opposition, this time between Levinas and deconstruction. The following subsection argues that this latter opposition is based on a series of further complicated, and unjustified, oppositions that Critchley constructs within Derrida's work.

Opposition 2: Critchley on Levinas and Derrida

Critchley discusses Derrida's reading of Heidegger's involvement with the Nazis (*l'affaire Heidegger*) in *Of Spirit*. He uses it as an example of a 'deconstructive reading [that] responds to political topics by giving a rigorous *clôtural* reading of a text (in the general sense)' (Critchley 1999, 199). For Critchley, *Of Spirit* gives a clôtural reading by responding to various critical analyses of Heidegger's politics. In and through his reading of Heidegger, Derrida, in a self-referential move, at the same time responds to those accusations that his own work 'avoids discussions of ethical and political responsibility' (Critchley 1999, 195–6). According to Critchley, however, Derrida's undecidable and clôtural reading of Heidegger actually 'opens' the question of responsibility and alterity (Critchley 1999, 198).

Of Spirit is just one example of Derrida's discussion of political topics: Critchley goes on to list topics as diverse as the law, nationalism, nuclear criticism, the university, apartheid, and so on. As a result of Derrida's deconstructive reading of these various topics (as well as his reading of Heidegger in *Of Spirit*), Critchley acknowledges that Derrida's thinking is dominated by the 'question' of politics. Critchley does concede that, as a means of political analysis, deconstruction is effective in that it can demonstrate an initial but important step in the subversion of a regime's legitimacy (apartheid, for instance) precisely by recognizing that the regime is based on an 'undecidable proposition' (Critchley 1999, 199). However, Critchley then asks, '[w]hat is the relation, in Derrida's work, between the rigorous and responsible undecidability of deconstructive reading and the

necessity for political decisions and political critique?', and 'how is one to
account for the move from undecidability to the political *decision* to combat
that domination?' (Critchley 1999, 199). How, in other words, does
deconstruction move from ethics to politics? The answer, for Critchley, is
that deconstruction cannot make this move, and thus there is an 'impasse'
of the political in Derrida's work (Critchley 1999, 43, 236). Undecidability
allows for political analysis but then fails to account for political action, and
Critchley attempts to demonstrate this through a discussion of Lacoue-
Labarthe and Jean-Luc Nancy's notion of the political. It is in this discussion
that Critchley's understanding of 'politics' and 'undecidability' (mentioned
in the above quote) is made explicit.

At the 1980 Cérisy colloquium on 'The Ends of Man', and then in
December of that same year in a paper given as the 'Ouverture' for the
'Centre for Philosophical Research on the Political', Philippe Lacoue-
Labarthe and Jean-Luc Nancy argued, according to Critchley, that there
was a strategy of 'withdrawal' in Derrida's deconstruction concerning
politics (*la politique*). This withdrawal, Critchley argues, meant Derrida
could refuse to attack the 'revolutionary force of Marxism in France'
(Critchley 1999, 202). Or, as Nancy Fraser argues when summarizing and
quoting Derrida's paper given at the Cérisy colloquium:

> So, for the sake of the traditional leftist aim of not splitting the left, Der-
> rida claimed to have adopted a 'complex', 'encumbered' strategy. He had
> refrained from a frontal attack while marking a series of 'virtual differ-
> ences or divergences' from the revolutionary project. This strategy was
> marked in his writings, he said, by 'a sort of withdrawal or retreat (*retrait*),
> a silence with respect to Marxism – a blank signifying . . . that Marxism
> was not attacked like such and such other theoretical comfort . . . This
> blank was not neutral . . . It was a perceptible political gesture.' (Fraser
> 1984, 133–4)

As Critchley explains, Derrida's strategy of withdrawal is a deconstructive
gesture that actually shows solidarity with Marxism (Critchley 1999, 202).[9]
Rather than go into the ins and outs of this deconstructive withdrawal, or
the arguments raised and positions taken at the Cérisy colloquium,[10] it is
enough to say that, according to both Critchley and Fraser, for Lacoue-
Labarthe and Nancy this deconstructive withdrawal (*retrait*) is, in fact, the
basis on which to rethink *la politique* via *le politique*. Critchley defines *la
politique* as the empirical, that is, the factical, ontic-based event of politics,
while *le politique* means the 'essence' of the political, which is the questioning

and interrogation of politics (*la politique*) by philosophy (Critchley 1999, 201). According to Critchley, for Lacoue-Labarthe and Nancy the philosophical interrogation of *la politique* by *le politique* is necessary because all areas of social life have become, in contemporary society, politicized, and this they define as 'totalitarian' (Critchley 1999, 202).

Critchley defines Lacoue-Labarthe and Nancy's notion of totalitarianism as a 'modern despotism in which the social is represented as something without anything beyond it . . . without any transcendence . . . it is the total immanence of the social in the political. It is politics without transcendence, without remainder or interruption; what Nancy calls "immanentism"' (Critchley 1999, 206). Thus, society is dominated by the factical, empirical event of *la politique*, to the point where society is homogenized and unified, and difference and division are denied because there is no questioning of politics. In order to counteract this totalitarianism, Critchley argues that two moves are made by Lacoue-Labarthe and Nancy. First, in order to think the essence of *le politique* they follow Derrida and 'withdraw' (retreat/*retrait*) from *la politique*. Second, they then attempt to retrace 'the political in its essence'. Critchley argues that while Lacoue-Labarthe particularly enacts this double movement, Derrida's withdrawal is limited to the first (*retrait*) and does not extend to the second (Critchley 1999, 206). We will return to this presently.

For Critchley there is good reason to question the distinction that Lacoue-Labarthe and Nancy make between *le* and *la politique* (Critchley 1999, 201). This is because what seems to be a distinction is actually an exclusion and, hence, a reduction of *la politique* to *le politique*. Critchley argues that this reduction then leads to 'a synoptic and transcendental vision of the political in which any trace of *la politique* must be excluded. But it is precisely this gesture that I want to question, because rejection of *la politique* means rejection of the very genre of political debate, of dispute and dissension, persuasion and the battle over *doxa*' (Critchley 1999, 215). Whether Lacoue-Labarthe and Nancy actually do reject *la politique* is an issue we cannot pursue here. The important thing is that Critchley puts into question this putative distinction (which he interprets as a reduction) by arguing that there 'remains a trace, or *grapheme*, of empiricity and facticity in the reduction of *la politique* to *le politique* that disrupts or deconstructs the possibility of such a reduction' (Critchley 1999, 215). Following the quasi-transcendental logic of undecidability, Critchley questions whether or not reduction is in fact possible given that a trace of *la politique* always haunts *le politique* and vice versa.

There appears to be, nonetheless, a more worrying dimension to Critchley's argument when he goes on to claim that the reduction of *la politique* is a refusal to enter into the empirical event of politics as struggle, dissension and negotiation. He asks, 'is not this reduction of *la politique* itself a refusal of the "dirty hands" that must accompany any intervention in political struggle? . . . Is not the desire for an interrogation of *le politique* a desire for clean hands? And is this not a classical philosophical desire in the Platonic sense: namely, to determine the essence of the *polis* without having to act (or, at best, act reluctantly) within that *polis*?' (Critchley 1999, 215). The accusation here is that philosophers such as Lacoue-Labarthe and Nancy are all talk and no action! Despite his argument that it is impossible to reduce *la politique*, it is at this juncture – when Critchley wants to save *la politique* being reduced to *le politique* in order to, in turn, save the factical and empirical event of politics – that the problem arises. In privileging *la politique*, by wanting to save it, Critchley re-establishes the distinction between *le politique* and *la politique* that he initially put into question (when he said that there is a trace of *la politique* in *le politique*). Moreover, in wanting to save *la politique*, and by his deconstructive argument that there is contamination between them, Critchley reduces – in an inverse move to the one he says Lacoue-Labarthe and Nancy make – *le politique* to *la politique*. In this inverse reduction, Critchley inadvertently confirms what he disagrees with: that is, Lacoue-Labarthe and Nancy's Heideggerian notion that 'everything is political' (Critchley 1999, 202).

Critchley argues that the withdrawal that Derrida enacts, and that Lacoue-Labarthe and Nancy follow, excludes *la politique*, and thus deconstruction remains within the realm of *le politique* which, in its philosophical questioning and interrogation, is the realm of the abstract, and the transcendental. For Critchley, remaining in the realm of *le politique* means that deconstruction cannot move into the empirical, factical and ontic terrain of political space, that is, the terrain in which the 'activity of questioning, critique, judgement, and *decision*' is made (Critchley 1999, 236.; italics mine). Consequently, deconstruction cannot move 'from undecidability to the decision, from responsibility to questioning, from deconstruction to critique, from ethics to politics' (Critchley 1999, 236). It is odd that Critchley uses deconstruction, specifically undecidability, to demonstrate the contamination between *le* and *la politique*, but then argues that deconstruction leads to a political impasse. However, this move could be seen as a consequence of Critchley's association of the 'quasi-transcendental delineation of undecidability' (which is the logic of contamination), with the ethical realm only. That is, for Critchley, in the ethical realm, the quasi-transcendental is what opens alterity. Yet, when it comes to 'politics' (*la politique*), undecidability loses its quasi-transcendental status and simply becomes transcendental, thus unable to move from ethics to politics (the empirical terrain). As Geoffrey

Bennington perceptively notes, wanting to save *la politique* is a result of Critchley's 'desire, in the name of politics, to oppose the empirical to the transcendental' (Bennington 2000, 200, fn. 20). As a consequence, under the rubric of deconstruction, Critchley constitutes a false opposition between 'undecidability', which he aligns with the transcendental (*le politique*), and the decision, which he aligns with the empirical (*la politique*).

Critchley argues that undecidability (and deconstruction in general) belong to the 'ethical' domain only, and this leads him to question whether or not Richard Rorty is right to argue that Derrida's work is 'a quest for ironical, private perfection which is politically useless and perhaps even pernicious?' (Critchley 1999, 200) The question is surprising, given that a few years prior to the publication of the second edition of his book Critchley objected to Rorty's reduction of Derrida to 'private irony'.[11] Paradoxically, then, Critchley disagrees with Rorty, arguing that *ethically*, deconstruction has public significance, but agrees with Rorty arguing that *politically* deconstruction is relevant only for 'private irony':

> Roughly, my disagreement with Rorty's interpretation is that, in so far as deconstruction is ethical – that is, in so far as it is a certain opening on to the Other – Derrida's work has an irreducibly public function by Rorty's own definition; that is, it is concerned with the suffering of the Other. On my reading, the *crucial distinction* to be drawn in relation to deconstruction is between the relation to the Other, or ethics, and the relation to others as a whole, or politics. (Critchley 1999, 242, fn. 21; italics mine)

The opposition constructed here between ethics and politics in Derrida's work is confirmed when Critchley poses the rhetorical question: 'in the rigorous, quasi-transcendental delineation of undecidability as the dimension of political responsibility, is there not an implicit refusal of the ontic, the factical, and the empirical'? (Critchley 1999, 200) We could ask Critchley, in turn, if undecidability is quasi-transcendental, then how can it refuse the ontic, the factical, the empirical; in short, what Critchley defines as *la politique*? If Critchley thinks undecidability does enact this 'implicit refusal', then how does he understand 'undecidability'?

By associating the 'decision' with *la politique*, Critchley implicitly defines decision as 'action'. That is, not only does decision determine action, but to act is to decide. Arguably, this construction of decision, which arises when Critchley reduces *le politique* to *la politique*, is based on a notion of the autonomous subject; one that has the freedom to act/decide autonomously, because decision as action requires a rationality and objectivity associated with a humanist subject. As Niall Lucy argues when defending Derrida against criticisms that his work does not address political decision-making, such criticisms 'suppose, uncritically, that action is the supreme justification of thought, and that doing comes before thinking. At any rate, it is to suppose that all thought is purposive in advance, and that knowledge is simply an available tool of some pre-existent economy or agenda, to be used as prescribed either ideologically or oppositionally' (Lucy 1999, 95–6). Thus, on the one hand, Critchley's notion of action aligns with precisely the definition that Lucy's criticizes, 'action' as 'purposive'. On the other hand, Critchley's understanding of decision also aligns with Hillis Miller's 'ethics as action' that Critchley rejects (Critchley 1999, 47–8).

Critchley's understanding of action leads him to argue that, in its quasi-transcendentality, 'undecidability' fails to allow for decision on the political, hence empirical, level: '[t]he rigorous undecidability of deconstructive reading fails to account for the activity of political judgement, political critique, and the political decision' (Critchley 1999, 190). However, this interpretation of undecidability is questionable for two reasons. First, because of its quasi-transcendentality, undecidability does not refuse decision. It does not mean there is an absence of decision (or even rules and laws) in the empirical realm; rather, every decision is based, and depends, on a moment of undecidability, a moment that is not a formulated law or rule. It is in the undecidable moment (when having to make a decision [or judgement] between two or more equally weighted choices, one does not know what to decide), that any proper decision can occur. Second, and to push the point further, this 'moment ' is not necessarily a present moment in a series of present moments ('nows'), as it might be if we took a conventional view of time. Rather, undecidability is an aporetic experience (Derrida 1993a, 15), or an aporia of time and space. This notion of the aporetic time of decision and undecidability is elucidated by Derrida in *Adieu*:

> As always, the decision remains heterogeneous to the calculations, knowl-
> edge, science, and consciousness that nonetheless condition it. The
> silence of which we are speaking, the one toward which we are above
> all attentive, is the elementary and decisive between-time, the meantime,
> the instantaneous meantime of decision, which unsettles time and puts it
> off its hinges ('out of joint') in anachrony and in contretemps. (Derrida
> 1999a, 116)

Analogously, if time and space are generally understood as the formulated cause and effect of decision as action, then undecidability unsettles and interrupts, without rejecting, decision. Derrida articulates aporetic experiences as hauntings (Derrida 1993a, 20). Thus, the interruption to the time of the decision is a consequence of the fact that undecidability haunts the decision. In opposing undecidability to decision, and defining decision as empirical and determinable action, Critchley implicitly associates undecidability with indecision, defined in the narrow sense as indecisiveness or hesitation. However, Derrida's explanation of the 'aporetic experience' as haunting reveals that undecidability is not simply a moment of hesitancy. That is, undecidability is not simply a present moment that occurs just before the decision (which is yet another present moment in a series of present moments). A decision can never be absolutely rational, objective and calculable because 'haunting' every decision is undecidability, just as archewriting 'traces' through, or 'haunts', writing. The consequence of decisions never being absolutely rational, calculable and objective is, as Bennington explains, that Derrida reinscribes 'the concept of decision away from the concept of the subject to which it is traditionally bound . . . this means it can no longer be quite *my* decision. On this view, decisions are taken *by the other*' (Bennington 2000, 27). What Bennington is suggesting is that events and decisions, thus politics, are determined not absolutely by me but by the arrival of the Other. Or, as Derrida phrases it, 'could it not be argued . . . decision and responsibility are always *of the other*? They always come back or come down to the other, from the other, even if it is the other in me?' (Derrida 1999a, 23).

If, as Critchley implies, there is an absolute separation, a space, between the undecidable and decision as action, then decision would become a political formula, a method, a law for action (simply a prescriptive ethics). Furthermore, decision as action (on Critchley's definition) would reduce the other, thus Other, to the same insofar as it would deny the singularity, the uniqueness and the quasi-transcendental logic of undecidability and, hence, the decision. It would align the decision with ethics as laws, rules and norms. But in fact this is not the case, because undecidability haunts the decision and ensures that it is always already unique and singular. Thus the decision is a transcendental *as well as* empirical moment. Inversely, the quasi-transcendentality of undecidability leaves the decision open to the singularity, the uniqueness of the situation or the 'event' requiring decision. Thus, it is not the denial of decision that characterizes undecidability. Rather, it is the denial of a fixed, absolute formula or application for how, where or when decisions are made. If decisions could be made in this way, this would not be ethical but simply a formulated law to follow (because no decision had in fact been made). It would not take account of the 'otherness' of the situation or event, or the otherness haunting the decision itself. Moreover, the decision as blind obedience to law would dissolve the responsibility of the subject making/enacting the decision.

The significance of this is that undecidability (and deconstruction in general) has, as Bennington suggests, 'an ethical import' in precisely the Levinasian sense that Critchley requires. (And in Chapter 4 this is elaborated in relation to the characters' ethical negotiations with each other in Todd Haynes' film *Far From Heaven*.) Consequently, undecidability is not a 'refusal' of the empirical, ontic, factical, as Critchley supposes. Rather, undecidability is precisely what makes possible the decision, the empirical, in the first place. And, since it does not deny the transcendental either, the empirical decision cannot become unified and homogenizing (or totalitarian in the sense given by Lacoue-Labarthe and Nancy). This, then, is the quasi-transcendental logic of undecidability, and other aporias of deconstruction, such as archewriting, différance, the trace, and so on, in their ethical import.

The oppositions Critchley constructs in the work of Derrida, between the transcendental and the empirical, undecidability and the decision, ethics and politics, have brought us full circle, back to Critchley's opposition between Derrida and Levinas. I am not objecting to distinctions generally, which are necessary, but to the way in which these distinctions in Critchley become oppositions. And they become oppositions as soon as hierarchies are involved, and hierarchies are never innocent. For instance, are not the oppositions that Critchley constructs perhaps the result of his privileging the political worth of Levinas' work over Derrida's? This seems to be the case, particularly when Critchley argues that the political 'lack' of deconstruction needs to be supplemented by a Levinasian politics (Critchley 1999, 190, 236). Furthermore, he argues, 'this supplement is necessary in order to prevent deconstruction from becoming a fail-safe strategy for reading – an empty formalism – which, as Rorty would have it, is a means to private autonomy that is publicly useless and politically pernicious' (Critchley 1999, 237). If Critchley means here that deconstruction should be supplemented by Levinasian politics, he does not adequately demonstrate how a Levinasian politics might be enacted in and by deconstruction. This is not to suggest that deconstruction cannot or should not be supplemented, as if there were only one deconstruction, or as if deconstruction is a formula or method to follow. But, by arguing that deconstruction 'lacks' what he believes Levinas' politics can offer (Critchley 1999, 237), Critchley sets up a hierarchy where, in relation to Levinas, deconstruction is understood as deficient by comparison. It is this supposed hierarchy, in turn, that determines Critchley's opposition between Levinas and Derrida.

This move of Critchley's raises the following questions. First, if deconstruction does not, in fact, refuse *la politique* (the ontic, the factical), if undecidability does not reductively mean 'indecision', and if undecidability is a quasi-transcendental relation, then what remains of the oppositions that Critchley constructs within Derrida's work? Second, assuming these oppositions are problematic, then doesn't this problematic also put into question Critchley's argument that deconstruction 'lacks' political effectiveness, and thus reaches a political impasse? Finally, if there is a contamination of ethics and politics, and therefore of Derrida and Levinas, then is Critchley's reading of deconstruction as ethical too Levinasian? These questions will be addressed in the following section through a discussion of the theme of contamination between same and Other/other (and hence ethics and politics) in Derrida's 'Violence and Metaphysics' and *Adieu*. Perhaps in this discussion we will experience the quasi-transcendentality of Derrida's deconstructive double reading of Levinas' *Totality and Infinity*. Regardless, this reading will enable us to expose the distinction Critchley establishes between the ethics of Derrida's deconstruction and Levinasian politics.

Derrida's Reading of Levinas

In 'Violence and Metaphysics', Derrida asks the following in relation to Levinas:

> We are wondering about the meaning of a necessity: the necessity of lodging oneself within traditional conceptuality in order to destroy it. Why did this necessity finally impose itself upon Levinas? Is it an extrinsic necessity? Does it not touch upon only an instrument, only an 'expression', which can be put between quotation marks? Or does it hide, rather, some indestructible and unforeseeable resource of the Greek logos? Some unlimited power of envelopment, by which he who attempts to repel it would always already be *overtaken*? (Derrida 1995a, 111–12)

When Derrida argues that Levinas attempts to interrupt the metaphysical tradition but can only do so via the discourse, the language, of that tradition, he articulates the 'problem of closure' within Levinas' work as well as his own. These questions, then, are not traditional criticisms of Levinas. Rather, as Bernasconi suggests, Derrida's essay 'Violence and Metaphysics' poses questions to Levinas that, in Derrida' s view, are already "'put to us by

Levinas"' (Derrida, quoted in Bernasconi 1991, 154). It is in posing these questions that Derrida also argues that we 'will try to remain faithful to the themes and audacities of a thought – and this despite several parentheses and notes which will enclose our perplexity' (Derrida 1995a, 84). If, as Bernasconi suggests (1987, 124, 136), Derrida does not criticize Levinas in the traditional way, then what he does do is perform a double reading of Levinas' text *Totality and Infinity*. As a result, the difficulty but ingenuity of 'Violence and Metaphysics' lies in its 'speaking several languages and producing several texts at once' (Bernasconi 1988, 16, 17). Derrida's thoughts regarding ethics and alterity are intertwined to a considerable extent with Levinas', and this produces a simultaneous dance of separation and contamination between them. Thus, the questions raised about Levinas' thought are also self-reflective, and this leads Bernasconi to ask whether or not the double strategy employed is 'brought to Levinas or is it already to be found there?' (Bernasconi 1988, 19).

This double reading of Levinas' text by Derrida works in the following way: on the basis of his initial reading, Derrida argues that Levinas' thought attempts to break with the 'Greek domination of the Same and the One (other names for the light of Being and of the phenomenon)', in other words, with the philosophy and metaphysics which, in Western European culture, goes back to its Greek source, and is the origin of all oppression (ontological and transcendental) in the world (Derrida 1995a, 83). Derrida argues that Levinas wants to rectify the Greeks' disregard of the other precisely by seeking the other in 'the ethical relationship', which as 'a nonviolent relationship to the infinite as infinitely other, to the Other ... [is] capable of opening the space of transcendence and of liberating metaphysics' (Derrida 1995a, 83). That is, Levinas calls upon ethics (defined as the moment when the Other/other puts the same, the ego, into question) to liberate us from Greek metaphysics. Derrida claims that 'Levinas seeks to raise up [metaphysics] from its subordinate position and whose concept he seeks to restore in opposition to the entire tradition derived from Aristotle' (Derrida 1995a, 83). However, the only way Levinas can do this is by using what he rejects: the philosophical language inherited from the Greek *logos*. For Derrida, Levinas cannot possibly succeed in achieving the nonviolent 'opening toward the beyond of philosophical discourse' while he continues to use this language (Derrida 1995a, 110). This is because every term that Levinas uses – for instance, the Face, infinity, Identity, the same, the Other/ other, Ethics, Totality, Light, Metaphysics, and so on – is unable to escape metaphysical language and meaning (*logos*). Derrida gives us an example when he argues that 'Light' is one of the primary metaphors used by

Levinas, and that Levinas' notion of the Face is in many respects determined by this metaphysical metaphor: 'Who will ever dominate it, who will
ever pronounce its meaning without first being pronounced by it? What
language will ever escape it? How, for example, will the metaphysics of the
face as the *epiphany* of the other free itself of light? Light perhaps has no
opposite; if it does, it is certainly not night' (Derrida 1995a, 92).

Derrida questions Levinas on this issue. Yet, in what appears to be an
about-turn (but is in fact part of what Critchley would call Derrida's
deconstructive double reading), Derrida also discusses Levinas' reworking
of these terms and concepts, demonstrating how Levinas dissociates them
from traditional understandings given by phenomenology, ontology and
metaphysics. For Derrida, while Levinas may not be able to escape the
metaphysical language he uses, he can, and perhaps does, use them 'under
erasure' (Derrida 1995a, 112). 'Under erasure' is Derrida's term, however,
and even though Derrida reads Levinas in this way he also reveals that, in
fact, Levinas' style, his writing, his use of terms, articulates this erasure by
progressing through 'negations, and by negation against negation'. Moving
in this way, Levinas' writing is not, as Derrida argues, 'an "either this . . . or
that" but of a "neither this . . . nor that". The poetic force of metaphor is
often the trace of this rejected alternative' (Derrida 1995a, 90).

An example of this negation in Levinas is his use of the term 'metaphysics'.
For Levinas, ethics as he defines it is the true metaphysics, and Greek
metaphysics (the *logos*) is false. This is not a denial of the latter, nor is it a
contradiction, because Levinas reworks an old term and uses 'tradition's
words, rub[s] them like a rusty and devalued old coin [so that] one can say
[for instance] that true exteriority is nonexteriority without being interiority,
and one can write by crossing out, by crossing out what already has been
crossed out' (Derrida 1995a, 112).

Derrida questions Levinas' use of philosophical language on the one
hand, and he shows how Levinas reworks that language through negation
on the other; a negation which we could argue entails violence (putting
under erasure therefore involves a violence of sorts). Yet, in a double
reading of a double reading, Derrida proceeds to further question Levinas'
negations and the implications it has for his ethics. Derrida argues that
Levinas is seeking the 'essence' of the ethical relation, not trying to
determine or propose moral laws and rules. However, Derrida ponders
what this essence of ethics 'is' given that Levinas does not offer a theory.
Importantly, then, what is in question for Derrida is an 'Ethics of Ethics'. He
adds, '[i]n this case, it is perhaps serious that this Ethics of Ethics can
occasion neither a determined ethics nor determined laws without negating

and forgetting itself. Moreover, is this Ethics of Ethics beyond all laws? Is it not the Law of laws?' (Derrida 1995a, 111). If the essence of Ethics is the relation between the same and Other, a relation structured by absolute alterity (or infinitely other), and if we can only think this essence in and through philosophical discourse, then how is it possible to think the 'essence' of Ethics, or the absolute alterity (infinitely other)? That is, if absolute alterity cannot be thought except through the language of philosophical discourse (metaphysics), then can absolute alterity (as that which exceeds language), actually be thought? A few pages on, an answer to these questions starts to emerge when Derrida proposes that absolute alterity or '[t]he infinitely Other would not be what it is, other, if it was a positive infinity, and if it did not maintain within itself the negativity of the indefinite, of the *aperion* [the infinite, boundless and limitless]' (Derrida 1995a, 114).

If there is a sense, a thought of the infinitely other, of absolute alterity, it is because the 'other cannot be what it is, infinitely other, except in finitude and mortality (mine *and* its). It is such as soon as it comes into language, of course, and only then, and only if the word *other* has a meaning – but has not Levinas taught us that there is no thought before language?' (Derrida 1995a, 114–15). When Derrida contends that the other (infinite other, absolute alterity) cannot be what it is except in finitude and mortality, he is arguing that any purity of the other is so precisely because it is contaminated by the finite, by Others. Thus, Bennington explains that 'Derrida's construal of alterity as *always less than absolute* in fact constitutes a thought of the other as *more other than the absolute other*' (Bennington, 2000, 44). In a quasi-transcendental logic, the contamination of the infinite by the finite (by mortality) radicalizes and extends Levinas' thought on separation and exteriority (that is, the difference between the same and Other). Derrida is not arguing against Levinas' theory of separation, but posits separation in contamination. Derrida elaborates on this in 'Violence and Metaphysics' by discussing Levinas' critique of Husserl on the other/Other.

This critique is part of a larger disagreement with what Levinas sees as the modern philosophers of ontology (Heidegger and Hegel in addition to Husserl). Without going into the details of Derrida's reading of Levinas' quarrel with Heidegger and Hegel, suffice to say that Levinas dissociates his ethics as first philosophy from the notion of ethics as it is determined by the Greek tradition of metaphysics to which Husserl, Heidegger and Hegel belong (Levinas 1996, 42–3). For Derrida, Levinas' 'thought calls upon the ethical relationship – a nonviolent relationship to the infinite as infinitely other, to the Other – as the only one capable of opening the space of transcendence and of liberating metaphysics' (Derrida 1995a, 83). Given this, Levinas argues that Husserl, Heidegger and Hegel, in their ontological theories, perpetuate the Greek domination of the same (totality) by disregarding the other (Levinas, 1996, 42–3). Therefore, according to Derrida, Levinas argues that 'by making the other, notably in the *Cartesian Meditations*, the ego's phenomenon, constituted by analogical appresentation on the bases of belonging to the ego's own sphere, Husserl allegedly missed the infinite alterity of the other, reducing it to the same' (Derrida 1995a, 123). Analogical appresentation means that we only ever have indirect perceptual presentation of an object or Other (another person). That is, an object or Other is mediated in and through the direct presentation of something else, for example, the presentation of the 'rear through the frontal aspect, or of other minds through their bodies' (Spiegelberg, 1978, 712). To put it another way, we can only see and experience the Other in part, and although we are not presented with the back of another's head (the rear) while simultaneously looking at the face (frontal), it is through the presentation of the face (front) that we can fill in the gap by imaging the person, the Other, as a whole. To do this is to make the Other an alter ego, which is why, according to Derrida, for Levinas, analogical appresentation neutralizes absolute alterity (Derrida 1995a, 123).

It is precisely on the basis of analogical appresentation that Derrida is able to defend Husserl,[12] arguing that, in *The Cartesian Meditations*, Husserl goes out of his way to describe how the other as alterity is 'presented to me' as 'originary nonpresence'. As Derrida points out,

> it is impossible to encounter the alter ego (in the very form of the encounter described by Levinas), impossible to respect it in experience and in language, if this other, in its alterity, does not *appear* for an ego (in general). One could neither speak, nor have any sense of the totally other, if there was not a phenomenon of the totally other, or evidence of the totally other as such. (Derrida 1995a, 123)

This 'evidence' is not a reduction of the Other to the same. Rather, because the Other can only be presented 'to me' (the ego) through analogical appresentation, this respects, and indeed confirms, Levinas' notion of separation between the same and the Other. That is, Derrida argues that it is only through analogical appresentation that the Other is in fact other, because 'if I attained to the other immediately and originally, silently, in communion with the other's own experience, the other would cease to be the other' (Derrida 1995a, 124). Here, Derrida is radicalizing Levinas' notion of separation and exteriority through Husserl's thinking on analogical appresentation. The repercussion of this is that the infinitely other is so only as it appears in the Ego, and the Other as alter ego. That is, the infinite is within the finite, alterity in the same and, as Bennington notes, this quasi-transcendental logic of Derrida's moves beyond Levinas' attempt to situate 'the ethical as such as "first philosophy", against ontology' (Bennington, 2000, 45). Derrida goes on to argue that the Other/other is not absolutely exterior to the same, therefore the same is 'not a totality closed in upon itself' (Derrida 1995a, 126). This makes clearer what Bennington meant when he argued that Derrida's notion of alterity is less than absolute. Derrida puts it this way: 'the other is absolutely other only if he is an ego, that is, in a certain way, if he is the same as I. Inversely, the other as *res* is simultaneously less other (not absolutely other) and less "the same" than I. Simultaneously more and less other, which means, once more, that the absolute alterity is the same' (Derrida 1995a, 127). If alterity is (in) the same, the same cannot be 'presence/present', therefore the same is also Other/other. This being the case, same and Other can never be reduced to one another, and can never become 'one and the same'. For reduction to be possible both the same and the Other would have to be simultaneously present to themselves in space and time. However, analogical appresentation ensures that this cannot occur. Thus, the same (as it appears as the ego, or subject) is always 'singular'.

In *The Gift of Death*, Derrida links singularity to alterity, and he encapsulates this link by the phrase *tout autre est tout autre*, which is translated as 'Every other (one) is every (bit) other' (Derrida 1995b, 82). For Derrida, '*tout autre est tout autre* signifies that every other is singular, that every one is a singularity, which also means that every one is each one, a proposition that seals the contract between universality and the exception of singularity' (Derrida 1995b, 87). That is, alterity as singularity haunts the Other (alter ego) and the same (ego). This does not mean that the singular, or singularity, is an essence in the humanist sense, rather the phrase *tout autre est tout autre* 'introduces the principle of the most irreducible heterology' (Derrida 1995b, 83). Derrida explains this heterology more fully in an interview with Jean-Luc Nancy, when he argues that singularity 'is not the individuality of a thing that would be identical to itself'. Instead, '[i]t is singularity that dislocates or divides itself in gathering itself together to answer to the other, whose call somehow precedes its own identification with itself, for this call I can *only* answer, have already answered, even if I think I am answering "no"'

(Derrida and Nancy 1991, 100–1). These remarks on singularity make apparent Derrida's ethical closeness to Levinas, in that they confirm Levinas' notion that the ethical relation (face-to-face) is dissymetrical.[13]

For Derrida, Levinas' ethical relation is dissymetrical because of the Other's transcendence, which is evident when the alterity of the Other calls the same into question and demands obligation. But being obligated is not a voluntary act by the 'I'. Rather, one is always and already obligated. Levinas explains that a 'calling into question of the same – which cannot occur within the egoist spontaneity of the same – is brought about by the other. We name this calling into question of my spontaneity by the presence of the Other ethics' (Levinas 1996, 43). Thus, '[t]he Other who dominates me in his transcendence is . . . the stranger, the widow, and the orphan, to whom I am obligated' (Levinas 1996, 215). So transcendence is the separation between the same and the Other, which, through a calling into question, is a dissymetrical (non-equal) separation. Transcendence is the infinitely other, it is alterity.

However, if Derrida confirms the dissymmetry evident in Levinas' notion of separation, he also draws out its implications, radicalizing Levinas further by arguing that it is only because of the 'symmetry' between same and Other that dissymmetry is possible. In 'Violence and Metaphysics', Derrida goes on to argue that the 'movement of transcendence toward the other, as invoked by Levinas, would have no meaning if it did not bear within it, as one of its essential meanings, that in my ipseity I know myself to be other for the other' (Derrida 1995a, 126). That is, as we saw in our discussion of Husserl, there is symmetry between the same and the Other because the Other is another Other, another ego. And this is why, Derrida argues, the Other, as face, can command, understand and speak to me. Or as Derrida formulates it, '[d]issymmetry itself would be impossible without this symmetry . . . This dissymmetry is an *economy* in a new sense; a sense which would probably be intolerable to Levinas. Despite the logical absurdity of this formulation, this economy is the transcendental symmetry of two empirical asymmetries' (Derrida 1995a, 126).

This radicalization of Levinas' notion of separation has implications for Levinas' ethics. The implications are illuminated in Derrida's discussion of the 'third party' (le tiers) in *Adieu*, where he argues that the dissymetrical relation is always already inhabited by the third party.[14] Derrida points out that the notion of the third is present in Levinas' *Totality and Infinity* before it is developed further in *Otherwise than Being* (Derrida 1999a, 110). In the former book Levinas construes the third as follows:

> The third party looks at me in the eyes of the Other . . . It is not
> that there first would be the face, and then the being it manifests or
> expresses would concern itself with justice; the epiphany of the face
> qua face opens humanity . . . The presence of the face, the infinity of
> the other, is a destituteness, a presence of the third party (that is, of the
> whole of humanity which looks at us), and a command that commands
> commanding. (Levinas 1996, 213)

In the face-to-face relation, and hence, in the eyes of the Other, we see the
third party, another Other, as well as humanity as a whole. It is because of
this 'third' that, for Derrida, the ethicality of the face-to-face is never pure
and is never simply a relation between the same and the Other (a symmetrical
relation in its dissymmetry). The third party introduces multiplicity into
this dual relation, and thus, there is contamination. While Levinas
acknowledges this later in *Otherwise Than Being*, by demonstrating that the
third party introduces 'justice', and thus politics, Derrida argues that
Levinas in *Totality and Infinity* wants to keep pure the limit between the face-
to-face (the ethical relation) and the third party (politics).[15] However,
Derrida argues that the 'limit' (or demarcation) between ethics and politics
cannot be maintained as '[t]he border between the ethical and the political
here loses for good the indivisible simplicity of a limit . . . the determinability
of this limit was never pure, and it never will be' (Derrida 1999a, 99). As
Derrida points out, not only is the purity of the face-to-face relation cast
into doubt by the third party, but the ethicality of the face-to-face relation
is, from the first, political (Bennington 2000, 45).

As we have seen in 'Violence and Metaphysics', and it is apparent also in
Adieu, Derrida sees Levinas' notion of separation as an ethical relation, a
relation Levinas renames 'metaphysics'. Derrida argues that because 'it
opens itself to – so as to welcome – the irruption of the idea of infinity in the
finite, this metaphysics is an experience of hospitality' (Derrida 1999a, 46).
Thus when Levinas in *Totality and Infinity* shows how an openness to, and
welcome of, the face occurs, this is for Derrida a discursive logic conveying
the notion of 'hospitality' (even though Levinas rarely uses the word). And
it is in this way, Derrida suggests, that Levinas 'bequeaths to us an immense
treatise of *hospitality*', because 'hospitality becomes the very name of what
opens itself to the face' (Derrida 1999a, 21).

However, Derrida asks Levinas what the relationship is between hospitality
as ethics (as first philosophy), and the hospitality of rights, laws and rules:
in other words, hospitality as politics (de Vries 2001, 174). In Derrida's
words, 'how can this infinite and thus unconditional hospitality, this

hospitality at the opening of ethics, be regulated in a particular political or juridical practice? How might it, in turn, regulate a particular politics or law?' (Derrida 1999a, 48). The quasi-transcendental logic of Derrida's answer, and his interpretation of Levinas, is that both hospitality as ethics and hospitality as politics enable each other through perjury [*parjure*] (de Vries 2001, 174). It is through this notion of perjury that Derrida draws out the implications of the notion of hospitality evident in Levinas' work. That is, it is in Derrida's notion of perjury that the limit (or demarcation) between the face-to-face relation (ethics) and the third party (justice, and thus politics) is revealed as contaminated. (Contamination is not simply a blurring of borders, which shows the impossibility of the purity of the ethical relation but, simultaneously, it is what allows for the possibility of purity (Bennington, 2000, 40). Without impurity no purity could exist.)

Taking up the theme of the 'economy of violence' that he articulates in 'Violence and Metaphysics', Derrida, in *Adieu*, argues that the purity of the ethical is one of violence because it becomes impossible in this dual face-to-face relation between the same and the Other to distinguish between 'good and evil, love and hate'. Therefore, Derrida wonders whether or not Levinas is actually 'trying to take into account this hypothesis of a violence in the pure and immediate ethics of the face to face' by insisting that the third (justice) is necessary? (Derrida 1999a, 32). However, Derrida argues that the third party is also a violence, one that perhaps, and paradoxically, protects the purity of the ethical. That is, the violence of the third is so because it enacts perjury. Meaning, the engagement with the Other, requires unconditional respect or fidelity – in and through my responsibility for the Other – but this is betrayed or perjured (made an infidelity) by the mediation of the third:

> Silent, passive, painful, but inevitable, such perjury is not accidental and secondary, but is as originary as the experience of the face. Justice would begin with this perjury . . . Henceforth, in the operation of justice one can no longer distinguish between fidelity to oath and the perjury of false witness, and even before this, between betrayal and betrayal, always more than one betrayal. (Derrida 1999a, 33–4)

So how does this violence of the third, in its perjury, protect the purity of the ethical? In answer Derrida argues that 'Good, Justice, Love, Faith – and perfectibility, etc.' are always at risk of being perjured and perverted (by bad intentions, bad will, by 'the worst') (Derrida 1999a, 35), but that this is necessary if there is to be the possibility of the goodness of unconditional hospitality (the purity of ethics). That is, perjury is inevitable if there is to be a 'chance of letting the other come, the *yes* of the other no less than the *yes* to the other' (Derrida 1999a, 35). Hospitality would cease to mean what it does if there was not inhospitality, perjury, and so on. This yes to the other is the 'welcome' of the Other as stranger. Thus, it is a yes to the possibility that the other/Other is the 'worst': bringing the worst intentions, bringing pain, destruction and violence (Derrida 1999a, 111–12; Bennington 2000, 42–3).

Bennington elucidates Derrida's notion of perjury in relation to the 'non-ethical' when he explains: 'Ethics, then, is ethical only to the extent that it is originarily comprised or contaminated by the non-ethical . . . The non-ethical opening of ethics . . . consists in just this: that the *chance* of ethics (i.e. its necessary possibility as non-necessary) lies in its hospitality to the possibility that the event to come is the worst.' And this 'worst' is brought by 'the other, the stranger, the *arrivant*' (Bennington 2000, 42–3). This worse is the pervertability of ethics. This notion of perjury, then, may perhaps clarify the meaning of Derrida's phrase 'non-ethical opening of ethics' with which this chapter began (Derrida 1976, 140). So not only is the 'non-ethical' the other of speech and language, that is, an otherness as archewriting, dissimulation, detour, difference, and so on, it is also 'the other' as Other who potentially encapsulates the 'worst' (pervertability/perjury), as violence that can be done to me (Bennington 2000, 43; Derrida 1999a, 111–12). Both senses of 'the Other/other' here overlap and haunt each other. Therefore, the Other/other not only haunts, but in its haunting perverts and interrupts the metaphysical determination of ethics (ethics as presence), leaving Derrida to demonstrate that, in being haunted by the 'non-ethical', ethics exceeds its traditional metaphysical-philosophical determination. Or, to put it another way, there is contamination between the ethical and non-ethical, which complicates the delineation of traditional metaphysical ethics, as that which is non-violent and brings order and happiness. As we will discover in Chapter 2, this ethical order (another form of violence) is constructed in and through what Nietzsche calls a language of antithesis. Given this, Critchley explains that for Derrida 'ethics is no ethics at all and is not even worthy to bear the name. Indeed, Derrida himself wonders whether the title "ultra-ethics" might not be a more fitting description of his own and Levinas' projects' (Critchley 1999, 18).

Having said this, the contamination between the same and the Other – evident in Derrida's radicalization of separation in 'Violence and Metaphysics' – also complicates Critchley's definition of the political as simply factical and empirical. For Critchley, in Levinas there is a passage from ethics to politics (Critchley 1999, 227, 233). But while Critchley suggests that this passage is 'not a passage of time, but rather a doubling of discourse' (Critchley 1999,

227), he contrasts this 'passage' in Levinas with Derrida, arguing that Derrida is incapable of making this 'passage from undecidability to the decision, from responsibility to questioning, from deconstruction to critique, from ethics to politics' (Critchley 1999, 236). However, this chapter so far has argued against Critchley's position in a number of ways: first, undecidability is not in opposition to decision; second, Derrida's radicalization of separation reveals the same and Other to be contaminated; and finally, the third party (politics) haunts the face-to-face (ethics), so that there is a contamination between the face-to-face and the third party and vice versa. This contamination is not a denial of the separation (as difference) between ethics and politics, but makes separation as difference possible.

On the basis of the radicalization of Levinas' theory of separation and exteriority, Derrida argues that '[e]thics enjoins a politics and a law: this dependence and the direction of this conditional derivation are as irreversible as they are unconditional' (Derrida 1999a, 115). Given Derrida's position here, it is obvious that one of the differences between Derrida and Critchley is the role they assign to politics, not only in Levinas' work, but generally. To reiterate, then: for Critchley, 'politics' is the empirical, the factical event of the decision. That is, by privileging *la politique* (politics) over *le politique*, he implies that *la politique* is a 'unified' empirical event only. Furthermore, by constructing an opposition between *la politique* and ethics, Critchley is able to oppose ethics and politics in Derrida's work, and this enables him to argue that deconstruction, while it is ethical (understood in the Levinasian sense), cannot make the move from ethics to politics in the way Levinas can (via justice) (Critchley 1999, 226). For Critchley, deconstruction needs to be 'supplemented' by a 'Levinasian politics of ethical difference' (Critchley 1999, xiv, 236). In suggesting that Derrida needs to be supplemented by Levinas, Critchley neglects the congruencies between Derrida's and Levinas' approaches to justice. The congruencies and differences between Derrida's and Levinas' thinking on justice will be explored further in the next chapter.

At this point we should note that for Derrida, unlike Critchley, there is not simply 'one' politics, one empiricism. Politics, like ethics, is never 'pure', as Derrida argues in the following passage:

[T]he political or juridical *content* that is thus assigned remains undetermined, still to be determined beyond knowledge, beyond all presentation, all concepts, all possible intuition, in a singular way, in the speech and the responsibility *taken* by each person, in each situation, and on the basis of an analysis that is each time unique – unique and infinite, unique but *a priori* exposed to substitution, unique and yet general, interminable in spite of the urgency of the decision. (Derrida 1999a, 115)

Like Levinas, Derrida does not offer an ethical model or theory, and given that he puts into doubt the purity of the ethical face-to-face relation (a doubt already latent in Levinas), it would be just as troubling to offer a political model. But this does not mean, as Critchley argues, that deconstruction excludes *la politique*, thus privileging, and limiting itself to, the realm of *le politique* (the realm of the transcendental in Critchley's account). Rather, for Derrida, as the above quote makes clear, the political event (*la politique*) is always singular, and thus is always yet to be determined: political action (which Critchley associates with 'decision') is determined by the singular context and thus is always already contaminated by undecidability. That is, the political/ethical for Derrida is structured by a quasi-transcendental 'logic': both politics and ethics are singular/unique and universal/plural at the same time (Derrida 1999a, 120). This, singular-plural, or quasi-transcendentality, undermines the arguable distinction Critchley tends to make between metaphysical determination(s) of ethics (represented in Critchley's critique of Hillis Miller) and Levinasian ethics discussed in the previous section. Derrida's reading of Levinas implies that the contamination of the purity of the ethical (in the Levinasian sense) by what Derrida calls the non-ethical, or by the other in ethics (revealed in and through perjury, or archewriting), actually casts doubt on the absolute and thus universal status of metaphysical forms of ethics. That is, if the purity of the ethical relation between the same and Other in face-to-face relations is contaminated by the third party, and if the purity of this ethical face-to-face relation guarantees the singularity of the political event/act (which is generally prescribed by laws and rules) then, by analogy, metaphysical, and thus universal, determinations of ethics (or the generality of the law) are contaminated by the singularity of the political 'event': since universality is contaminated by singularity, universality is put into question. The consequences of this contamination of metaphysical (universal) forms of ethics by the singular ethical and political relation will be taken up in more detailed discussion under the heading of 'ethics under erasure' in chapters 3 and 4.

Dancing with Derrida

Is Critchley's reading of the ethical significance of deconstruction too Levinasian? Let us accept Critchley's, following Derrida's, argument that the text, or writing, is inhabited by archewriting, which is 'the opening of ethics' within the text (or in Critchley's terms, 'clôtural reading'). Let us also agree that the type of ethics that is opened involves the infinitely other, or Transcendence, which is the 'ethics of ethics' for Levinas. Under these conditions, Critchley's reinscription of Derrida's deconstruction is *not* too Levinasian. After all, Derrida is convinced by Levinas' articulation of the ego and the same, same and other: 'If one is not convinced by these initial propositions authorizing the equation of the ego and same, one never will be' (Derrida 1995a, 94).

Having said this, Critchley's reading *is* too Levinasian when he suggests that both the ethical and political dimensions of Derrida's deconstruction must be supplemented by Levinas. In arguing this, Critchley privileges Levinas' thinking on ethics and politics above Derrida's. In addition, he does not seem to take full account of Derrida's influence on Levinas, and pays insufficient attention to the congruencies and differences between them, which will be discussed in detail in Chapter 2. For instance, as argued earlier, for Critchley, archewriting and undecidability (or deconstruction in general) are significant, but only insofar as deconstruction enables what Critchley calls 'clôtural reading', and only to the extent that its ethical demand can be read through Levinas' ethics. However, by not acknowledging the *congruencies* between Derrida and Levinas' notion of the 'politics of ethical difference', Critchley is led to argue that deconstruction cannot move from the ethical (the transcendental realm) to the political (empirical realm), and thus that deconstruction is politically ineffective. At the same time, Critchley does not acknowledge the *differences* between Derrida and Levinas, and therefore fails to take account of Derrida's radical development of Levinas' ethical/political position. Without denying the obvious influence of Levinas on Derrida, it is important to recall that 'Violence and Metaphysics' contributed significantly to the insights in *Totality and Infinity* being reformulated in *Otherwise than Being*. As Bernasconi argues, when Levinas in *Otherwise than Being* 'allows that his language is a thematization, he is doing more than repeating a point he had already conceded in *Totality and Infinity*. He is now entering into a dialogue in which Derrida is his main interlocutor' (Bernasconi 1991, 154).[16]

In this sense there is a dance of separation and contamination, of congruence and difference, between Derrida and Levinas. And what this interplay, or 'dialogue', between them reveals is that Derrida, through his discussion of analogical appresentation in 'Violence and Metaphysics', draws out the contamination between ethics and politics, same and Other/other, that is latent in Levinas' *Totality and Infinity*. Thus, to suggest, as Critchley does, that Levinas makes the move *from* ethics *to* politics which deconstruction cannot make (despite recognizing that in Levinas politics begins with ethics), is to reify an opposition that deconstruction complicates. The aporetic quasi-transcendentality of deconstruction questions precisely the purity of the separation or limit between ethics and politics that is the basis of Critchley's critique. Following the logic – or more aptly the (il)logic – of deconstruction, then, we can say that ethics is already politics and vice versa. This is not to deny the separation between them: after all, there would be no contamination if there were not separation (which is ontologically distinct from opposition). Given this, the question of whether or not deconstruction can make the move from ethics to politics is somewhat redundant.

Thus, Critchley, while he privileges the Levinasian ethical aspect of deconstruction, and argues that deconstruction opens ethics, does not place enough importance on the quasi-transcendentality of deconstruction that contaminates ethics and politics. To put it another way: in deconstruction, via Derrida's notion of perjury, the contamination of ethics and politics that Levinas begins to articulate via the third party in *Totality and Infinity* is drawn out and developed. That is, not only does archewriting, or 'the other' (alterity), open ethics in Derrida's work (discussed by Critchley in terms of clôtural reading) but, building on 'Violence and Metaphysics', Derrida, in *Adieu*, argues that what opens ethics is a 'quasi-transcendental or originary, indeed, pre-originary, perjury' (Derrida 1999a, 34). Although *Adieu* was published after Critchley's book, it is in *Adieu* that Derrida confirms, through 'perjury', the contamination between ethics and politics, and Levinasian ethics and ontology, initially outlined in 'Violence and Metaphysics'. Yet despite the contamination between these oppositions which problematizes oppositionality per se, 'Violence and Metaphysics' reveals that the quasi-transcendental logic of contamination respects, not opposition, but separation (difference). From this we can conclude that when Derrida argues that Levinas' thought is not that of an '"either this . . . or that", but of a "neither this . . . nor that"' (Derrida 1995a, 90), this is as valid, if not more, for Derrida's deconstruction, and his thought generally. In 'Violence and Metaphysics', the quasi-transcendental logic that casts doubt on the distinction (as opposition) between ethics, politics and ontology, answers the question Derrida poses at the end of his essay:

Are we Jews? Are we Greeks? We live in the difference between the Jew and the Greek . . . Are we Greeks? Are we Jews? But who, we? Are we (not a chronological, but pre-logical question) *first* Jews or *first* Greeks? . . . And what is the legitimacy, what is the meaning of the *copula* in this proposition from perhaps the most Hegelian of modern novelists: 'Jewgreek is greekjew. Extremes meet'? (Derrida 1995a, 153)[17]

Perhaps, in this questioning, Derrida is also referring to the 'contamination' between Levinas' Jewish but also Greek thinking, which Derrida argues is most apparent when Levinas' thought coincides with Husserl, Heidegger and Hegel. And *perhaps* Derrida is also referring to the distinction Levinas (as a Jewish philosopher) makes between his ethics as first philosophy and the ontological thought of those modern 'Greek' (but also German) philosophers Husserl, Heidegger and Hegel (Jewgerman, Germanjew, or, Jewgentile, Gentilejew, perhaps?) John Llewellyn is right to claim that Derrida, while acknowledging 'the idea that extremes meet', is by no means saying that extremes meet in some neutral, middle ground: 'for example, a higher or deeper synthesis [*Aufhebung*] such as is posited by the aforementioned Hegelianism' (Llewellyn 2002, 143).

Derrida, as we have seen, thematizes the quasi-transcendental logic in his discussion of ethics, politics and ontology in relation to Levinas' *Totality and Infinity*. In 'Violence and Metaphysics', Derrida also enacts this logic through a double reading of a double reading of Levinas. Because of this, Derrida intentionally and continually moves in and out of the contamination and separation between his own and Levinas' thinking. Consequently, as Bernasconi argues, Derrida deconstructs the ethical and in doing so 'enacts the ethical' in textuality itself (Bernasconi 1987, 125). The thematization and enactment of the quasi-transcendentality of deconstruction in 'Violence and Metaphysics' casts doubt upon Critchley's argument that deconstruction does not move from ethics to politics and that, therefore, deconstruction reaches a political impasse.

Given that Critchley associates politics with 'the decision' (as action), given also that he opposes this politics to ethics (so that politics becomes fixed and unified into a decisive empirical act), then *should* and *would* we want deconstruction to be able to make this move? Deconstruction would cease to be deconstruction if it *did* make the move Critchley suggests. As Bennington argues in relation to the political demand made of Derrida: 'if Derrida were ever to simply *answer* to that demand, to provide an answer which that demand could hear and accept, then his own thinking could safely be located in the metaphysical tradition he has always claimed to outflank' (Bennington 2000, 23). Moreover, if politics as a pure empirical act is deconstructed in and through Derrida's discussion of perjury and its production by the third party, then, as Niall Lucy observes, 'the question . . . arises as to where a presumption of Derrida's lack of any real political

conviction comes from, since such a "lack" cannot be found "in" his writing'
(Lucy 1999, 92). Thus, if deconstruction 'enacts the ethical' in textuality as
Bernasconi suggests (Bernasconi 1987, 125), and if the ethical is
contaminated by politics, as Derrida argues in 'Violence and Metaphysics'
and *Adieu*, then so too is the political enacted in textuality and reading.

If Critchley's reading of Derrida's deconstruction is too Levinasian in the
way I have argued, then is his reading adequate? As part of his justification,
Critchley claims that Derrida subscribes to everything Levinas thinks, albeit
differently. (Once again, although Critchley claims that 'the two thinkers
are evidently not identical' (Critchley 1999, 12), he does not elaborate on
the difference in their positions except negatively when he argues that
Derrida's work needs to be supplemented by Levinas' politics.) However,
this justification is too simple, because Derrida while he subscribes to
Levinas' ethics also radicalizes Levinas (as Derrida's discussion of analogical
appresentation in 'Violence and Metaphysics' attests). That is, while
Derrida is often linked to Levinas' ethical position, his radicalization makes
it impossible for deconstruction to be subsumed into Levinasian ethics, or
simply supplemented by a Levinasian 'politics of ethical difference'. Rather,
this radicalization of Levinas' ethics opens up other ways of reading the
ethical significance of Derrida's work. This is because the quasi-
transcendental (non)structure of deconstruction reveals the influences of
other philosophers besides Levinas on Derrida's work. The best example
of this is Derrida's neologism 'différance', where he outlines in his article
'La Difference' all the formulations of difference articulated by Saussure,
Freud, Nietzsche, Heidegger and Levinas. Thus, in the same way that
Derrida's voice, his congruence with and difference from Levinas, is heard
in the interplay between his discussion on Levinas and Husserl's notion of
the Other/other in 'Violence and Metaphysics', différance has developed
from the nexus between 'the difference of forces in Nietzsche, Saussure's
principle of semiological difference, differing as the possibility of [neurone]
facilitation, impression and delayed effect in Freud, difference as the
irreducibility of the trace of the other in Levinas, and the ontic-ontological
difference in Heidegger' (Derrida 1973, 130; see also Bernasconi 1988,
13). This suggests that there are other philosophers through which it is
possible to 'read' Derrida's work in relation to the ethical. Levinas is not
the only way.

Given this, Chapter 2 focuses on Derrida's formulation of difference via
Nietzsche (rather than Heidegger, Saussure or Freud) because, as
elaborated in the Introduction, many of the post-modern and/or nihilistic
interpretations of Derrida's work are based on an unjustified reduction of

Derrida to Nietzsche. Chapter 2, then, argues that Derrida's intersection with Nietzsche, through his articulation of différance, does not lead to some form of 'infinite undifferentiated textuality', and that neither Nietzsche nor Derrida are nihilistic and unethical, as some critics argue. Chapter 2 attempts to neutralize these accusations by contesting them at the site (the work of Nietzsche) on which they are largely based. This means rethinking the ethical evident in, and enabled by, deconstruction, through Nietzsche *as well as* Levinas. In particular, one of the aims of the next chapter is to rethink ethical (im)possibilities that are revealed by deconstruction, by combining Nietzsche and Levinas, and thus attempts to take a different direction to Critchley. Therefore with Nietzsche, Chapter 2 elaborates another, or different, way (but certainly not the only way) of thinking the ethical in and through Derrida's deconstruction.

Chapter 2

Ethical (Im)possibilities

But the relation to the singularity of the other also passes through the universality of the law

–*Derrida*, Politics of Friendship, 276

*

When talking about a deconstructive process of writing in 'The Ends of Man', Derrida argues that 'what we need, perhaps, as Nietzsche said, is a change of "style"; and if there is style, Nietzsche reminded us, it must be *plural*' (Derrida 1986, 135). On his debt to Nietzsche, Derrida remains elusive, although it is obvious that there are many manifestations of Nietzsche's presence throughout Derrida's writings.[1] As this quote implies, if there is not a similarity of style between Derrida and Nietzsche's texts, there are some definite congruencies between their modes of interrogation and enquiry. Although their arguments are far more intricate than a discussion of their congruencies can outline, this chapter will argue that Nietzsche's concept of 'perspectivism' has affinities with Derrida's concept of 'différance'.

The first aim of this chapter, then, will be to argue that in 'perspectivism' and 'différance' a notion of 'play' deconstructs the traditional concept of the subject but, in doing so, allows for ethical possibilities. This will be the focus of the first two sections. Section one, entitled 'The Subject as Play', argues that in Nietzsche's 'perspectivism' and Derrida's 'différance', there is a refusal to hypostasize the subject, and that this refusal is evidenced in both Nietzsche and Derrida's playing with the 'proper name'. The second section, entitled 'Ethical Possibilities' argues against those critical readings of Nietzsche and Derrida which, because of their switching of styles and their manipulation of the subject, label their writings irresponsible and nihilistic. Instead, this chapter argues that it is precisely because of their subversive techniques that ethical possibilities are generated. The second aim is dealt with in the third, fourth and fifth sections, '(Im)possibility', 'The (Im)possibility of Justice', and 'Nietzsche↔Derrida↔Levinas', respectively. Here it is argued that Derrida's notion of impossibility runs through possibility, and therefore allows for an elaboration of 'ethical possibilities' discussed in section two. This notion of (im)possibility also informs Derrida's discussion of 'justice', a discussion which reflects both Nietzsche's and Levinas' influence. Given this, the chapter concludes that there is a contamination between Nietzsche and Levinas in Derrida's elaboration of 'justice', and it is in this way that my argument diverges from Simon Critchley's ethical interpretation of deconstruction.

The Subject as Play

Let's begin with a passage from *Beyond Good and Evil* that epitomizes Nietzsche's view of metaphysics as it also sets the scene for an understanding of his concept of the 'subject as play'. He argues that metaphysicians 'concern themselves' with a knowledge which they believe to be, or have at least 'baptized', 'the truth'. However, Nietzsche challenges this concept of 'truth', defined by metaphysicians, as *'the faith in antithetical values'*. He argues that 'it may be doubted, firstly whether there exists any antitheses at all, and secondly whether these popular evaluations and value-antitheses, on which the metaphysicians have set their seal, are not perhaps merely foreground valuations, merely provisional perspectives' (Nietzsche 1986, 16). This is fighting talk! We have not only a challenge to the role of antithesis in constituting metaphysical knowledge, but Nietzsche then goes on to argue that the faith in antithetical values is simply one of many interpretations and evaluations. That is, he is arguing against 'the truth' as constituted through antithetical knowledge and, instead, puts forth his idea of the plurality of meaning, which is generated by multiple interpretations: what he calls 'perspectivism'.[2] In this challenge to metaphysical language, Nietzsche undermines the concept of the humanist subject. For Nietzsche, the subject perpetuated by metaphysics is a subject that is constructed by antithetical language. Even the title of his book, *Beyond Good and Evil*, hints at the dichotomous structure of Western metaphysics. But the title also suggests that the concept of the humanist subject, *itself* structured by 'antithetical values', is a subject that evaluates and acts prescriptively and normatively. Implicitly then, Nietzsche attacks the prescriptive ethical evaluations perpetuated by this antithesis, and the second section of this chapter will develop this in more detail.

Meanwhile, in *The Will To Power* Nietzsche declares that the 'world with which we are concerned is false, i.e., is not a fact . . . it is "in flux", as something in a state of becoming, as a falsehood always changing but never getting near the truth: for – there is no "truth"' (Nietzsche 1968, 330). There is no absolute truth but only interpretation and evaluation, and this idea of multiple interpretations through which the subject as a state of becoming appears permeates his writings. Nietzsche is claiming that the subject is not 'fixed' but in its changing, its shifting, its fleetingness, is perpetually becoming. To demonstrate this, Nietzsche 'performs' this becoming by contaminating the boundary between content and style. In this sense, content cannot be separated from Nietzsche's style, which in his writings are actually many styles, because '[g]ood style *in itself* he says is 'a piece of pure folly', mere 'idealism', on a par with the 'beautiful *in itself*', the 'good *in itself*', the 'thing, *in itself*' (Nietzsche 1992, 44). If there is no absolute truth, only interpretation and evaluation, then this concept of multiple styles cannot be separated from his concept of the subject. Referring to himself in *Ecce Homo* Nietzsche declares, 'the multiplicity of inner states is in my case extraordinary, there exists in my case the possibility of many styles' (Nietzsche 1992, 44). In considering himself extraordinary, is Nietzsche here setting himself up as the Overman over and against the herd or the norm, and/or is he extrapolating on subjectivity overall? For Nietzsche, subjectivity more generally is constituted in and through multiple interpretations and evaluations. This is evident when, through his style(s), Nietzsche radicalizes 'interpretation' and 'evaluation' to the point where his writings themselves do not manifest one single unified 'meaning'.[3] There is, then, no absolute truth; no foundation or origin behind interpretation and therefore no true essence underlying the subject, because as Nietzsche declares:

> The assumption of one single subject is perhaps unnecessary; perhaps it is just as permissible to assume a multiplicity of subjects, whose interaction and struggle is the basis of our thought and our consciousness in general? . . . *My hypothesis*: the subject as multiplicity . . . The continual transitoriness and fleetingness of the subject. 'Mortal Soul'. (Nietzsche 1968, 270–1)

The multiplicity of the subject is an effect of the movement from one interpretation to another and the struggle between them: in other words, the play of ever changing surface. So by saying in *Ecce Homo* that 'consciousness *is* a surface' (Nietzsche 1992, 35), Nietzsche is claiming that there is nothing more than appearance as a state of becoming.

Furthermore, Nietzsche is arguing that the subject is not only the 'play' of multiple interpretations but also the difference that this generates. This subject as the 'play' of multiplicity is a result of a movement away from a single interpretation and evaluation that is not unlike Derrida's concept of différance as a 'play of differences' in language (Derrida 1973, 130). In fact, Nietzsche's subject as a 'play' of multiplicity 'contributed', Derrida argues, to the 'liberation of the signifier from its dependence or derivation with respect to the logos and the related concept of truth or the primary signified' (Derrida 1976, 19).

Discussing the notion of 'play' in *The Ear of the Other*, Derrida argues that philosophy typically conceives 'play' as an 'activity' where the subject 'manipulat[es] objects' (Derrida 1988a, 69). However, this activity of play is positioned as less serious, less economical, than 'work'. Play conceived in this way constructs a metaphysical dichotomy (or antithesis, as Nietzsche would say) between play and work, where the space of play is 'dominated by meaning' and 'by its finality', and consequently, between being and non-being, subject and object, subject and Other. Yet, because the metaphysical concept of play is that which is enacted in a 'contained' and 'present' space, a concept of the humanist subject as unified and autonomous, that exists within and by this space, is therefore privileged as the 'presence of the present' and as the 'present of presence' (Derrida 1988a, 69).[4] Derrida explains that:

> In order to make apparent a play that is not comprehended in this philo-sophical or scientific space, one must think of play in another way. Indeed, this is what I am trying to do within what is already a tradition – that of Nietzsche, for example – but one which also has its genealogy. On the basis of thinking such as Nietzsche's . . . the concept of play, understood as the play *of* the world, is no longer play *in* the world. That is, it is no longer determined and contained by something, by the space that would comprehend it. (Derrida 1988a, 68–9)

One of the ways in which Derrida thinks of 'play' away from a philosophical and scientific space is through the deconstructive process he terms 'différance'. In doing so, he opens up a concept of the subject that is not *only* contained by this traditional space.

Différance disrupts the privilege given to presence in the sign. However, différance is what makes the 'presentation of being-present possible'. That is, the presence of the present is manifested, exposed, and it exists, only because of différance that produces differences through an endless movement of differing and deferral from one signifier to another. In 'La Differance' Derrida explains:

What we note as *differance* will thus be the movement of play that 'produces' (and not by something that is simply an activity) these differences,
these effects of difference . . . Since language (which Saussure says is a
classification) has not fallen from the sky, it is clear that the differences
have been produced; they are the effects produced, but effects that do
not have as their cause a subject or substance, a thing in general, or a
being that is somewhere present and itself escapes the play of difference.
(Derrida 1973, 141)

The subject as 'play', then, is one that is produced by the differences in
language. (Re)temporalizing the subject as a differing and deferring
movement disrupts the traditional concept of cause and effect, where the
subject has come to be experienced as fixed (and therefore unified) in time
and space, in other words, as the subject of the presence of the present.
This becomes clearer when it is related to Derrida's discussion of deconstruction in general. He says that deconstruction is not about 'passing from one
concept to another', and it does not *just* practise an 'overturning' of classical
oppositions, rather

an opposition of metaphysical concepts (for example, speech/writing,
presence/absence, etc.) is never the face-to-face of two terms, but a hierarchy and an order of subordination. Deconstruction ... must, by means
of a double gesture, a double science, a double writing, practice an *overturning* of the classical opposition *and* a general *displacement* of the system.
(Derrida 1986, 329 n. 3)

In this way, différance, as a deconstructive process, resists all oppositions
such as the sensible and the intelligible, speech and writing. Instead,
différance takes place in the *between* of oppositions. Yet, while différance
disrupts the privilege of unity and totality given to the sign, différance does
not necessarily disregard unity altogether nor does it simply favour
multiplicity. Différance is neither pure unity nor pure multiplicity but is
both and neither simultaneously. In this sense, Derrida disrupts the unity
and autonomy of the subject, but because the subject as presence is
produced through the play of differences, he does not therefore abandon,
as some critics have suggested, the subject altogether.

In metaphysics, the 'proper name' has come to exemplify the 'presence
of the present', that is, the subject unified by a particular scientific and
philosophical notion of time and space, cause and effect. The proper name
as a noun is a result of ascribing characteristics such as unity and constancy,

and thereby 'fixing' the subject through this type of representation. However, this traditional concept of the proper name (and as a corollary the subject as presence) is destabilized by Derrida's concept of différance. And yet, paradoxically, the proper name only arises because of the system of differences with which it is 'inscribed'. Thus Derrida claims,

> if an idiom effect or an effect of absolute properness can arise only within a system of relations and differences with something else that is either near or far, then the secret proper name is right away inscribed – structurally and a priori – in a network where it is contaminated by common names . . . There may be effects of a secret proper name, but they could not possibly occur in a pure state because of the differential structure of any mark. (Derrida 1988a, 107)

Derrida argues that through his play with proper names 'Nietzsche attempted something which . . . was, precisely, of a "deconstructive" type' (Derrida 1988a, 85). And it is evident that in many of Nietzsche's writings he alludes to himself, not in terms of a single 'proper name' with particular unchanging characteristics, but rather with multiple names.

For instance, in *Ecce Homo*, Nietzsche says that he is his mother, his father (Nietzsche, 1992, 8), a Pole and a German (Nietzsche 1992, 11), Julius Caesar and Alexander (Nietzsche 1992, 12). He is Zarathustra and Wagner, Dionysus and the Crucified (Nietzsche 1992, 104). Furthermore, he says that he is a *décadent* and also its antithesis (Nietzsche 1992, 10). So what do these names signify? They do not 'signify' anything (if signifying is conceived in terms of 'presence'), because these names come and go in and out of his texts. And the fact that he is also the 'antithesis' of all the names of history points to Nietzsche's name as being none of these multiple names at the same time. Rather, the name of Nietzsche exists in the beyond of all oppositions. What is significant here, is that this dissemination of the proper name in Nietzsche's writings brings into question a metaphysics of absolute truth; Being as pure essence; of a single unified meaning behind interpretation, behind the subject as 'proper name' and hence as presence.

The differing and deferment of différance is evident in Nietzsche's play with his proper name. Likewise Derrida is also suspicious of the meaning of truth underlying the/his proper name, with which he also plays. However, one may ask: if playing with the proper name is something the subject 'does' then does this pose a problem for a critique of a traditional conception of cause and effect? Especially since Derrida argues that 'playing' with the proper name is a process that is not dominated by, but is the dissemination of, meaning. To a large extent this dissemination is not controlled like an activity, because the 'very structure of the proper name sets this process in motion' (Derrida 1988a, 76). Play as a movement that produces differences *does not*, he insists, 'have as their cause a subject or substance' (Derrida 1973, 141). Paradoxically, at the same time that Derrida wants to put his name into play, to lose and disseminate it, he argues that he only ends up making his name 'more and more intrusive . . . and as a result my name gains more ground'. In other words, Derrida argues that through dissemination he is able to put language to 'one's own use' (Derrida 1988a, 76–7), thereby claiming that 'playing with one's own name, putting it in play, is, in effect, what is always going on and what I have tried to do in a somewhat more explicit or systematic manner for some time now and in certain texts' (Derrida 1988a, 76).

An example of where the play with the proper name occurs, elliptically, is in *Spurs: Nietzsche's Styles*.[5] Derrida argues that 'the English *spur*, the *éperon*, is the << same word >> as the German *Spur*: or, in other words, trace, wake, indication, mark' (Derrida 1979, 41), and that 'style might be compared to that rocky point, also called an *éperon*, on which the waves break at the harbor's entrance'. In putting forth his idea of a 'spurring' style, Derrida points out that Nietzsche's heterogeneous styles 'seem to advance in the manner of a *spur* of sorts (*éperon*). Like the prow, for example, of a sailing vessel, its *rostrum*, the projection of the ship which surges ahead to meet the sea's attack and cleave its hostile surface' (Derrida 1979, 39). Nietzsche's heterogeneous, spurring style(s) put into question the idea that there may be an underlying truth in his writings. We could perhaps conclude from this that there is no such thing as Nietzsche's proper name.

Both Nietzsche's and Derrida's arguments are far more complex than the congruence on which I choose to focus might indicate. However, if the spur, as Derrida describes it, is something which 'might be used in a vicious attack against what philosophy appeals to . . . an attack whose thrust could not but leave its mark' (Derrida 1979, 37), then could it not be said that Derrida's 'différance' and Nietzsche's 'perspectivism', and their subversions of the sign (and of the subject as logos through the proper name) is for both a spurring style? That is, what is played with or 'spurred' is the idea that there is a single meaning or truth behind interpretation. In talking about Nietzsche's writings, as well as his own, Derrida, in *Spurs*, comments playfully:

[T]he text will remain, if it is really cryptic and parodying (and I tell you that it is so through and through. I might as well tell you since it won't be of any help to you. Even my admission can very well be a lie because there is dissimulation only if one tells the truth, only if one tells that one is telling the truth), still the text will remain indefinitely open, cryptic and parodying. (Derrida 1979, 137)

Is Derrida's text *Spurs* a parody: is it cryptic or not? He tells us it is so, but here, like Nietzsche, Derrida plays with interpretation, and in this playing with the truth and lie of the text Derrida is breaking out of the enclosure of interpretation, of the proper name. By switching the reader's perspective between Nietzsche's style(s) and his own, conflating and confusing these styles, Derrida ensures that the proper name behind a single interpretation is thwarted and instead left open for questioning. In other words, Derrida's text 'folds' and 'unfolds' (like an 'umbrella') into the name of Nietzsche, so that both the names of Derrida and Nietzsche 'veil' and 'unveil' each other's texts. Who is Nietzsche? He is all, but also none, of the names he refers to in his writings. But then, who is Derrida in this veiling and unveiling in the text of *Spurs*? Is he, *and* is he not, perhaps, Nietzsche?

Ethical Possibilities

The radicalization of the subject as multiplicity or as a 'play of differences ', in Nietzsche and Derrida, has been used to justify readings that have reduced their writings to an 'anything goes' philosophy of textual freeplay exemplified by Richard Rorty's form of postmodernism. As argued in the Introduction to this book, this is a narrow interpretation of Derrida's arguments in particular, seeing them as an assault on traditional metaphysics, which he uses to justify a 'freeplay' of textual interpretation and to dispense with the subject altogether. Equally unjustified has been the tendency among more orthodox critics, like Habermas and Searle, to label both Nietzsche and Derrida's writings irresponsible, unethical and nihilistic. There are many ethical dilemmas produced by a concept of the subject as the 'play of differences', and these will be discussed more fully at a later point in this chapter. Nevertheless, in direct response to these accusations of irresponsibility and nihilism, in what follows it is argued that there are ethical possibilities that can be 'unveiled' in Nietzsche's and Derrida's concepts of subjectivity.

At the start of the previous section a quote from *Beyond Good and Evil* introduced Nietzsche's view of metaphysics as constructed on antithesis; also discussed was Nietzsche's challenge to this antithetical structure of language on which the humanist subject is formulated. Building on this, further on in the same passage, Nietzsche also attacks a certain mode of evaluation, and the mode attacked is precisely an ethical one. He says that '[i]t is no more than a moral prejudice that truth is worth more than appearance; it is even the worst-proved assumption that exists . . . Indeed, what compels us to assume there exists any essential antithesis between "true" and "false"?' (Nietzsche 1986, 47) Here the dichotomy between 'true' and 'false' exemplifies Nietzsche's general criticism of an antithetical language structure which perpetuates particular value interpretations and moral prejudices. In challenging antithesis in general, Nietzsche undermines a form of ethical evaluation that supports prescriptive and normative ethics. Through the oppositional hierarchy of Western language, Nietzsche argues, a normative grammar is produced which, by its antithetical structure, limits ethical interpretation and evaluation to prescriptive and normative responses in terms of either good or evil, right or wrong, true or false. The subject's capacity for ethical response is recuperated within these binary oppositions, and this creates a normative subject. Nietzsche's attack on the antithetical structure of language is not, therefore, only an attack on a normative and prescriptive ethics, but a rejection of the formation of the ethical subject along these dichotomous lines.

Nietzsche also challenges the ethical autonomy of the subject. He declares, '[t]hat things possess a constitution in themselves quite apart from interpretation and subjectivity, is quite an idle hypothesis: it presupposes that interpretation and subjectivity are not essential, that a thing freed from all relationships would still be a thing' (Nietzsche 1968, 302–3). If interpretation and subjectivity is not essential, then for Nietzsche the subject is formed by its relationship to the social semiotic. That is, the ethical subject is formulated in and through relations with the Other. Thus when Nietzsche argues that morality should be 'something questionable, as worthy of question marks' (Nietzsche 1986, 139), he is challenging the restricting aspects of normative, prescriptive ethics that plays down the ethical singular response to, and importance of, the Other. We can conclude from this that a language of antithesis, then, limits the potential for responsive differences to develop from ethical dilemmas and conflicts. To put it another way, in a language of antithesis there is little room for a difference generated by, and encountered in, the ethical dilemmas and conflicts arising from the subject's singular relation to Others.

Nietzsche believes that ethical evaluations or interpretations are 'no more than moral prejudices' that compel us to think that there is an 'antithesis between "true" and "false"' (Nietzsche 1986, 47) and good and evil. In doing so, they construct the subject's responses in terms of normative criteria.

According to Nietzsche, in order to subvert this type of ethical evaluation what needs to be overcome, what we need to be liberated from, are those 'old valuations that dishonor us in the best and strongest things we have achieved' (Nietzsche 1968, 521). This liberation requires that the subject rise above the values associated with the antithetical structure of language, in other words, 'above the belief in grammar' (Nietzsche 1986, 48). Moreover, this entails what he calls a 'courageous becoming', where the subject is not 'fixed' by, but is able to move *beyond*, this dichotomous rubric of good and evil. What is ultimately needed, Nietzsche claims, is a revaluation of all values (Nietzsche 1968, 3), '[b]ecause the values we have had hitherto thus draw their final consequence; because nihilism represents the ultimate logical conclusion of our great values and ideals . . . We require, sometime, *new values*' (Nietzsche 1968, 4). Far from endorsing nihilism, Nietzsche is attempting to overcome the nihilism that he sees inherent in the normative and prescriptive ethical evaluations produced by the antitheses of language.

As the title of his book suggests, Nietzsche attempts to go *beyond* good and evil. Yet what does this going beyond good and evil, *beyond* antithesis, actually entail for him? Does this 'beyond' simply mean for Nietzsche a (re)construction of values through an inverting of oppositions, or is he attempting to go beyond dichotomous language, and therefore language itself? Either way, Nietzsche falls into a metaphysical system, that is, dichotomous language structure, which he attempts to subvert. And the question then arises: is Nietzsche, in his attempt to go beyond, or transcend, language, perpetuating a concept of the transcendental subject? If so, then this would contradict his notion of the subject as a 'play of multiplicity' and 'becoming' as appearance. But then, is/are not Nietzsche's style(s) deliberately contradictory?

It seems that Nietzsche, while he is able to rise above the *belief* in grammar, cannot actually rise above grammar itself. This is a criticism often levelled at Derrida. However, Derrida does not believe there is a 'beyond' grammar, and does not attempt a going 'beyond' in the way that Nietzsche does. Rather, Derrida is well aware of the problems that this type of attempted transcendence involves. In 'La Differance' he argues:

> [T]o prepare ourselves for venturing *beyond* our own logos, that is, for a differance so violent that it refuses to be stopped and examined as the epochality of Being and ontological difference, is neither to give up this passage through the truth of Being, nor is it in anyway to 'criticize', 'contest', or fail to recognize the incessant necessity for it. (Derrida 1973, 154; italics mine)

Différance, in fact any deconstructive process of Derrida's, is not about destroying metaphysics, or reconstructing it for that matter, because a reconstruction cannot take place outside the system one attempts to subvert. Instead, deconstruction attempts to displace or dismantle metaphysics. It does this not simply to invert one opposition for another, but in order to expose, through this inversion, the privileging of presence in the sign. This is a subversion that once again has attracted criticism of Derrida's ideas as unethical or anti-ethical. In contrast, I want to propose that it is precisely this aspect of différance that allows for ethical possibilities.

Derrida is aware of the problems of going 'beyond' language, and so conceptualizes différance not as the beyond (as a pure transcendentalism) but as the *between* of oppositions (although we must be careful not to see this word 'between' as a synthesis of opposites). It is différance as the between, not the beyond, of these oppositions that allows for ethical possibilities. In arguing that différance is not unethical is not to suggest that we reduce différance to the 'ethical' side of the ethical/unethical opposition. To think of his writings as either one or other of these opposites is to do exactly what différance – and deconstruction in general – does not do, and that is simply to invert one term in an oppositional hierarchy for another. Rather, différance is neither anti-ethical nor ethical but both anti-ethical and ethical at the same time. In *Speech and Phenomena* Derrida makes it clear that différance 'can therefore no longer be conceived within the opposition of finiteness and infinity, absence and presence, negation and affirmation' (Derrida 1973, 102). It is in this *between* state of either/or and neither/and, that there arises 'ambiguity'. That is, différance, in opening up 'possible' responses away from prescriptive ones, produces potential uncertainty, and the moral dilemma endemic to ambiguity. Moreover, this ambiguity, generated by différance, and existing in the 'between' of all oppositions, transgresses (without transcending) by its very (*non*)structure, the reduction of ethical response to prescriptive and normative choices.

Différance allows for a subjectivity that is not fixed and unified by a certain concept of time and space and, in doing so, not only challenges the idea of the subject as an 'originary source' but, in conjunction, puts into question its ethical autonomy. To argue that Derrida abandons metaphysics and hence the subject would be to miss the point of the deconstructive process of différance. In fact, Derrida argues that 'the speaking or signifying subject would not be self-present, insofar as he speaks or signifies, except for the play of linguistic or semiological differance' (Derrida 1973, 146). Without rejecting the subject altogether, Derrida's challenge is to think of the subject other than as 'presence', the privileged conceptualization in traditional Western metaphysics. In posing the following question Derrida acknowledges this difficulty:

> How can we conceive of differance as a systematic detour which, within the element of the same, always aims at either finding again the plea-sure or the presence that had been deferred by (conscious or uncon-scious) calculation, and, *at the same time*, how can we, on the other hand, conceive of differance as the relation to an impossible presence . . . ? (Derrida 1973, 150)

Further questions arise from this. For example, how does one, without abandoning the subject altogether, avoid the transcendental and liberal humanist subject? If there is no transcendental subject, then who decides, and how are decisions made? Furthermore, how does one conceptualize ethics apart from 'presence' without simply falling into the negativity of its opposite? There are no necessary answers to these questions (because différance precludes answers). Nevertheless, the posing of these questions is vital to any understanding of how a subject of différance might inform ethical possibilities.

It was suggested that différance generates ambiguity. Let us go further and suggest that it is precisely this ambiguity that is ethical. This is because différance does not reduce the subject's responses to the following of prescriptive and normative ethical rules. Rather, différance opens the way for ethical possibilities, which allows for a free response within a system of differences. In other words, ethical possibilities can be defined as those free responses, questions and choices that ambiguity creates, and for which différance in general allows. This free response is not, however, identical to the liberal humanist concept of freedom that assumes the subject's ethical choices are absolutely autonomous. This is because différance, at the same time that it allows for 'free' response within a system of differences, is constrained by this very system. Response is constrained within and by language, for example by dichotomous structures (antitheses) and more specifically by context. For Derrida, context opens possibilities because '[o]ne sentence can have two meanings, and two effects', that is, context cannot be saturated, and is always 'open and mobile' (Derrida 2002, 24). At the same time, however, context constrains differences, ambiguity, and hence, possibility.[6] Because context is open and mobile, constraint can only delineate and limit, not close down openness or possibilities. It is precisely because of context as constraint that Derrida can argue that the 'multiplicity of contexts and discursive strategies that they govern' are not necessarily relativistic (Derrida 2002, 363). Therefore, while a language of antithesis restricts any 'possibility' of responsive differences, language is also structured by différance, which produces ambiguity. Within language, then, there is an oscillation between constraint and differences (which produces ambiguity), such that constraint and ambiguity occur simultaneously.

As a result of the constraining aspects of context, normative ethics and the normative responses it encapsulates cannot be abandoned altogether. Indeed, Derrida acknowledges 'norms are necessary' (Derrida 2002, 199). Furthermore, because 'presence' (and thus the subject) is constituted by a system of differences, and these differences are constrained by context, and because, as Derrida argues, there is 'nothing outside context' (Derrida 1997a, 136), then it is impossible to abandon the subject. Any criticism arguing that différance is a licence for 'textual freeplay' and an 'anything goes' philosophy fails to see the circumscribing effects that the 'presence' in language has on 'free response' and the subject in general. Likewise, any suggestion that the play of differences within language (and the general text) is a version of nihilism, and is unethical, fails to understand how the ambiguity arising from the play of differences opens, rather than closes, ethical possibilities. Both criticisms ignore the paradox of différance. Precisely because of the dilemmas and questions raised by this paradox, différance allows for, and opens, the possibility of an ethics that is other than but also normative. Given that the subject is largely constituted by this ethical-normative metanarrative, différance also allows for a simultaneous reconceptualization of subjectivity that is not, or is not only, founded on a liberal humanist philosophy and ethics.

(Im)possibility

In *Psyche: Inventions of the Other* Derrida warns that the notion of 'possibility' is in danger of falling into an absolute empiricism, and thus, relativism. He argues that the term 'possibility' is synonymous with the word 'invention'. The latter word means to make something 'new' and 'different': to foresee and imagine a future that can be achieved through calculation. He links this definition of invention to 'possibility' by suggesting that what we foresee and imagine is what is possible. This is the reason why possibility is empirical, because it does not allow for a future that is absolutely unknown (wholly other), or can never be known. Rather, it only opens onto, or allows for, a future that can be anticipated and made known. Consequently, possibility is in danger of becoming simply the 'available set of rule governed procedures, methods, accessible approaches' (Derrida 2007b, 15) that are determined by social and legal institutional frameworks, and which legitimate the possible as empirical (tangible) future horizons and events. In other words, because possibility 'makes known', it also reduces the future as possibility to the present, so that possibility as invention comes to exist within a 'fixed future horizon' (Derrida 2007b, 15). However, this danger produces another: that the 'other' is conceived simply as possibility in this conventional sense. If possibility works and exists only within and through a fixed horizon, then not only is possibility an invention of the 'same', but the Other is thereby also the same. Derrida claims that:

> 'A singular situation. Invention is always possible, it is the invention of the possible, the *teckhnē* of a human subject within an ontotheological horizon . . . it is the invention of the law, invention according to the law that confers status; invention of and according to the institutions that socialize, recognize, guarantee, legitimize; the programmed invention of programs; the invention of the same through which the other comes down to the same'. (Derrida 2007b, 44)

Despite the new, different, non-normative and multiple responses and decisions called 'ethical possibilities', these possibilities still operate within an empirical future horizon. That is, these ethical possibilities are ethical 'inventions'. If Derrida is right about the empirical structure of possibility, then ethical possibilities can do nothing more than reinstitute norms and values, adding nothing new. The danger for ethical possibilities, then, is falling into the trap of the same by anticipating and imagining *new* ethical responses that are achieved within a fixed future horizon. Is this really the only way we can think ethical possibilities? Are these possibilities doomed to forever repeat the normative, albeit in new and novel ways?

Yes and no. The previous section argued that ethical possibilities are based on différance. Différance constitutes the possible, through nominal and hence empirical structures and events (future horizons). In fact, Derrida defines différance as 'the play which makes possible nominal effects, the relatively unitary and atomic structures that are called names' (Derrida 1986, 26). While it constitutes the possible, Derrida also insists that différance is not a 'pure nominal unity'. For this reason he argues it is 'unnameable' (Derrida 1986, 26). Therefore, nominal effects are made possible precisely by the differing and deferring movement of differences that, in turn, allows for, and contains the trace of, the 'impossible'. So if ethical possibilities are based on différance, then ethical possibilities are a result of, and contain, the impossible.

Again in *Psyche*, in an argument that initially appears to contradict his definition of possibility, Derrida suggests that impossibility is an event that is *un*determinable, *un*anticipated, *un*foreseeable, *un*imaginable, and *in*calculable. Thus, impossibility is not entirely empirical, because it cannot be solely determined by, and within, an economy of the same. Impossibility is that which is always 'to come', which means it will never come, never arrive, because it is 'wholly other'. Having established this definition, Derrida then goes on to argue that the 'only possible invention' is the 'invention of the impossible' (Derrida 2007b, 44). In other words, if possibility as invention is to be genuinely possible, it must contain the trace of impossibility. Paradoxically this impossibility is what makes possibility possible. In his essay 'As If It Were Possible', Derrida elucidates this paradox of the (im)possible:

> When the impossible *makes itself* possible, the event takes place (possibility *of* the impossible). This is, irrecusably, the paradoxical form of the event: if an event is only possible, in the classic sense of the word, if it is inscribed in conditions of possibility, if it does no more than make explicit, unveil, reveal, accomplish what was already possible, then it is no longer an event. For an event to take place, for an event to be possible, it must be, as event, as invention, the coming of the impossible. (Derrida 2002, 360–1)

Here, in a deconstructive double move, Derrida argues on the one hand that 'the other is not the possible' (Derrida 2007b, 44) because the other is always coming, or about 'to come'. That is, the other is not the possible because it cannot be invented and thus is impossible. On the other hand, Derrida argues that we have to 'reinvent invention itself, another invention, or rather an invention of the other that would come, through the economy of the same' (Derrida 2007b, 44).

Despite the apparent opposition in Derrida's original definitions, this latter quote clearly demonstrates that the invention of possibility is not to be opposed, indeed is not opposable, to the event of impossibility. This is because the impossible is 'more than impossible'. What Derrida means is that 'the most impossible possible [is] more impossible than the impossible if the impossible is the simple negative modality of the possible' (Derrida 1995c, 43). In other words, impossibility is not simply the negative, the opposite, of the positive term possibility. This being the case, then impossibility is not absolutely outside possibility, because they are not absolutely antithetical, one to the other. Rather, impossibility contaminates possibility. As suggested in

Chapter 1, contamination is not the conjoining or the conjunction of two opposed terms because, like spectral haunting, or infidelity, impossibility 'runs through possibility and leaves in it the trace of its withdrawal' (Derrida 2002, 362). This trace is not simply the 'appearing' of the impossible as such. The trace is the *experience* of what is 'to come' but will never come. In relation to the performative success and failure of possibility, Derrida explains how the trace of the impossible contaminates the possible:

> [T]he possibility of failure is not only inscribed as a preliminary risk in the condition of the possibility of the success of a performative (a promise must *be able not to* be kept, it must risk not being kept or becoming a threat to be a promise that is freely given, and even to succeed; whence the originary inscription of guilt, of confession, of the excuse of forgiveness in the promise). The possibility of failure must continue to mark the event, even when it succeeds, as the trace of an impossibility, at times its memory and always its haunting. (Derrida 2002, 362)

This quote goes a long way towards answering the question Derrida himself poses early on in his article: how is the impossible possible?; or 'how is it possible . . . that that which makes possible makes impossible the very thing that it makes possible?' (Derrida 2002, 361). The impossible makes possible (and impossible) precisely because possibility is marked by the trace of impossibility. If it were not, then possibility would not allow for the experience of the singularity of the Other/other 'to come'. (It would not allow for the future that would never arrive.) Instead, it would do 'nothing but deploy, explain, actualize what was already possible' (Derrida 2002, 362). Thus, the failure of possibility to be absolutely and purely possible is what enables the possible itself to allow, and to prepare, for the event (unknowable future) as 'wholly other'.

For Derrida, 'destabilizing foreclusionary structures' (Derrida 2007b, 45), such as the rules and norms that structure and delineate texts[7] and language, reveal the ambiguity inherent in those structures. It is precisely through this destabilization of structures that we can experience the failure of possibility. In *Psyche*, Derrida suggests that specific linguistic or rhetorical features can destabilize the structure of performative and constative language, and he uses Francis Ponge's 'Fable' as his example. He demonstrates how destabilization operates through the performative repetition of the word 'with' that occurs in the first line of this poem: 'With this word *with* commences then this text'.[8] Derrida argues that in the repetition of the word 'with', the first line of the poem constates itself as a performative while it takes place:

Not all performatives are somehow reflexive, certainly; they do not all describe themselves, they do not constate themselves as performatives while they take place. This one ['Fable'] does so, but its constative description is nothing other than the performative itself. *'With the word* with *commences then this text'*. Its beginning, its invention or its first coming does not come about before the sentence that recounts precisely this event. The narrative is nothing other than the coming of what it cites, recites, constates, or describes. (Derrida 1992a, 323)

As Derrida implies in this quote there is a double strategy at work in 'Fable'. The repetition of the word 'with' institutes a reflexivity that '*deconstructs* the oppositional logic that relies on an untouchable distinction between the performative and the constative' (Derrida 2007b, 13), but without totally undoing the distinction. Then, because the distinction is not altogether dismantled, the word 'with' unfolds back into itself, thus repeating the 'invention of the same, at the very instant when it takes place' (Derrida 2007b, 11). Paradoxically, not only does the repetition of the word 'with' disturb without entirely disabling the distinction between the performative and the constative (or the other rules and norms structuring the text), but also it is only by operating within the rules and norms that these very rules and norms can be repeated (iterated), and hence destabilized. Iteration is destabilizing because while repeating, and therefore respecting, the same, it does so differently. Thus, it is only by operating within the same, within 'foreclusionary structures', that we can prepare for the possibility of the experience of impossibility. In other words, it is in the rules of repetition that we can bring about the singular event, an event that is not just possible, but one that allows, *through the possible*, for the coming of the other: for the impossible.

What Derrida's destabilization works to reveal is the ambiguity already and always inherent within texts and language. That is, ambiguity is not brought to the text from outside, which is why Derrida argues that the 'performance of the "Fable" respects the rules, but does so with a strange move . . . This move consists in defying and exhibiting the precarious structure of its rules, even while respecting them, and through the mark of respect that it invents' (Derrida 2007b, 44). The performative contamination of the constative and vice versa, in 'Fable', is an example Derrida uses to demonstrate how impossibility marks or haunts the possible. As we have seen, if possibility was not haunted, then the event of possibility would be reduced to a programme, a general rule, and an invention in the conventional sense. Instead, impossibility saves possibility from an absolute empiricism. The irony, however, is that without this 'danger' of simply following a programme, and hence, of falling into the same, impossibility would not only not be possible, it would not be 'impossible', it would not be other. That is, the other would be nothing but *another* 'possible': calculable, foreseeable, containable within a determined future horizon, and thus, the same.[9]

We have seen, then, how différance not only constitutes the possible, producing ethical possibilities, but also dislocates the possible through a differing, deferring movement. A movement, moreover, that opens the possible to the 'experience' of the impossible, and that makes both the possible and impossible a quasi-transcendental logic. This quasi-transcendentality is what Derrida calls the condition of possibility and impossibility. From this it can now be deduced that ethical possibilities are an opening to different and multiple empirical events, which produce new rules and norms. What can now also be argued is that the ambiguity generated by the contesting and conflicting multiplicity of ethical (empirical) possibilities, opens and produces ethically singular events and situations that are not normatively governed, precisely because they contain the trace of impossibility. Thus, if singular events are marked by the impossible, and if those singular events are produced by ethical possibilities, then the ethically normative contains the trace of impossibility. From this we can further deduce that ethical possibilities are marked by the trace of the impossible, making ethical possibility a quasi-transcendental relation. Therefore, it would be more apt, from this point on, to refer to the quasi-transcendentality of this ethical condition, not as 'ethical possibilities', but as 'ethical (im)possibilities'.

The (Im)possibility of Justice

We have seen how the distinction between the performative and the constative is contaminated through the repetition of the word 'with' in Ponge's poem, and we have seen that Derrida uses this contamination to demonstrate the condition of (im)possibility. However, despite this example of language, the condition of (im)possibility still begs the question: how do the differences and constraints of language more generally, and the contamination between the performative and the constative more specifically, actually relate to '(im)possibility' in a *larger cultural context?* While Derrida does not pose this question explicitly, or at least not in this way, the answer can be found in his essay 'Force of Law: the "Mystical Foundation of Authority"' (1992b), where he links the performative aspect of language to justice. By making this link, Derrida locates (im)possibility within the larger cultural context of Western legal institutions.

From the start of his essay it is clear that Derrida does not conceptualize 'justice' in the conventional way. Instead, it is understood as the 'experience of the impossible' (Derrida 1992b, 16). By this Derrida means justice is 'infinite, incalculable, rebellious to rule and foreign to symmetry, heterogeneous and heterotropic' (Derrida 1992b, 22). This experience of the impossible is what Derrida argues is 'justice without law', to be distinguished from 'justice as law (*droit*)' (Derrida 1992b, 16, 22). From now on, and for simplicity, these terms 'justice' and 'law' will be used as shorthand to refer to 'justice without law' and 'justice as law', respectively. For Derrida 'law' (justice as law or right) is 'the element of calculation' (Derrida 1992b, 16), a 'system of regulated and encoded prescriptions' (Derrida 1992b, 22), which are universalizing, and thus stabilizing, statutory and legitimate. Justice as law (*droit*) is the law of right and legality.

In answer to the question posed above, Derrida links justice to the performative structure of speech acts, arguing that speech acts illuminate and constitute the operation of justice and of law (*droit*), as well as the distinction between them. However, the performative speech act is constituted by an aporia. This is because the structure of the performative means that it can only be 'just'

> by founding itself on conventions and so on other anterior performatives, buried or not, it always maintains within itself some irruptive violence, it no longer responds to the demands of theoretical rationality. Since every constative utterance itself relies, at least implicitly, on a performative structure (. . .) the dimension of *justesse* or truth of the theoretico-constatie utterances (. . .) always thus presupposes the dimension of justice of the performative utterances, that is to say their essential precipitation, which never proceeds without a certain dissymmetry and some quality of violence. (Derrida 1992b, 27)

The aporia is that the justice of the performative utterance is based on convention: in other words, it is constituted by the constative. So while the constative can always be 'right' (*droit*) in the sense of 'truth' (*justesse*), it can never be just (justice), *except* when it relies on the performative, that is, on the justice of the performative utterance for its rightness and its truth. The reason the performative is a 'dimension' of justice is because the urgency (the immediacy, the spontaneity) of the performative utterance reveals that the future horizon cannot be calculated or anticipated. The urgency of the performative, in other words, does not correlate with 'theoretical rationality'. In this way, Derrida sees the immediacy and spontaneity of the performative as analogous to justice. For Derrida, justice *is* urgent.

This notion of 'urgency' is only one of the three aporias of justice that Derrida outlines in 'Force of Law'. Closely connected to urgency are the aporias of decision and singularity. Now, the urgency of justice is related to 'decision' in the following way. Justice is urgent because it does not calculate or take account of knowledge (the rational) to make a 'just decision'. Rather, a just decision (justice) is always thoughtless and unconscious. It always goes through the 'ordeal of the undecidable'. If it did not, then Derrida claims it would not be just, simply legal. This is because a decision, like 'possibility', would only follow a legal programme, a universal rule. This 'irreducible thoughtlessness and unconsciousness', which is the structure of performativity as urgency, and thus of justice, is the 'undecidable' that paradoxically structures and enables the decision to take place. So the aporia here is that the decision turns on undecidability. That is, while the decision 'must follow a law or a prescription, a rule' in order to be a decision, it must do so without simply being an act that applies a rule or follows a programme. Thus, Derrida argues:

> [F]or a decision to be just and responsible, it must, in its proper moment if there is one, be both regulated and without regulation: it must conserve the law and also destroy it or suspend it enough to have to reinvent it in each case, rejustify it . . . Each case is other, each decision is different and requires an absolutely unique interpretation, which no existing, coded rule can or ought to guarantee absolutely. (Derrida 1992b, 23)

Here Derrida explains that undecidability not only haunts the decision, but allows for every decision to be singular. Singularity, then, is the final aporia of justice. Undecidability, that which makes the decision singular, contaminates the generality that is characteristic of that very decision. As Caputo argues, the decision has to account simultaneously for every particular case, for every singularity (Other), and also for 'the generality of the law' (Caputo 1997a, 211). So singularity has to conform to the general law while still remaining singular.

These aporias demonstrate that the distinction between the performative and the constative, the impossible and the possible, the singularity and the generality (universality) of the law, is unstable and that the terms, apparently oppositional, contaminate one another without dismantling the distinctions altogether. Now all these 'pairs' are homologous with every other pair and, what is more, each and every pair is homologous with justice and law. Derrida, in fact, makes it clear that these aporias, or discourses on performativity, undecidability, and singularity, as well as on the gift, différance, the incalculable, and so on, are *all* 'obliquely discourses on justice' (Derrida 1992b, 7). Given the homology between the structure of justice and law and all these discourses (pairs), Derrida is able to demonstrate that justice is aporetic, because there would not be justice without the law and vice versa:

> Everything would still be simple if this distinction between justice and *droit* were a true distinction, an opposition whose functioning was logically regulated and permitted mastery. But it turns out that *droit* claims to exercise itself in the name of justice and that justice is required to establish itself in the name of a law that must be "enforced". (Derrida 1992b, 22)

In other words, if we simply followed a law, applied a rule, then this would not be justice, because we would be reducing the singularity of a 'case', or event, to a system of rules, to the universal law. Inversely, without following the universality of the law, the singular event, or decision, would not be singular. Rather, it would give away its singularity by, once again, applying a rule or 'enacting a program' (Derrida 1992b, 23).

Nietzsche↔Derrida↔Levinas

John Caputo argues that 'without underestimating the serious debt of Derrida to Nietzsche's critique of metaphysics and of its "faith in opposites", such a characterization misses the profoundly Levinasian affirmation of the *tout autre*, the "wholly other", in deconstruction' (Caputo 1997b, 127). We have seen how critics like Rorty have *over*emphasized Derrida's debt to Nietzsche, and they have done so without taking account of the differences between them, leading to a misinformed conclusion that Derrida's work endorses a textual freeplay. This has lead various critics to an unwarranted assumption that Derrida either perpetuates a Nietzschean reactionary politics and a Nietzschean-based nihilism and unethicality, or reaches a political impasse because deconstruction's aesthetic contextualism, utopianism, or infinite deferment makes it unable to produce political action. Understandably, in response to these accusations, some defenders of Derrida have tended to *over*emphasize or privilege the Levinasian aspect of Derrida's deconstruction. However, as the quote from Derrida at the end of Chapter 1 makes explicitly clear, deconstruction is influenced by several philosophers at once (such as Nietzsche, Saussure, Freud, Levinas, Heidegger, to name only five), and this influence is evident in all areas of his work. As a result, an argument, that Derrida is *either* Levinasian, *or* Nietzschean, *or* Heideggerian, and so on, is unsustainable. This contamination between Derrida's thinking and the ideas of other philosophers is rather a performative gesture, fundamental to Derrida's deconstruction.

This chapter's discussion of 'perspectivism' and 'différance' has made it possible to compare the congruencies and differences between Nietzsche and Derrida. This has led us, in the first two sections of this chapter, to modify, in significant ways, the position adopted by Rorty and Habermas on the extent and nature of Nietzsche's influence on Derrida. Nor is there any need to deny the obvious influence of Levinas: I agree with Caputo's argument here (quoted above). Nonetheless, we can rethink the ethical (im)possibilities evident in and enabled by deconstruction through Nietzsche as well as Levinas, and therefore this chapter will conclude by suggesting that in Derrida's concept of 'justice' there is a contamination between Nietzsche and Levinas.

Let us start with Levinas. As we saw in Chapter 1, for Levinas the 'third party' introduces justice into the purity of the face-to-face relation. Derrida argues in 'Violence and Metaphysics' that, as much as Levinas might want to, he cannot maintain a pure distinction between ethics as the face-to-face, and justice. Not wanting to reject Levinas' position, Derrida radicalizes it, by demonstrating that separation is only possible because of contamination. In other words, this contamination (perjury, or infidelity) is what ensures the separation between the face-to-face, and justice. This radicalization is also evident in 'Force of Law', where Derrida argues that justice is the experience of the impossible (Derrida 1992b, 15–16). Thus, Levinas' notion of the singularity of the face-to-face ethical relation is evident in this concept of justice as the singular event, as the experience of the impossible. On the other hand, what Derrida calls 'justice as law (*droit*)' is similar to Levinas' notion of the third party (what Levinas calls 'justice').

In the same way, then, that 'perjury' demonstrated that the purity of the face-to-face is contaminated by the 'third party' (by justice), so too does Derrida's condition of (im)possibility reveal that justice enables, indeed constitutes, law (as possibility): in other words, Derrida's notion of justice reflects the influence of Levinas' face-to-face relation. In fact, in 'Force of Law' Derrida says that he is 'tempted, *up to a certain point*, to compare the concept of justice – which I'm here trying to distinguish from law – to Levinas's, just because of this infinity and because of the heteronomic relation to others, to the faces of otherness that govern me, whose infinity I cannot thematize and whose hostage I remain' (Derrida 1992b, 22; italics mine). Note that it is *only* 'up to a certain point' that Derrida is tempted. This is because Derrida questions the purity of the ethical relation that Levinas attempts to institute. So, in order to save justice from being a pure transcendentality, Derrida radicalizes Levinas, demonstrating that justice and law are contaminated by each other. The irony for critics of Derrida is that Nietzsche's critique of the metaphysical faith in opposites is evident in Derrida's radicalization of Levinas, and of justice, as he outlines it not only in 'Violence and Metaphysics', but also in 'Force of Law'.[10] For example, we can see Nietzsche's influence when Derrida, in 'Force of Law', argues that there is 'an analogy between "the undecidability (*Unentscheidbarkeit*) of all the problems of *droit*" and what happens in nascent language . . . in which it is impossible to make a clear, convincing, determinant decision . . . between true and false, correct and incorrect (*richtig/falsch*, "right/wrong")' (Derrida 1992b, 50). What Derrida is suggesting here is that there is a connection between the *aporias* of justice and the ambiguity of language evident in the contamination of the oppositional logic of distinctions, here the distinction between ethical values. That is, there can never be a clear-cut decision between the normative categories of true/false, correct/incorrect, right/wrong, and so on. This is not to say that decisions cannot be made, or that these moral distinctions are not made; it is just that they are not absolute or fixed. This is obviously reminiscent of Nietzsche's critique of normative language outlined in the first two sections.

Again, as argued earlier, this contamination of ethical values in language has implications for subjectivity. If the subject is largely constructed in and through language, then the ambiguity of language complicates the subject as presence: the subject can never be fixed or absolutely autonomous. However, what we know as the 'humanist subject' is so because it is structured by 'antithetical values'. That is, through the ethically normative structure of language, our choices, responses and decisions are made normative to some extent. Therefore, despite Nietzsche's claim that the subject is 'perpetually becoming' the subject is still fixed, made 'present/presence', by being reduced by language to the ethically same. This is why Nietzsche wanted 'new values', and why Derrida thinks the empirical structure of 'possibility' is dangerous, because it reinstitutes *only* ethical norms and normative responses. Questioning the validity of the humanist subject is not the same as claiming there is no subject, or effects of subjectivity. Neither is

Derrida denying that the subject has no autonomy or freedom, for how could there be justice without them? Derrida argues precisely this in 'Force of Law':

> [T]o be just or unjust and to exercise justice, I must be free and responsible for my actions, my behavior, my thought, my decisions. We would not say of being without freedom, or at least of one without freedom in a given act, that its decision is just or unjust. But this freedom or this decision of the just, if it is one, must follow a law or a prescription, a rule. In this sense, in its very autonomy, in its freedom to follow or to give itself laws, it must have the power to be of the calculable or programmable order. (Derrida 1992b, 22–3)

Freedom follows a law or prescription, but without conformity to this 'programmable order'. Thus, as this quote suggests, Derrida does not endorse, or perpetuate, the humanist notion of autonomy and freedom. Rather, the autonomy of the humanist subject, or the effect of autonomy, is constituted through norms and universal laws that, in turn, are made possible through the condition of (im)possibility. There can only be autonomy and freedom within the 'context' of law, of language, of undecidability, of différance, and so on. This notion of autonomy will be discussed further in Chapter 4.

In the same way that questioning possibility does not mean, for Derrida, that we abandon subjectivity, autonomy and freedom, Nietzsche's 'new values' do not reject normativity, or law. That is, while it could be argued that Nietzsche's 'new values' invert the normative structure, therefore staying within the same and simply perpetuating the norms he wants to question, this would be to assume that Nietzsche wants to, or thinks he can, reject norms. In an interview with Richard Beardsworth entitled 'Nietzsche and the Machine', Derrida suggests that in the same way that possibility contains, and is made possible, by the trace of impossibility, Nietzsche's 'new values' presupposes law, and hence norms:

> Nietzsche's genealogy of morality implies an affirmation of law, with all the attendant paradoxes that being-before-the-law implies. Whatever these paradoxes, there is always law [*il y a de la loi*]. The law, or this 'must', can, indeed, be read in all the prescriptive modalities of Nietzsche's discourse. When he speaks of the different hierarchies of force and of difference of force, there must also be law. The *reversal of values* or their hierarchical ordering presupposes law – hence the foolish simplicity of aligning Nietzsche's thought with relativism. (Derrida 2002, 223–4; italics mine)

This quote unveils not just Nietzsche's but also, more subtly, Levinas' influence on Derrida's discussion of justice and law. For Derrida, 'justice without law' *does not* constitute an *ought*, or a *must*, characteristic of normative ethics: universal laws and prescriptive rules. Rather, justice as the experience of the impossible 'traces through', or haunts, the normative structure of law (of ethics) itself. This is evidence of Levinas' influence. At the same time, we can see Nietzsche's influence when Derrida argues that justice ensures the singularity of the decision through contamination with the law, and also when he claims that the 'universalization of *droit* is its very possibility, it is analytically inscribed in the concept of justice' (Derrida 1992b, 51).

Possible Manifestations

In conclusion, let us restate the reasons for discussing 'Force of Law'. First, through its articulation of the institution of law, Derrida's essay gives a much more culturally contextualized example of the manifestation of (im)possibility. Second, 'Force of Law' makes clear that, through contamination, or the condition of (im)possibility, justice is 'enjoined' to and by law. In turn, the specificity of justice and law are linked to metaphysical (and normative) ethics. As Derrida argues elsewhere, there is 'a *relation* between ethics and politics, ethics and justice or law. *This relation is necessary*, it must exist, it is necessary to deduce a politics and a law from ethics' (Derrida 1999a, 115).

This leads to the final reason for discussing 'Force of Law' that has not been previously outlined: if justice and law are an example of how (im)possibility operates, and if ethics enjoins justice and law, then metaphysical ethics, too, must be constituted by the condition of (im)possibility. What follows from this condition of (im)possibility is what I call 'ethics under erasure'. As will be elaborated in more detail in the next chapter, for Derrida 'under erasure' (*sous rature*) means to retain a concept or word while simultaneously demonstrating its inaccuracy. I take a further step by bringing together Derrida's notion of 'under erasure' with ethics to form the term 'ethics under erasure'. There is congruence between the condition of (im)possibility – as Derrida articulates it through law and justice – and 'ethics under erasure'. Nonetheless, it is in the way that 'ethics under erasure' *manifests* itself that it develops its singularity and difference from the (im)possibility of law and justice (and from Derrida's 'irresponsibilization', discussed in the Introduction).[11]

So how is 'ethics under erasure' manifested? By analogy to the condition of (im)possibility outlined above, it could be suggested that in everyday life, in our experiences, interactions and relations, metaphysical and normative ethics is constantly put under erasure. Even the term 'ethical norms' is inaccurate, because the everyday situations in which subjects find themselves require responses that do not necessarily, or only, obey and follow prescriptive rules and laws of ethical systems. These responses do not reject ethical systems and norms either, for they cannot. Rather, they constantly negotiate, and mediate in, by, and with, normative ethics. Thus, 'ethics under erasure' reveals that metaphysical and normative ethics is a constant oscillation and negotiation with singular situations requiring singular responses (possibilities) which simultaneously reshape, reconstitute, reinvent norms. 'Ethics under erasure' reveals that, through singular responses, the perceived universal and unifying position of metaphysical and normative ethics is constantly being undermined, is shifting and forever changing.

Nevertheless, because these singular responses are possibilities in the empirical sense, we can say that singular responses do not dispense with norms per se. And, because these responses are empirical possibilities, they are constantly contesting and competing possibilities, and so norms are constantly reinvented through erasure. However, it is precisely because these possibilities (responses, decisions, and so on) *are* contesting and competing that we can also say that within possibility (the empirical) something other (the impossible, the transcendental) is called for and opened. Given this, under what conditions is ethics under erasure manifested in everyday practice? The multiplicity of possibilities suggests that there are many manifestations. However, in Chapter 4 an example of this manifestation is provided in the exploration of how taboos of sexuality, race and class in personal relations are (re)presented (or rather iterated) through the cultural context of Western film in Todd Haynes' *Far From Heaven*. In my analysis of the film, what is argued is that Western discourses and representations of these taboos end up, sometimes deliberately, mostly inadvertently, conveying how every day we all enact and live 'ethics under erasure'. Meanwhile, in the next chapter, it is in and through Derrida's term hauntology, as he outlines it in *Specters of Marx*, that the phrase 'ethics under erasure' is articulated. In other words, hauntology is important for understanding Derrida's 'quasi-transcendental' neologism 'under erasure', and consequently Chapter 3 forges a connection between hauntology (and spectrality) and under erasure, in order to attempt to elucidate the link made between 'under erasure' and ethics.

Chapter 3

Ethics Under Erasure

'There is no inheritance without a call to responsibility.'
— *Jacques Derrida,* Specters of Marx, 91

Prelude: A Discourse on Inheritance

'We all live in a world, some would say a culture, that still bears, at an incalculable depth, the mark of this inheritance, whether in a directly visible fashion or not' (Derrida 1994, 14). So says Derrida in relation to the legacy of Marx in his book *Specters of Marx* (1994), a book that Derrida elsewhere identifies 'as a book on inheritance'(Derrida 1999c, 231).[1] Derrida defines the condition of inheritance as a mode of haunting exemplary of the spectre (ghost), which he in turn explains can be understood as that which exceeds (in a similar quasi-transcendental logic to différance, the trace, the aporia, and so forth) the dialectical/binary logic that constitutes the discourses on visibility and appearance, ideality, and 'being'.[2] Written in the plural, the word 'Specters' in the title conveys, further, that it is not a 'who' that we necessarily inherit: Marx, for instance. We do not, in other words, simply inherit a proper name and an unmediated truth and meaning associated with the proper name as noun (presence of the present). There is no '*pure* spirit'[3] of Marxism. Rather, we inherit more than one inheritance; '*more than one* form of speech' (Derrida 1994, 16), and thus there is more than one translation and interpretation of a tradition or inheritance. And therefore, there are multiple spectres and spirits of Marxism.

Derrida's discussion of 'Marx' and Marxism, throughout his book, serves as a pivot around which he politically and ethically complicates the ways in which philosophy predominantly deals with its spectres: exorcism being the method of choice. The exorcism of the spectre occurs in and through the construction of binary oppositions, categories and objectivity, critical analysis, and the creating of distinctions between one philosophy, one philosopher and another. This is why for Derrida

[a] traditional scholar does not believe in ghosts – nor in all that could be called the virtual space of spectrality. There has never been a scholar who, as such, does not believe in the sharp distinction between the real and the unreal, the actual and the inactual, the living and the non-living, being and non-being ('to be or not to be', in the conventional reading), in the opposition between what is present and what is not, for example in the form of objectivity. (Derrida 1994, 11)

It is easy to believe in the *spirit* as that which is unreal, inactual and non-living; as that which is invisible (see endnote 3), and it is also easy to believe in life, that is, everything perceived to be real, actual and living (the body or living flesh). It is easy to construct this philosophical binary opposition. But it is more difficult believing in the spectre as that which is the 'undecidability between flesh and spirit' (Laclau 2007, 68), that which is, in other words, neither spirit nor body, but 'the carnal apparition of the spirit, its phenomenal body, its fallen and guilty body . . . The ghost [spectre] would be the deferred spirit, the promise or calculation of an expiation'. The difference between spectre and spirit, then, is a 'différance' (Derrida 1994, 136): a differing and deferral between one and the other. For Derrida, Marx (the man and his work) serves as an example of this traditional philosophical-metaphysical manoeuvre to exorcize spectres by creating a very sharp distinction between spirit and living flesh/body.[4]

Two instances of Derrida unveiling how Marx too attempts to exorcize his inheritances can be seen, first, in Marx's constructed opposition between Hegel's dialectical *idealism* or *Geist*, and his own dialectical *materialism*. Second, Marx critiques Max Stirner for failing to exorcize his philosophical ghosts, but ironically attempts to exorcize the spectre of Stirner by showing how he himself is the expert in ghost exorcism. Marx effects this exorcism by distinguishing between Stirner's abstract and egological appropriation of the spectre, and his own realist (material and practical) actuality. Derrida shows that for Marx, if one doesn't take this course of exorcism then 'you will have conjured away only the phantomality of the body, not the body itself of the ghost, namely, the reality of the State, Emperor, Nation, Fatherland, and so on' (Derrida 1994, 142). This is to suggest as Marx does that spectres can be exorcized in and through material presence (use-value and production), which he opposes to exchange-value and the commodity form. Thus, Marx creates a sharp distinction between use and exchange value in order to distinguish his work from Stirner's. However, as Derrida argues, if '[t]he commodity thus haunts the thing' so that 'its specter is at work in use-value' (Derrida 1994, 151), then what is it exactly that serves the distinction for Marx? Or as Derrida puts the question, what makes 'a use-value purified of everything that makes for exchange-value and the commodity-form?' In answer Derrida goes on to explain:

It is not a matter here of negating a use-value or the necessity of refer-ring to it. But of doubting its strict purity. If this purity is not guaranteed, then one would have to say that the phantasmagoria began before the said exchange-value, at the threshold of the value of value in general, or that the commodity-form began before the commodity-form, itself before itself . . . Just as there is no pure use, there is no *use-value* which the pos-sibility of exchange and commerce . . . has not in advance inscribed itself in an *out-of-use* – an excessive signification that cannot be reduced to the useless. (Derrida 1994, 159–60)

In creating this opposition between materialism and idealism, between use-value and exchange-value, Derrida argues that Marx wants to 'denounce, chase away, or exorcise the specters but by means of critical analysis' (Derrida 1994, 47). Complicating this metaphysical manoeuvre Derrida reveals how Marx perpetually conjures that which he tries to exorcize. That is, the more Marx constructs oppositions in order to distance his work from his spectres (for example, Hegel and Stirner), the more he makes them appear. This is because Marx has to reintroduce them, reappropriate them; incorporate and interiorize them; gather them into appearance before he can dismiss them and pretend to make them disappear (Derrida 1994, 128–9). Just as there is no presence without absence and vice versa, there is no disappearance without appearance, no invisibility without visibility, and so on, and therefore we cannot, as much as we might want to, fly from our spectres, our inheritances. And whether we know it or not, we constantly borrow from our heritage. Derrida insists upon this when he demonstrates that Marx's unwanted debt to Hegel and Stirner highlights further spectres in a philosophical lineage: Marx is indebted to Hegel (and Engels) who is indebted to Kant (and others) who is indebted to Rousseau (and others) who is indebted to the moral philosophy of the Enlightenment, all of whom are indebted to further literary, philosophical, economic traditions; and all of whom, in turn, are indebted to Plato and Aristotle, as well as to the whole tradition of European- and Judeo-Christianity.[5]

In this spectral unveiling of Marx's philosophical heritage, Derrida inter-weaves into the fabric of his own book his own inheritances from Husserl, Heidegger, Blanchot, Benjamin, Levinas, Merleau-Ponty, L. J. Austin, Shakespeare, Valery, Freud and Nietzsche, not to mention Marx, and so on.[6] In doing so, Derrida's point is that all inheritances are never simply a direct passing on of the philosophical, political, ethical or ideological batons from father to son, brother to brother; as if ideas (spirit), spectres, people are never 'transformed' in the exchange; as if what is exchanged occurs without 'iterability' that comes in interpretation and translation; as if one can simply, without complication, claim to be a philosophical heir, and the only heir, as Derrida has been accused wrongly of attempting in relation to Marx.[7]

In *Specters of Marx*, Derrida is not claiming to be Marx's heir and thus claiming the baton for himself. Rather, in the same way that we saw him playing with the/his 'proper name' in the previous chapter, Derrida performatively plays with more than one spectre; his book(s) assumes more than one 'filiation and affiliation' (Derrida 1999c, 230), more than one inheritance. This is why, while Derrida invokes the authority of Marx in *Specters*, he also explains in 'Marx and Sons' that 'it can also happen that, having spoken "for him", I also speak "against him": in the *same* book' (Derrida 1999c, 230–1). As we have seen with Levinas and Nietzsche in previous chapters, Derrida in fact speaks for and against all his spectres, which can be seen performatively in the way in which he plays with style(s) of writing and argument, where, as Joanna Hodge interestingly puts it, his discussions of 'one theoretical construct often masks an address to another, or to a conjunction of the first with the second' (Hodge 2007, 16). As will be discussed later in the chapter, this performativity is not simply a rhetorical aesthetic device but encapsulates a responsibility for inheritance, and for the Other/other.

In and through the multiplicity of, and play between, both Marx and Derrida's spectres, we can begin to understand the impurity Derrida introduces into the concept of 'Marx' and Marxism, and thus into the notion of inheritance. If inheritance is about what is passed between life and death, the living (material) and non-living (the immaterial), reality and illusion, spirit and spectre, and so on, then Derrida reveals the instability of the 'dividing line' that constructs these oppositions, and which inform the concept of inheritance (or the inherited concept of inheritance), while at the same time respecting and demarcating their differences. In so doing, Derrida throws into crisis the conceived teleological linearity underpinning an inheritance of patrilineage, 'one whose consequence can be measured by the constancy of an immense tradition, or rather one must say of the philosophical *patrimony* such as it is handed down, through the most parricidal mutations, from Plato to Saint Max, to Marx and beyond. The lineage of this patrimony is wrought, but never interrupted' (Derrida 1994, 147).

This 'constancy of an immense tradition' has been accomplished, completed, made possible, in a word 'wrought', in the habitual and performative act of constantly passing on the patrilineal characteristic of this tradition of inheritance. This, Derrida claims, has not been interrupted; not enough to ever break what is now its concrete foundation in metaphysics, subjectivity, ethics, and so on. Yet Derrida's deconstructive double move (achieved in the play of multiple spectres), while not fully interrupting, certainly exposes 'impossibility' as that which makes the tradition possible. As discussed in Chapter 2, the impossible (the unknowable 'to come'; the alterity of the 'to come') makes an event, an inheritance, of Marx for instance, both possible and impossible simultaneously. Long after *Specters of Marx*, Derrida writes that the 'possibility of failure must continue to mark the event, even when it succeeds, as the trace of an impossibility, at times its memory and always its haunting' (Derrida 2002, 362). (Im)possibility, for Derrida, can be conceived as a haunting, what he refers to in both *Specters of Marx* and 'Marx and Sons' as 'hauntology' (Derrida 1994, 161; 1999c, 244). Thus, the possibility of patrilineal inheritance is always already a consequence of an 'impossibility' tracing through, or haunting, its very condition, and yet at the same time, it is impossibility that also enables the 'deconstruction of that heritage itself' (Derrida 1995a, 282). Furthermore, hauntology makes impossible and possible a metaphysics of ontology that structures inheritance along linear coordinates in time and space, cause and effect, which in turn (in)forms the presence of the subject as a 'certain temporality: identity to self, positionality, property, ego, consciousness, will, intentionality, freedom, humanity' (Derrida and Nancy 1991, 109). Impossibility, then, is not only that which makes presence possible, but is what delays the 'arrival' of the full presence of Being, and this is why Derrida also insists that the presence of the subject is also a 'fable' (Derrida and Nancy 1991, 100). This notion of delayed arrival (that which haunts: the *revenant*) enables Derrida to reposition ontology as hauntology (Bouman 2007, 264).

As a 'discourse on spectrality' (Derrida 1999c, 219), hauntology is important for understanding Derrida's quasi-transcendental neologism, 'under erasure', because hauntology makes 'apparent' how and why our ethical inheritances (which includes philosophical ethical theories), cannot easily, nor should they necessarily, be abandoned. Given this, there are two predominant aims to this chapter: first, to forge a connection between hauntology (and thus spectrality), and 'under erasure', in order to, second, attempt a further link between 'under erasure' and ethics – to form 'ethics under erasure'. This is in the hope of resituating (without 'forgetting') the hauntological logic of 'under erasure' as originally outlined in *Of Grammatology* and *Dissemination,* into another heritage: the metaphysical-philosophical ethical tradition.

This resituating will enable me to argue that ethics is always already under erasure. In other words, when Derrida insists that we cannot simply exorcize our inheritances, our spectres, he suggests instead that '*one must* reckon with them' (Derrida 1994, xx). If 'we must reckon with' our inheritances, our spectres, then *how* do we do this responsibly? The argument of this chapter is that 'reckoning with' not only calls for responsibility towards our inheritances, our spectres, but also the reckoning itself *is* a form of responsibility. And this is because it requires a negotiation with an ethical inheritance that has to account for difference and sameness; a negotiation between ethical universality (normativity) and particularity (singularity). 'Reckoning with', in other words, requires putting ethics 'under erasure', precisely because it entails responsibility that moves away from one that simply follows ethical laws, rules and prescriptions, by taking into account the singularity of each and every event and person, but without falling into potential nihilism. Thus what this chapter aims to demonstrate is that ethics under erasure ensures that ethical singularity, that is, the responsibility for the singularity of the other that deconstruction calls for, does not perpetuate some form of moral and ethical nihilism. We will return to a detailed discussion of singularity in the final section.

This chapter, then, does not intend a detailed explication of Marx's texts, or of Marxist and economic theories as such, or of Derrida's reading of Marx. Rather, it attempts, both an exposition of, and interposition on, Derrida's notion of spectrality in relation to inheritance. My interposition is to argue that there is a hauntological logic evident in 'under erasure' which captures this necessity of ethical responsibility ('of reckoning with'): hence my joining of 'ethics' with Derrida's 'under erasure' to form *ethics under erasure.* In order to provide a stepping stone to a more detailed discussion of ethics under erasure much later in the chapter, the following section attempts to provide the connection between hauntology and 'under erasure', in turn drawing on and expanding Derrida's notion of 'justice without law' outlined in the previous chapter.

Hauntology: a discourse on 'erasure'

Derrida explains that the 'form of the chiasm, of the χ, interests me a great deal, not as the symbol of the unknown, but because there is in it . . . a kind of fork (the series *crossroads, quadrifurcum, grid, trellis, key,* etc.) that is, moreover, unequal, one of the points extending its range further than the other: this is the figure of the double gesture, the intersection' (Derrida 1982a, 70) between the calculable and incalculable, visible and invisible, past and future, material and immaterial, being and non-being, presence and absence, appearance and disappearance, and so on. Derrida's (re) interpretation of the Greek chiasm as a 'double gesture' of deconstruction is employed across much of his work in and through the forms of his neologisms and palaeonymys. The most obvious example of this employment of the chiasm is in what Derrida calls 'under erasure' (*sous rature*). As Spivak famously elucidates in the 'Introduction' to *Of Grammatology*, Derrida's notion of 'under erasure', which takes the form of the chiasm, means 'to write a word, cross it out [using the symbol of the chiasm: χ] and then to print both word and deletion. (Since the word is inaccurate, it is crossed out. Since it is necessary, it remains legible)' (Spivak, 1976, xiv). For example, to put the word 'is' under erasure it would look like this: i̶s̶, thus conveying both 'is' (presence) and 'is not' (absence). It works, argues Derrida, as a 'double register of production and nonproduction, without it being possible to privilege one of the two terms over the other' (Derrida 1982a, 68). Thus, under erasure marks what is produced, that is, the old word and concepts and meanings that we inherit, without privileging the transformation that occurs in the process of putting under erasure. In other words, for Derrida, this chiasm that conveys 'under erasure' is the physical mark or manifestation, in written form, of the more abstract notion of 'how writing [the general text] structurally carries within itself (counts-discounts) the process of its own erasure and annulation, all the while marking what *remains* of this erasure' (Derrida 1982a, 68).

Derrida borrows, he inherits, this crossing-out (under erasure) from Heidegger, who uses the chiasm (χ) in the *Question of Being* to attempt to dismantle the metaphysics of Being. Contrary to the metaphysical position on Being (ontology) handed down from Aristotle (and made famous by Descartes *cogito ergo sum*) where Being is conceived as detached from the world of objects (from materiality), or as that which is not *in* or *of* the world, Heidegger argues that 'Being' is instead the mode of existence of consciousness, which can only be understood as something that is located in the world; a locatedness Heidegger names 'being-there' (*Dasein*). To convey this Heidegger uses the chiasm to cross out B̶e̶i̶n̶g̶ in order to 'repel . . . the almost ineradicable habit of conceiving "Being" as something standing by itself' (Heidegger 1958, 81). By doing this, Heidegger conveys how 'the symbol of crossed lines can, to be sure . . . not be a merely negative symbol of crossing out' (Heidegger 1958, 83), because in the crossing-out we can 'transform' the ways we use language (Heidegger 1958, 73). It is the means by which Heidegger tries not to forget the language he was attempting to transform (by keeping it legible in the crossing-out) (Spivak 1976, xv).

Derrida argues that while Heidegger attempted to free language of its metaphysical foundations (origin), and to convey Being as that which is not simply present in and through the use of the chiasm, he nonetheless makes Being that which is before all concepts, and thus an origin. For instance, when Heidegger claims 'that the essence of man is a part of that which in the crossed intersected lines of Being puts thinking under the claim of an earlier demand' (Heidegger 1958, 83), he is constructing Being as a 'transcendental signified' because, as Derrida insists, the 'word "being", or at any rate the words designating the sense of being in different languages, is, with some others, an "originary word" ("*Urwort*"), the transcendental word assuring the possibility of being-word to all other words' (Derrida 1976, 20). What Derrida is arguing here is that while Heidegger erases 'Being' in order to 'de-limit' 'onto-theology, the metaphysics of presence and logocentrism, this last writing is also the first writing' (Derrida 1976, 23). It is, in other words, the origin of origin, because everything, all other questions, all meaning, refer to Being. Despite Spivak then reminding us that 'Heidegger makes it clear that Being cannot be contained by, is always prior to, indeed transcends, signification' (Spivak 1976, xvi), for Derrida this transcendentality of Being is an ontotheological position, and thus once again, metaphysical.

Although borrowing from Heidegger, Derrida argues that his own notion of 'under erasure' extends that of Heidegger, and thus in turn, transforms Heidegger's use of the chiasm. This transformation is especially evident when, in the opening pages of *Specters of Marx*, Derrida quotes Shakespeare's Hamlet saying: 'The time is out of joint' (I, 5), and in turn, invoking later,[8] Hamlet's famous soliloquy: 'To be, or not to be, that is the question' (III, 1). Recalling Hamlet's notion of time as that which is out of joint, Derrida is able to transform Heidegger's notion of 'being-there' (*Dasein*) away from what is still a presence in the world, into a relation of différance. Thus Derrida redefines 'being-there', not only as presence in the material world, but as differing and deferring; a différance that replaces autonomy with heteronomy, and ontology with hauntology. This is why Derrida writes that

> 'ontico-ontological' are, in an original style, *derivative* with regard to difference; and with respect to what I shall later call *différance*, an economic concept designating the production of differing/deferring. The ontico-ontological difference and its ground (*Grund*) in the 'transcendence of Dasein' . . . are not absolutely originary. Differance by itself would be more

'originary', but one would no longer be able to call it 'origin' or 'ground', those notions belonging essentially to the history of onto-theology, to the system functioning as the effacing of difference. (Derrida 1976, 23)

Bringing together the two passages from Hamlet, Derrida conveys in and through différance that 'to be' means to be 'out of joint'. Therefore, it is not about being or non-being. That is *not* the question. Rather, Being is constituted in and through both being and non-being, and thus it is a spacio-temporal relation, which is as a result 'out of joint' because it is never absolutely in the present moment, but always already differed (and delayed). It is always already the past and future, and thus differing. Given this, Being, and thus the subject, is spectral (*revenant*, and thus always 'to come'). The question then is not 'to be, or not to be', but instead, how to 'live *with*', how to 'reckon *with*', the spectral: with the ghosts of ourselves and others, with our inheritances?

For Derrida, not only are 'the questions on the subject of being or of what is to be (or not to be) . . . questions of inheritance' (Derrida 1994, 54), but they are also ethical questions. Thus Derrida shifts this question of inheritance from a purely ontological one to an ethical one (along, but not entirely, Levinasian lines) when he answers the question of how to live *with*, to be-with, spectres entails learning to live justly.[9] And to live justly is to learn to live *with* the other in ourselves and outside ourselves (other people, animals, things), and with(out) the absolute other: alterity (the difference produced by the past and the future 'to come'). To put it another way, Derrida transforms Heidegger's being-there and being-with as not simply individual presences located *there in* the material world *with* others, but as learning to live with(out) others: dead, living and to come. Learning to live with spectres, then, means living

in the upkeep, the conversation, the company, or the companionship, in the commerce without commerce of ghosts. To live otherwise, and better. No, not better, but more justly. But *with them*. No *being-with* the other, no *socius* without this *with* that makes *being-with* in general more enigmatic than ever for us. And this being-with specters would also be, not only but also, a *politics* of memory, of inheritance, and of generations. (Derrida 1994, xviii–xix)

Notably, for Derrida, what traces through or haunts every concept, word, language, experience is that which is not 'presence, origin, master' (Derrida 1976, xv), but instead is a differing and deferring that produces a spectral relation (out of joint), and thus hints at that which is absolutely other. This spectral relation is justice itself; it is what Derrida calls 'messianicity without messianism'. Messianicity is not the transcendentality of Being, it is not a traditional onto-theological position, and it is therefore not metaphysical; it is rather a promise that Derrida links to justice without law, which in turn he links to democracy 'to come':

> [W]hat remains irreducible to any deconstruction, what remains as undeconstructible as the possibility itself of deconstruction is, perhaps, a certain experience of the emancipatory promise; it is perhaps even the formality of a structural messianism, a messianism without religion, even a messianic without messianism, an idea of justice – which we distinguish from law or right and even from human rights – and an idea of democracy – which we distinguish from its current concept and from its determined predicates today. (Derrida 1994, 59)

Derrida thus defines the messianic as a promise, 'not this or that particular promise, but the promise implicit in an originary opening to the "other", to the unforeseeable, to the pure event which cannot be mastered by any aprioristic discourse', to the promise as the 'general structure of experience' (Laclau 2007, 73).

We will return later to this discussion in order to address some criticisms of messianism (and hence différance, the trace, arche-writing and Derrida's neologism's more generally) as simply another metaphysical foundation but in the form of a *negative metaphysics*, and thus the question raised by this: how would one know that an act towards the Other was 'just' if one couldn't refer it to a specific code of law? However, at this point, a range of other more pressing questions raise themselves in relation to the spectral and hauntology: in materially conveying this spectral logic in and through the mark of the chiasm, is this an attempt to bring the other into presence? That is, how does, or how can, the subject (in its presence) enable an 'opening' to something other (as alterity; as that which is unknowable) without violently reducing the appearance of the opening to the present (by virtue of the fact that this 'putting' under erasure would be a manoeuvre characteristic of metaphysics)? Is being 'aware' of an 'opening' to otherness simply a negation of this other as alterity? That is, does the other cease to be other once we are aware of it, because in being aware, we bring it into presence and thus reduce it to the 'same': an identification? The following section will attempt to answer these questions by embarking on a discussion of how 'under erasure' is, for Derrida, in at least two ways, a 'strategic necessity' that attempts from within the metaphysics of closure an *opening* to the other (alterity) without reducing it to the same, or without negating the potential sameness and thus understanding of the Other. This strategic necessity enables *transformation*. It is also in this discussion that the connection between hauntology and under erasure will be developed in more depth.

Opening and Transformation: Two Strategic Necessities

Opening

Under erasure is what we (you or I) do to something (such as a word or concept). But we not only put something under erasure graphically; we can and do this metaphorically and abstractly, as we would in putting a particular experience under erasure. If we take a traditional position, this suggests, however, that there is not only a 'who' doing the erasing, but that this 'doing' is an acting upon something, which requires a who that is objectively distinguished from objects and others. And as we saw in Chapter 2, Derrida argues that in traditional science and philosophy, to do, to act, to 'play', requires a disinterested and distanced (autonomous) observer; a subject positioned outside or apart from the object:

> Philosophy has always made play into an activity, the activity of a subject manipulating objects. As soon as one interprets play in the sense of playing, one has already been dragged into the space of classical philosophy where play is demarcated by meaning, by its finality, and consequently by something that surpasses and orients it. (Derrida 1988a, 69)

Doing, or 'to do', or playing with something, requires putting oneself in or into a particular place or space in order to perform that action. It is therefore to constitute the subject as that which enters a space, which in turn constitutes not only an inside/outside opposition (between one space and another), but at the same time constitutes the subject as distancing and objective, and hence autonomous. Consequently, the subject (the 'who') is experienced as the presence of the present, thus what is perpetuated is the metaphysical conception of Being and ontology discussed earlier.

However, Derrida reformulates the concept of 'doing' and 'playing' away from the classical conception outlined here and in Chapter 2. He explains that '[t]his play is not like a game that one plays with', rather the notion of play should be 'understood as the play *of* the world', not 'play *in* the world'

(Derrida 1988a, 69). On the one hand, to be 'in' something is to perform an action, and to construct 'a difference or interval between two things'. This 'difference' is a structural difference of comparison and contrast that operates to permanently fix, and make unchanging, the interval or space between two things. It also means to be enclosed (the significance of which will become apparent shortly), which encapsulates an opposition between inside and outside, place and space, and thus constructing a causative relation or function. On the other hand, to be *of* the world is to be associated, in accord, assimilated: and what these synonyms suggest is that play *of* the world is a play that is always already a disseminating process that haunts (differs and defers) the constructed boundaries between 'play' and 'work', and subject and object, subject and Other. To rethink play in this way is to simultaneously play with one's proper name, thereby disseminating the notion of an autonomous subject from one that 'does' the playing to one that is a continual process of play; it is to move from autonomy to heteronomy, from 'auto-affection' to 'hetero-affection' (Derrida 1998, 28). In Derrida's rethinking of 'autonomy' in *Resistances of Psychoanalysis*, he argues,

> the deconstructive necessity drives one to put into question even this principle of self-presence in the unity of consciousness or in this auto-determination, this logic of *Selbstbewegung*, or this immanence of the presupposition (*Voraussetzung*) that is constantly required by the Hegelian dialectic.
>
> Basically, what resists both the Kantian analytic and its dialectical critique is still an analysis, to be sure, but it is an analysis of the presence of the present that cannot not give in to the necessity and the affirmation of the hetero-affection in the system of auto-affection and of the living present of consciousness. (Derrida 1998, 28)

Here we can see Derrida's inheritance of Freud's notion of the unconscious to question the perpetuation of the unity of consciousness in the transcendental phenomenology of Husserl, the dialectics of Hegel, and the analytics or aesthetics of Kant. However, when Derrida puts the unity of consciousness into question it is not to deny unity altogether. Rather, Freud's notion that there are several 'doers' within the same subject (the ego, super-ego, id: all 'other' to each Other), attests to the continual move to and from (*fort/da*) autonomy and auto-affection to heteronomy and hetero-affection, respectively, and that without heteronomy there would be no need for autonomy: it is to affirm 'hetero-affection in the system of auto-affection'.

In fact we could conclude that otherness comes to consciousness, aware-ness, as a result of another Other.

In the same way that he plays with the proper name,[10] Derrida's use of the chiasm to graphically mark the (il)legibility of a concept or word is also a play with language. And to answer the questions posed earlier, while under erasure is a means by which to mark graphically, and thus bring to aware-ness the other, what is called forth in this awareness is not the full presence of the other, but rather the 'absence of presence, an always already absent present, of the lack at the origin that is the condition of thought and experi-ence' (Derrida 1976, xvii). What is 'opened' in and through 'under era-sure', then, is neither absence nor presence (absence would cease to be absence otherwise), but that which emerges in the between state, and as a result of presence and absence, appearance and disappearance, legibility and illegibility, visibility and invisibility, being and non-being, and so forth. What is 'opened', then, is heteronomy; the hetero-affection of thought and experience that makes auto-affection possible, and which, in turn, produces the ethical mode of questioning: how to 'live *with*' these Others/others; with heteronomy? This is a question that will be addressed later in this chapter and in Chapter 4.

To further understand this 'opening' to the other means returning briefly to a discussion on Derrida's deconstruction of the metaphysics of closure in Chapter 1. There it was argued that this 'opening' does not exist outside of, or transcend, metaphysics, as if there is an inside; a closure; like a cage from which we can simply escape. There is no outside of metaphysical closure; no outside language; '*nothing outside of the text*' (Derrida 1976, 158); there is no play *in* the world that is so neatly opposed to play *of* the world. But this is not to say there is no opening. It is more accurate to say that this opening is not an 'outside' of closure, and thus cannot be set in opposition to closure, because the 'outside bears with the inside a relationship that is, as usual, anything but simple exteriority. The meaning of the outside was always pres-ent within the inside, imprisoned outside the outside, and vice versa' (Derrida 1976, 35). This opening, then, can only be experienced as the haunting of the inside and outside. It is in the haunting that there is pro-duced a 'glimmer', an 'opening', of something other. Or as Derrida describes it, there is an 'unnameable glimmer beyond the closure [that] can be glimpsed' (Derrida 1976, 14).

My proposition here is that this opening is a result of hauntology itself: that which we can gain a sense of, but can never fully grasp. It is the haunt-ing of non-being within being, absence within presence, outside within inside, and vice versa. In other words, we can therefore potentially be aware of the opening to the other because, like a spectre, the other haunts us: it makes visible as it makes presence possible. What we are aware of, then, is not the Other as such (as full presence or full absence) but the presence of a non-presence, or the trace of the trace; the trace of the other (alterity). At the same time we cannot grasp the other, because it is also invisible, precisely because it is a trace of the trace. And therefore, we cannot entirely reduce the other (or the Other) to the same, to absolute presence. And yet, at the same time, the Other as other can be understandable, can be grasped, not by reducing it to the same, but as discussed in Chapter 1, through indirect perceptual presentation (analogical representation). If this was not the case then '[o]ne could neither speak, nor have any sense of the totally other, if there was not a phenomenon of the totally other, or evidence of the totally other as such' (Derrida 1995a, 123).

Returning now to Derrida's use of the chiasm to graphically mark language as 'under erasure', we can perhaps see that this use is a means by which to visibly demonstrate the hauntology, and thus spectrality, at work within the sign and the metaphysics of closure itself. In the context of his early writings, in particular *Of Grammatology* and *Dissemination*,[11] under erasure deconstructs not only the phonocentric tradition, but also the logocentrism encapsulated in 'semiology', what Derrida defines as a linguistic model that distinguishes between signifier and signified in a series of present 'nows', which thus structures language (and writing) as teleological; where in the classical conception the sign (origin) points and leads to meaning (end). Meaning, then, is produced by the relationship between the signifier and signified, which culminates in the referent. The referent in traditional semiology is believed to refer to an unchanging reality, because the referent (a word, for instance) is believed to capture and represent accurately and purely (without contamination of other signs) the one, true and permanent and essential meaning of the thing/object.[12] Thus traditional semiology assumes there is an intrinsic connection between a thing (in the world) and a word (in language). Words are not just names for things and objects (which is what they also are), but words also 'name', or 'stand in directly' for (represent), what is absent. As a result, traditional semiology constitutes a binary opposition between presence and absence.

However, Derrida deconstructs this 'incessant deciphering for the disclosure of truth as a presentation of the thing itself' as established by traditional semiology, and instead offers a ciphering 'without truth, or at least a system of ciphers not dominated by truth value', and which he calls 'différance'. Derrida further describes différance as 'this "active" (in movement) discord of the different forces and of the differences between forces which Nietzsche opposes to the entire system of metaphysical grammar' (Derrida 1973, 149). In and through this deconstruction of metaphysical grammar Derrida is arguing that there is no 'origin' and no end, no primary signified from which these significations, and thus interpretation and meaning, come and go. As already discussed, this is not to suggest, as Habermas and Rorty do, that Derrida thinks all meaning to be an 'undifferentiated textuality', or that we can, or would want to, dispense with the metaphysical tradition. Instead, Derrida wants to deconstruct this tradition: 'Western metaphysics, as the limitation of the sense of being within the field of presence is produced as the domination of a linguistic form. To question the origin of that domination does not amount to hypostasizing a transcendental signified, but to a questioning of what constitutes our history and what produced transcendentality itself' (Derrida 1976, 23).

Derrida questions this history and heritage by strategically replacing semiology with grammatology. The latter is that which conveys how the sign is always already haunted by other signs, to which it inevitably refers, but which never fully appear (Derrida 1976, xxxix). Grammatology is thus the movement of différance within the sign; within language. The chiasm marks this movement. It does this through a paradoxical process of simultaneously conveying the legible and illegible, visible and invisible, and so on. This is the process of putting under erasure. In this way, the chiasm (the mark or symbol of putting 'under erasure') is a means by which to demonstrate that not only do binary oppositions haunt each other (thereby keeping the philosophical, cultural and metaphysical history legible while transforming it); and not only does this then enable a questioning of the Western tradition or heritage to which we belong, and by which our subjectivity is constructed, but to put 'under erasure' also disturbs the teleology of language and signification, precisely by conserving 'the values of legibility and the efficacy of a model and thus disturbs the time (tense) of the line or the line of time' (Derrida 1976, xc). Chapter 4 attempts to show that 'under erasure' is not only grammatology,[13] but both conveys, and is, our ethical experience.

This brings us full circle to the discussion at the start of this section: what and 'who' is doing the erasing? To summarize the argument thus far: grammatology as the movement of différance, and under erasure as grammatology, suggests that the 'who' doing the erasing is not in and of itself absolutely 'present/presence'. Rather, the 'who', or the subject, is always another absent present. That is, the subject is constituted by the other – alterity – to which it refers, in the same way a sign refers to other signs. Therefore the other is not entirely outside the system. Thus, the 'who', as we have seen, is heteronymous. Given this, to graphically mark language with the chiasm is a metaphorical 'play' for the way in which the subject is always already 'under erasure', and this is precisely because there is no play as objective activity that produces final meaning without différance. The sub-ject is thus both present and absent; it is in fact spectral. In the following paragraphs this notion of the spectral subject is discussed in connection with hauntology and inheritance as a lead-into the next section on the second strategic necessity of under erasure. But first, underpinning this connection between hauntology and inheritance is différance.

First articulated in *Of Grammatology* and then in his essay 'La Differance', the notion of différance pervades Derrida's *oeuvre*. However, in his later work we can see différance being contextualized, particularly in *The Post Card*, and more politically and ethically in *Specters of Marx*. In the latter book, 'inheritance', as a discourse on hauntology, extends the notion of the possibility of delayed arrival (deferral) as a means of interrupting his-tory understood as teleology and presence. Consequently, to inherit, *to be* 'heirs does not mean that we *have* or that we *receive* this or that, some inheritance that enriches us one day with this or that, but that the *being* of what we are *is* first of all inheritance, whether we like it or know it or not' (Derrida 1994, 54). Of course, Marx is Derrida's example of this contex-tual process of inheritance: of how capitalist democracies are haunted by Marx and Marxism ('an abbreviation for communism') (Laclau 2007, 70). Inheritance, then, is not simply objects or goods and concepts handed down from one generation to the next in a teleological line, where objects mean the same thing from one person to another. For Derrida, hauntol-ogy serves to complicate this traditional conception of inheritance that Marx, too, for instance, attempts unsuccessfully to perpetuate in and through his realist ontology: the idea that we can 'know' our present reali-ties without recourse to our intellectual, philosophical, cultural, social and historical inheritances (the past). And this realist ontology that Marx espouses is the basis for his demarcation and opposition between objec-tive and material realities (the present), and immaterial realities (the past); between being (as presence in the world) and non-being, respec-tively. But as Laclau observes, this is a result of 'the spectres of Marx that visited Marx himself and prevented him from establishing a non-haunted ontology' (Laclau 2007, 70).

However, as we have seen in the discussion of différance, the boundaries between past, present and future cannot be so easily demarcated, and thus spectres (that which displace the linearity of time) cannot be so easily exor-cized. Therefore, what différance conveys is that the potential or possible arrival of the absolute other may not arrive at all. We will never know because we cannot calculate the future. Derrida does not define 'future' as 'future present': what may be more or less accurately planned for tomorrow (although it is that, too). Rather, the future means the unanticipated, uncalculated, unexpected, unknown event or experience 'to come'. The future is in part defined by the past and present past, and yet is always to come because it is unknowable. Furthermore, as we move into the future, the past, and the various ways it may or may not be interpreted, is always yet to be determined, and as a result the past too is always 'to come'. This raises several issues about translation, interpretation and inheritance of the past and future, which we will return to shortly.

Hauntology, therefore, as a 'discourse on the spectre', is strange and unfamiliar. The spectre is neither living nor dead, present nor absent, past nor future, here nor there (Derrida 1994, 51). It is 'the frequency of a certain visibility. But the visibility of the invisible' and is therefore 'beyond being'. It is the trace of something absolutely other that haunts our experiences, our languages, writings, thoughts, lives; it is something we know without knowledge, sense without sensing, because even though we might not see it, we 'feel that the specter is looking . . . The specter is also, among other things, what one imagines, what one thinks one sees and which one projects – on an imaginary screen where there is nothing to see' (Derrida 1994, 100–1). The spectre is, to invoke Freud as Derrida does, an 'uncanny' relation of and to time and space. Neither there nor not-there, present nor absent, conscious nor unconscious, hauntology conveys the metaphysics of presence as a chance occurrence, and thus as an ephemerality made possible only by hauntology. Or as Derrida writes: 'There is no *Dasein* of the specter, but there is no *Dasein* without the uncanniness, without the strange familiarity (*Unheimlichkeit*) of some specter' (Derrida 1994, 100). This uncanniness is a result of what the spectre introduces: a *contretemps* into the modalized presents ('past, present, actual present: "now", future present') of which it makes possible (Derrida 1994, xx). In other words, the spectre 'makes this presence possible only on the basis of the movement of some disjoining, disjunction, or disproportion: in the inadequation to self' (Derrida 1994, xix). As Derrida clearly suggests here, hauntology not only deepens the notion of différance as disjointed spacing, but adds to it by revealing the *contretemps* (out of joint) of time that conditions every ego, and every experience. This is why Derrida concludes that because 'the phenomenal form of the world itself is spectral', so too, then, is 'the phenomenological *ego* (Me, You, and so forth)' (Derrida 1994, 135). We are, all of us, spectres, for this *living individual* would itself be inhabited and invaded by *its own specter*. It would be constituted by specters of which it becomes the host and which it assembles in the haunted community of a single body. Ego = ghost. Therefore 'I am' would mean 'I am haunted': I am haunted by myself who am (haunted by myself who am haunted by myself who am . . . and so forth). (Derrida 1994, 133)

We are not only the hosts for the spectres that come to us from the past and future-to-come (the dead and not-yet-living), because we will be, and are already, for those to come (future), spectres of the past; but we too haunt the future and past-to-come, just as much as we serve, in the present, as the hosts of spectres (Derrida 1994, 133). The implications of being 'host' to spectres in which the spectre resides as 'the non-living present in the living present' (Derrida 1999c, 254) is that the spectre as that which is immaterial is also at the same time living and material. That is, the spectre 'lives on' in the living, and thus the spectre becomes materialized as we embody the ideas, philosophies and philosophers, ethics, politics, and the socio-cultural and historical traditions we inherit.

Moreover, and to return to the opening paragraph of this chapter, if there is more than one spectre, and if we are all spectres, then we are also multiple spectres, which is why Derrida insists that what we inherit 'is never gathered together, it is never one with itself' (Derrida 1994, 16). This is because, as we have seen, inheritance is disjointed by the hauntology (the spectres) that structure it, and therefore what we inherit comes back to us differently each and every time. An example of this is Derrida claiming that there is no 'pure' spirit of Marx that can be passed on down the genealogical and patrilineal line accurately and unchangingly, to its heirs. Rather, because inheritance is always already structured by hauntology, by *contretemps*, the spectre, thus inheritance, is *iteration*. In *Specters of Marx* Derrida defines iteration in the following way: 'Repetition *and* first time, but also repetition *and* last time, since the singularity of any *first time* makes of it also a *last time*. Each time it is the event itself, a first time is a last time. Altogether other' (Derrida 1994, 10).

The iteration, and thus heterogeneity, of inheritance suggests something else: that there are multiple translations and interpretations of our inheritances; or, to put it another way, iteration is what thwarts the homogenization of the unity of interpretation. Inheritance, then, is *open* to multiple interpretations. Given this, there is, Derrida asserts, an injunction to choose. We must choose, we must make a decision, we have no choice but to choose (because in not choosing we are also choosing), between differing inheritances, which even a single spectre (a name such as Marx) evokes. However, even though Derrida argues inheritance is 'never gathered together' there is a 'presumed unity'. This is because to make a decision, to decide among all possible choices, is also to create an effect of unity, an effect of presence. This is not to suggest that this effect is not real or not experienced as real, but rather this effect is made possible in the act of choosing between interpretations, which due to *contretemps*, is always differing and deferring. By 'choosing', Derrida means

> *one must* filter, sift, criticize, one must sort out several different possibles that inhabit the same injunction. And inhabit it in a contradictory fashion around a secret. If the readability of a legacy were given, natural, transparent, univocal, if it did not call for and at the same time defy interpretation, we would never have anything to inherit from it . . . The injunction itself (it always says 'choose and decide from among what you inherit') can only be one by dividing itself, tearing itself apart, differing/deferring itself, by speaking at the same time several times – and in several voices. (Derrida 1994, 16)

Derrida's argument that in 'choosing' we are always having to decide between 'several different possibilities', means that rather than creating oppositions between spectres, or within an inheritance, we have to 'reckon with' spectres, and thus with the 'necessary *heterogeneity* of inheritance' (Derrida 1994, 16), and with 'heteronomy' that is oneself.

To summarize so far, this heterogeneity of interpretations enables an *opening*, an 'unnameable glimmer beyond the closure' of an attempted homogenization of interpretation: the universal meaning of a spectre or inheritance (transcendental signified) (Derrida 1976, 14). Furthermore, it is because of this heterogeneity of inheritance that what we inherit is not a transmission of content unchanged and passively received by an heir, and why, in turn, 'translations themselves are put "out of joint". However correct and legitimate they may be, and whatever *right* one may acknowledge them to have, they are all disadjusted' (Derrida 1994, 19). The disadjusted (*contretemps*) nature of interpretation and translation of an inheritance produces 'undecidability' endemic to choice-taking and decision-making. Interpretation is never simply about the passing on of a universally true unchanging meaning. Rather, interpretation involves exchange between the 'who' that interprets (a '*who*' that is heteronymous), the *context* in which the interpretation takes place, and that which is *interpreted* (an inheritance: Marx, for instance). As a result of this exchange, two further aspects to

Derrida's notion of inheritance are introduced: that interpretation is inevitably iterative, and at the same time, interpretation is a performative act. Both iteration and performativity lead to transformation (of the past, and hence the future). Transformation is the second 'strategic necessity' of under erasure. The following section will unravel how transformation of an inheritance encapsulates responsibility and justice.

Transformation

Transformation is traditionally defined as a radical change or alteration: radical because what is changed is replaced or substituted, in a word, transformed so completely that the previous 'thing' (object, event, concept, word, experience, and so on) is unrecognizable. In contradistinction, for Derrida, transformation is not a radical alteration of a 'thing' or break with inheritance. Instead, transformation is a process involving interpretation, which in turn, is always already iterative. To transform, then, is a repetition of the past (and thus an acknowledgment and recognition of that which we inherit) but with difference. Transformation is the process of becoming something other to that which has gone before, and out of which it has arisen. Analogously, under erasure is the material and/or abstract marking of the transformative process. In rendering inheritance illegible, while retaining its legibility (and thus its analysability) via the metaphorical and/ or graphical mark of the chiasm, under erasure repeats with difference. Under erasure is an iteration, and thus a transformation, of a metaphysical tradition or inheritance.[14] In the same way as iterability, as that which enables but perturbs analysis by resisting binary oppositions, under erasure does not erase a concept entirely, and nor does it perpetuate a binary between that which is erased and that which the erasure points to: between the illegibility and legibility of a word, concept, experience. Instead, like the iterative process, under erasure contaminates and thus haunts this potential opposition so that what is produced is transformation rather than 'binary and hierarchized oppositions' (Derrida 1998, 31).

Because transformation is both iterative and a consequence of iteration (which is always already *contretemps*), then this means that every event, every inheritance, is singular. And because transformation produces singularity, a future event or an outcome can never be absolutely calculated. In other words, interpretation involves choosing, it means 'deciding' between inheritances, between other interpretations, and so on. Yet in choosing we cannot ever calculate or have absolute knowledge (in the Hegelian sense) of what the material or abstract outcomes will be; we cannot 'know' what it means for the future, 'for the future is no future if it corresponds to conventions and can be indicated by means of a conventional code' (Hamacher, 1999, 189). And we cannot know, because tracing through the materiality of our choices and decisions is the immateriality, the unknown, an alterity that involves any decision-making process in a 'reckoning-with', in a process of responsibility. Behind every decision and interpretation is undecidability and thus spectrality (Derrida 1994, 55). Decisions and interpretations are spectral because they are *haunted* by that which makes them possible: undecidability. This spectrality that haunts interpretation, and that produces iteration and thus transformation, is not simply 'metaphysical' and 'abstract' (Derrida 1999c, 244).[15] Rather, transformation, because made empirically manifest in and through the material 'who' that interprets, is able to 'produce events, new effective forms of action, practice, organisation, and so forth' (Derrida 1999c, 245).

Moreover, this is why Derrida insists in 'Marx and Sons' that the 'spectral logic I appeal to in *Specters of Marx* and elsewhere, is, in my view, not metaphysical, but "deconstructive". This logic is required to account for the processes and effects of . . . metaphysicalization, abstraction, idealization, ideologization and fetishization' (Derrida 1999c, 244–5). Derrida is not denying abstraction because, as he also argues, he is attempting to account for the possibility of abstraction, and therefore 'we should not shrug off abstraction as if it were nothing to speak of ("that's just an abstraction"), as if it were the insubstantiality of the imaginary, and so on' (Derrida 1999c, 245). Given this, we can think of transformation as simultaneously empirical and transcendental, and therefore as quasi-transcendental: transformation involves the evolution from the old to an uncalculated coming to presence (that is, to the materiality) of the 'new', which is inhabited by a *contretemps*, a spectrality, that makes the transformation process absolutely other, and that which is transformed, singular. It is in this iterative process of transformation, which produces the singular, that there resides the 'promise' to the future to come, a notion that will be elaborated on shortly.

As we have seen, inheritance does not involve a 'passive' transmission of information or objects from one heir to another in a genealogical-teleological line. Rather, what is received is not only already interpreted and translated by a tradition and context, but continues to be 'actively' translated and interpreted in the receiving, making interpretation a performative act. Derrida's notion of the performative act is neither the metaphysical-philosophical-scientific notion of 'action' discussed earlier in relation to 'play', nor does it entirely conform to the traditional definition as '"form[s] of rhetoric", "affectivity", [or] "tone"' (Derrida 1999c, 230). Performativity is this, but it also contains an excess that deconstructs its traditional role. Derrida confesses that his book *Specters of Marx* is performative in this traditional sense. Yet despite this confession I would suggest that his notion of the performative takes his text beyond merely aesthetic form or a rhetorical game because there is in the act of performativity, a call or promise to the future and thus to the other to come that exceeds any traditional interpretation and definition. In other words, the performative act is not simply behaviour or conduct, or a textual procedure or form operating within the limitations of a 'theoretical determination within the categorical frame', that is, within and by certain rules and conventions (Hamacher 1999, 193). Rather, as the following paragraphs will elucidate, the performative contains a messianic promise: a call to the unknown future and thus to a disjointed, unknown time of the other. Consequently, like inheritance, the performative is not a structure of cause and effect following the form of a traditional linear trajectory.

Examples of the performative can be seen in *Specters of Marx* when Derrida conjures the spectres that Marx attempts to exorcize, contaminating them with his own spectres, transforming the spectres of Marx, and the spirit of Marxism in the process. Spectre upon spectre haunts Derrida's text forming threads of multiple interpretations that, in the process of simultaneously interweaving and unravelling from each other, produce a performative 'style', a 'tone', an 'affect' and aesthetic form. Yet it is precisely in and through the traditional sense of the performative that Derrida in the conjuring of spectres upon spectres saturates his text with a haunting; a call to multiple spectres, and thus a call to the pasts and futures to come. His book, in other words, performs *contretemps* (out of joint), and calls (makes a promise) to an unknown other (another spectre, interpretation, future, spirit). In and through the traditional performative act, Derrida's book becomes hauntological, enabling Derrida to move beyond traditional performativity into a notion of 'performance as transformative'. That is, his book reveals that there is always something other and more (an excess) to come, and in this way the performative process is a transformative one, because it is not limited to a calculated future outcome or a 'categorical frame', which is produced by *constative* language. As Hamacher explains, this promise 'must play itself out in a mode of saying which corresponds to nothing given, nothing present, nothing extant and therefore can in no way be placed under the logic of representation, imitation or mimesis' (Hamacher 1999, 189).

In 'performing' the encapsulation of the promise within the traditional performative act itself, Derrida reworks the traditional notion of the performative act as it is developed by Austin in his theory of speech acts. For

Derrida, then, his reworking of the notion of the performative as 'interpretation that transforms the very thing it interprets', 'is a definition of the performative as unorthodox with regard to speech act theory as it is with regard to the 11th Thesis on Feuerback ("The philosophers have only *interpreted* the world in various ways; the point, however, is to *change* it")' (Derrida 1994, 51). For Austin, performative speech acts indicate what is actually 'performed' when uttering words or a sentence, such as promising, demanding, and so on. For instance, marriage vows are 'performed'. Furthermore, the performative act directly affects its hearers or readers: for instance, a marriage vow or 'performance' might make someone cry with happiness or jealousy or pity, and so on. The constative, however, is defined as the indicative mood: the mood of plain statements, facts and questions, and conveying no special stance on the part of the speaker.

As Derrida points out, according to speech act theory, a promise can only be 'successful', and held accountable, if it follows certain rules and laws associated with the performance. A marriage vow is not considered successful if it is not performed in front of witnesses, a celebrant or priest, and the signing of a legal document. And then of course there are the expectations or expected outcomes of a performance, because all speech acts (locutionary, illocutionary and perlocutionary, and including Austin's previous notion of the constative) are rule-governed. So, for example, the expectations, and thus assumptions, associated with the marriage performance include a promise to act in particular ways in the future (to love your husband or wife in the possible event of sickness, for instance). This in turn requires a belief on the part of the speaker and listener that a promise or request will be performed. Thus the future is determined by the expectations associated with the performative present.

However, for Derrida the idea that the constative and the performative can be so easily separated means that theorists of speech act theory fail to account for not only the way the performative and constative modes imbricate each other, but how this imbrication reveals that the rules that attempt to fix the demarcation between the performative and constative, the present and future, cause and effect, are never secure. Thus for Derrida 'what remains irreducible to the constative, to knowledge (which a certain Marx called, sharply limiting the notion, "interpreting": interpreting the world, when the point is to "change" it)' is 'the coming of an event' (Derrida 1999c, 257). As Hamacher perceptively elucidates, it is 'an event which with every occurrence discloses other rules, discloses other conventions, other subject forms and other performances, alterformances, alterjects, allopraxes. If language is a promise, it is always the other who speaks. And this other cannot be an alter ego, but only the alteration – and alteralteration – of every possible ego' (Hamacher 1999, 193). The performative act, as Derrida redefines it, therefore exceeds rules and conventions that frame the act within the here and now (the present). In disclosing and pointing to other rules and conventions, the 'promise', instantiated by the performative act, is a call and promise to the future (and thus the past) to come. Moreover, the possibilities of other rules, conventions and alterations inherent in every performative act, reveals the spectrality/hauntology of the performative itself.

Thus, for speech act theory, the notion of the performative is that which defines the future according to rules and conventions, so that the future can be anticipated and calculated, or made known, in other words conceived as a 'fixed horizon' or a 'future present'. Derrida's notion of the future to come, instead, is an (im)possible event because it is *un*determinable, *un*anticipated, *un*foreseeable, *un*imaginable and *in*calculable. The future to come cannot be determined by, and within, an economy of the same, consequently it never arrives as anticipated, thereby a call to the future to come is a call to the impossible arrival of the wholly other. To put it another way, the promise, as a performative, is not only spectral, but spectralizes: makes real and unreal simultaneously (Hamacher 1999, 191). And it is this spectrality of the performative that allows for the affirmation of the unknowable or the absolute other. Given this, 'interpretation that transforms the very thing it interprets' is, as Michael Dillon argues, a messianic appeal to the 'aporia of the (im)possibility of justice' (Dillon 2007, 90): it is a 'promise' of unconditional welcoming of the unknowable 'to come'. Transformation is justice in the most unconventional sense.

Justice: Again, and Again

For Heidegger, justice is characterized by the 'law' of jointure, that is, the conjoining to oneself and to the Other in and through an accord, a 'correctness [*justesse*]'. But as we have seen, Derrida links hauntology and transformation (and thus the *contretemps*, the out of joint, of time) to justice, allowing him to argue that Heidegger's jointure or adjoining always presumes 'the calculated gathering up of oneself, coherence, responsibility' so that the notion of jointure is conceived as the foundational basis, emergence and perpetuation of Being, as presence. Derrida questions this, asking 'if adjoining in general, if the joining of the "joint" supposes first of all the adjoining, the correctness [*justesse*], or the justice of time, the being-with-oneself or the concord of time, what happens when *time itself* gets "out of joint", dis-jointed, disadjusted, disharmonic, discorded, or unjust? *Ana-chronique?*' (Derrida 1994, 22). In the form of a question, Derrida answers this, a few pages later, by claiming that justice, and Being as presence, can only proceed; can only come about, in and through anachrony. Thus, in the process of this questioning, Derrida transforms Heidegger's notion of justice (*Dikē*):

> [D]oes not justice as relation to the other suppose on the contrary the irreducible excess of a disjointure or an anachrony, some *Un-Fuge*, some 'out of joint' dislocation in Being and in time itself, a disjointure that, in always risking the evil, expropriation, and injustice (*adikia*) against which there is no calculable insurance, would alone be able to *do justice* or to *render justice* to the other as other? A *doing* that would not amount only to action and a *rendering* that would not come down just to restitution? (Derrida 1994, 27)

While Derrida argues that justice based on anachrony risks evil and injustice because it has to allow for the worst to come (and in taking this risk actually *does* justice by allowing the Other to be other); arguably Heidegger's justice as jointure ('of the event as coming into presence, of Being as presence joined to itself' (Derrida 1994, 27)), which for the sake of harmony, or the 'synthesis of a system', entails a much greater risk. Jointure risks justice 'being reduced once again to juridicial-moral rules, norms, or representations, within an inevitable totalizing horizon' (Derrida 1994, 28), precisely because justice, and hence the promise, is linked to a traditional notion of the performative and 'fixed future horizon', which in turn attempts to render the singularity of the Other (event, person, context) to the same.

Reducing justice to juridicial-moral rules and norms requires a conception of *responsibility* as an accountability of one's actions and decisions in relation to universal and metaphysical foundational ethical principles. That is, to be accountable means being judged and determined by the 'fairness' or the 'rightness' of those actions as they accord with, or conform to, the law. The law can be defined as those 'rules' of conduct instituted by custom, social practice, moral values and legal, institutional and governmental authorities. Furthermore, rules of conduct involve general principles that are considered universal across time and place (ethics): do not kill another person, do not steal, and so on. In turn, these principles constitute normative social behaviours and values in culture. Because the law is universal, justice for past wrongs or actions can be tried in a court of law in the present.

An example might be when evidence is uncovered 30 years after a murder, enabling a murderer (still alive) to be convicted. This example of the universality of the law can be used to highlight further what Derrida means by claiming that jointure risks justice 'being reduced . . . to juricial-moral rules, norms . . . within an inevitable totalizing horizon'. That is, using this example, we can infer, from what Derrida argues, that justice for past actions or events is always brought to presence in the present time, so that singularity of the actions or events occurring in the past is reduced to the same, in other words, to the rules and conventions of justice as law (*droit*) in the present.

So while taking responsibility in this conventional and traditional sense means that 'responsibility as accountability' and 'justice as law' is achieved according to socio-cultural conventions, and while Derrida does not deny this universality or its necessity, he suggests that this form of responsibility and justice as jointure risks not being just to the singularity of every event, context and person. (Although this is not to suggest that for Derrida openness to the other and singularity requires ethical nihilism, and we will return to this in relation to the work of Ernesto Laclau and Alain Badiou later.) Justice as law (metaphysical ethics) is then the short-cut to 'right action', precisely because ethics operates deductively: if one acts responsibly by following prescribed rules, then a specific conclusion will be achieved, that is, justice as restitution. Conventionally it is assumed that the law leads to justice, and that the law is justice. As we saw in Chapter 2, and as we will see in a moment, there are several problems with this assumption.

If ethics operates deductively, and deduction is a process of reasoning, and reasoning a characteristic of metaphysics, then, ethics appeals to rationality.[16] In operating deductively, this conventional notion of responsibility as accountability to the law is a 'time'- (not to mention an emotional- and psychological-) saving device, precisely because ethical and just responses becomes normative ones as they are delineated along dichotomous lines of good/bad; right/wrong, respectively, and in doing so closes all disjoinings and *contretemps* that may lead or open to a 'justice without law'. In summary, ethics is prescriptive, and thus avoids the singular moral responses to singular moral events. The irony is that the prescriptive response not only denies the reasoning (on which justice as law is based) required of a subject in a particular context, but also exorcizes the heterogeneity, difference, the anachrony, and thus the potential injustice inherent in the singularity of every event, but which makes justice possible.[17] Arguably, justice as law (ethics) does not always serve to take responsibility for the singularity of the Other, whether in the past or present, but instead constitutes and benefits, in the present, the subject following the law by ensuring that the subject does not have the pain of going against the status quo. If this is the case, then justice as law is not about a care for the Other, so much as care for the self. Given this, how can one ethically respond to Other; is it at all possible? Furthermore, ethics (justice as jointure) thereby perpetuates the 'effects' of the subject as the presence of the present and vice versa (an autonomous subject), while taking away autonomy and reason through prescriptivism, which can work to deny the undecidability inherent in every ethical decision.

Derrida deconstructs a notion of Reason that founds justice as law, by showing how 'right action' (responsibility as accountability) is aligned and associated with obedience to the principles of an ethical system. In ethical theory and systems, the status of an action, behaviour or response taken in relation to a situation or event that calls for it, is dependent on the principle of the ethical theory/system one might be applying or following. This principle is conveyed by the word 'must' or 'ought', which, as will be explained further on, is the principle of Reason itself. Furthermore, one's ethical response is determined by how the 'must' or 'ought' is defined by a particular ethical system. In what follows two dominant ethical systems of Western society will be briefly elucidated. This elucidation will attempt to prepare for the later discussion on – while also making clear the significance and implication of – Derrida's deconstruction of Reason for thinking ethics under erasure.

First, utilitarian philosophy states that someone performing an action needs to account for the consequences it will have on others. Therefore, what our actions *must* or *ought* to produce is the best outcome, not simply for oneself, but for the majority. To put it another way, action *must* depend on the goodness or badness of the consequences for the welfare of all human beings.[18] This means that action is based on rationality, where rationality serves as a means to the end or outcome. So it is the alignment of action with consequences which is considered 'responsible' behaviour according to this theory. Second, deontology, of which Immanuel Kant is a famous proponent, is a system of ethics that does not worry about the consequences of our actions, so much as appeal to conformity with certain rules of duty. If we obey the rule of duty then the right consequences will follow. For example, telling the 'truth' is a duty regardless of what we think should be the outcome or consequence. For Kant in particular, what is important about action is not the end or the outcome achieved, but the 'reason' for the action. This is what Kant calls the 'categorical imperative',[19] and is famously summarized by one of his maxims: 'Act only according to that maxim by which you can at the same time will that it should become a universal law' (Kant 1959, 39). This of course has led to the arguments that Kant's 'duty' is in fact utilitarian, because it can be applied universally to achieve the maximum benefit or happiness for the largest number of people. But for Kant, acting according to duty (obeying the 'must' or 'ought') is a 'good in itself'. We will return to addressing why this is so for Kant shortly; suffice to say that for deontology, the alignment of action with duty is responsibility.

What both these ethical systems have in common, then, is the construction of principles based on reason and that regulate action. Reason, and rationality, is the origin, the foundation upon which all actions and principles are based.[20] For utilitarianism, ethical principles are based on rational decision-making in relation to the norm. As J. J. C. Smart argues, for individuals this means that 'the rational way to decide what to do is to decide to perform one of those alternative actions open to us . . . which is likely to maximize the probable happiness or well-being of humanity as a whole, or more accurately, of all sentient beings' (Smart and Williams, 1996, 42). In a nutshell, utilitarianism not only provides rules and laws, but the 'must' or 'ought' is based on reason: to act in accordance with reason – that is, to base our ethical response on rational decisions – is the 'right action'. For utilitarianism, reason leads to right action, which leads to the best ends or outcomes: the maximum happiness or well-being of a community, or of humanity, as a whole, and which is determined by the general moral attitude of what any given society thinks constitutes its happiness or well-being.

There are a number of flaws with utilitarianism, the most obvious being that the rights of minorities are often overlooked in favour of the majority (and that majority may be made up of a dominant ethnic or religious group). That is, what is good is considered that which produces the greatest happiness for the greatest number of people, therefore, it is the majority that determine what is considered good or 'happiness'. Controversially, it could be argued that what the majority may think is good may not actually be good for the majority. Finally, if society's notion of happiness changes over time and across communities and states, then the moral attitude, and thus the ethical system, is revealed to be not universal, but contingent and contextual. If the rules change, this then suggests that there is no grounds for happiness apart from what the majority want (happiness or the good is based on norms). This is the problem, according to Kant, of ethical knowledge as *a posteriori*, or what Kant calls 'empirical idealism'. As we will see, Kant privileges Reason as *a priori*. Meanwhile, the bigger problem with a utilitarian notion of Reason is that it is end-orientated. That is, it is pragmatic, strategic and objectively focused 'in view of its utilization' (Derrida 1983, 11). Derrida suggests that utilization is potentially a problem because 'thinking' or 'thought' in general, and by implication ethical response, becomes simply a techno-scientific programme producing or authorizing particular discourses that serve 'technopolitical' powers (Derrida 1983, 18). (Or as Marx would put it, these discourses are a result of particular classed ideology, so that ethics and morality is simply an ideology of the bourgeois, for example, that functions to perpetuate their economic interests. For Marx then, the founding principle of ethics is purely economic.)[21]

In suggesting reason to be *a priori*, Kant is arguing that there are grounds for Reason, and that the ultimate ground or principle is Reason itself. Like Kant, Leibniz believed, too, that reason is the principle of reason, because '"[n]othing is without reason, no effect is without cause"' (Leibniz in Derrida 1983, 7). For Leibniz, as Derrida interprets him in his essay 'The Principle of Reason', what makes reason the principle of reason is, first, that reason can be 'rendered', and second, that reason is founded on the principle of non-contradiction. Derrida defines the former principle as that for which 'any truth – for any true proposition, that is – a reasoned account is possible' (Derrida 1983, 7). Furthermore, Derrida argues that the 'question of this reason cannot be separated from a question about the modal verb "must" and the phrase "must be rendered". The "must" seems to cover the essence of our relationship to principle, it seems to mark out for us requirement, debt, duty, request, command, obligation, law, the imperative. Whenever reason can be rendered (*reddi potest*), it must' (Derrida 1983, 8). Returning to the second principle, it is through his notion of 'duty' that Kant demonstrates how the principle of non-contradiction operates. He argues that to tell the 'truth', for instance, is to act out of duty:

> Suppose that someone followed the maxim that he might tell a lie if thereby he could acquire a big profit. Then ask whether this maxim could exist as a universal law. It is then to be assumed that no one would tell the truth to his own loss, and in that case no one would trust [anyone] anymore. The liar in that case could not come to be in a position to deceive through his lie. The law would thus defeat itself by itself. (Kant 2003, 657)

Kant argues here that happiness for all humanity cannot be beneficial if it is based on or requires deceit or lying, precisely because to lie can't be based on Reason. It may be rational in a particular context, but it is not based on 'reason as the principle of reason'. This is why, for Kant and deontology in general, utilitarian rationality is not sufficient. (But, then, one common argument made against Kant's position, for example, is that on occasion it may not be possible to keep a promise and tell the truth at the same time. Leaving aside whether or not this is a correct interpretation of Kant's notion of reason, this criticism attempts to reveal the contingency – not the universality – of reason as the foundation or principle of reason.)

It is only because reason is the principle of reason that it can be independent of all empirical, aesthetic (moral feeling) and religious influence, and which is why, for Kant, in the individual 'the principle of autonomy is thus the self-possessed legislation of the power of choice through reason' (Kant 2003, 659). The principle of autonomy leads to the obedience of the moral law, in and through which humanity attains freedom and Enlightenment. Any legislation that rests on grounds other than the 'freedom of reason' is, Kant insists, 'heteronomy'. Thus, for Kant, autonomy is achieved only in and through acting morally, and is not simply about mere individual 'wilfulness' or 'independence' (O'Neill 1994, 179).[22]

We saw earlier Derrida's problem with utilitarian end-orientated reason as producing techno-scientific 'thought'. But now we see that the principles of 'rendering' and 'non-contradiction', which draws on the logic of cause and effect, deduction and inference, to move from one universal truth, or true proposition, to another, privileges particular forms of knowledge (philosophical for instance), and so, too, leads to a comparatively narrow understanding of what it means to 'think'. Thinking, in other words, is limited to deductive and logical reasoning associated with argumentative-theoretical evidence. This form of reasoning privileges, or at least attempts to produce, a subject objectively and autonomously distanced (temporally, psychologically and affectively) from, and also from its response to, others. It is precisely this objective reasoned-based response that Derrida deconstructs. Given this privileging of reason, what is at risk of being marginalized is the 'affective' and the 'sensuous', and thus the subject's embodied experience in knowledge production.[23] Therefore, despite the differences of both ethical theories, in utilitarianism and deontology this form of end-orientated reason subjugates to reason (a mind-body split in fact) the subject's experiences within historical, cultural, political and social contexts, and thereby the raced, gendered, sexed and classed embodied positions in which subjects are situated and from which subjects are not autonomous. In the same way that Derrida argues that while there is an effect of presence, the subject as presence is a fable, and given the contextuality of subject positions just outlined, so too then is the notion of a metaphysical ethics of presence a fable. To suggest this does not mean, however, a rejection of forms of moral reasoning altogether, but it may enable us to question why privilege is accorded to a rational-based ethical decision-making process.

While to give a reasoned account means to draw on the logic of cause and effect, deduction and inference, Derrida nonetheless insists that there is a responsibility involved in *how* we 'respond to the call of the principle of reason' (Derrida 1983, 8). Derrida notes that traditionally 'the response to the call of the principle of reason is thus a response to the Aristotelian requirements, those of metaphysics, of primary philosophy, of the search for "roots", "principles", and "causes"' (Derrida 1983, 8); it is a response, in other words, that utilizes a dimension of technical, scientific and philosophical reason or thought. Importantly, for Derrida, responding to this call does not mean either obeying or disobeying this principle. Rather, response entails a broader definition of thought, one that 'would interrogate the essence of reason and the principle of reason, the values of the basic, of the principle, of radicality, of the *arkhe* in general, and it would attempt to draw out all the possible consequences of this questioning'; it is a form of thought that unmasks 'all the ruses of end-orientated reason' in order to produce, in turn, new '"thought" – a dimension that is not reducible to technique, nor to science, nor to philosophy' (Derrida 1983, 16). If, as Derrida argues, responding to the call does not mean obeying or disobeying the principle of reason, it is because '"[t]hought" requires *both* the principle of reason *and* what is beyond the principle of reason' (Derrida 1983, 18–19), because, after all, 'reason is only one species of thought – which does not mean that thought is "irrational"' (Derrida 1983, 16).

Once we move away from conventional or metaphysical notions of what is defined as thought, or even reason, and take account of the permeable boundary between the affective and the conceptual, Derrida's question of responsibility, or how to respond to the Other, becomes more interesting, but also more difficult to answer. In *Politics of Friendship* and *Specters of Marx*, Derrida does perhaps offer an answer, albeit obliquely. It is, then, to Derrida's 'question of responsibility' that we will now turn, because Derrida's deconstruction of reason, and of responsibility informed solely by the principle of Reason, reveals the need to acknowledge the role of both dimensions (that is, universal rules, codes and prescriptions on the one hand, and the context in which prescriptions occur, and in which the subject is situated, on the other) in the production of, not only knowledge and 'thought', but ethics and morality as well. This in turn will lead into thinking 'ethics under erasure'.

To answer for, before, to the other: the question of responsibility

Derrida argues that the 'must' in metaphysical ethical systems is tied to the principle of the 'autonomy of reason'. In the *Politics of Friendship* Derrida further deconstructs this 'must', and in doing so, addresses 'the question of responsibility' and what it might mean to respond ethically to the Other beyond duty and beyond the 'force of law' (law as justice; the rules of justice). For Derrida, 'response' contains (grammatically, syntactically and performatively) at least three modalities: 'to answer for', 'to answer before', and 'to respond to'. The first two modalities correspond closely to 'justice as law', and thus align themselves with both utilitarian, deontological and metaphysical conceptions of responsibility. Derrida describes these two modalities as such: '"One *answers for*", for self or for something (for someone, for an action, and thought, a discourse), *before* – before an other, a community of others, an institution, a court, a law' (Derrida 1997b, 250). Thus these two modalities presuppose an autonomous subject, one that is not only unified and 'gathered' to or within itself and in autoaffection, in the Heideggerian sense, but also one that is a result of the principle of reason in the Kantian and Leibnizian senses. In other words, these two modes of response require subjects with 'proper names', because without proper names there is no 'I' and thus no accountability (responsibility to the law):

> 'I' am assumed to be responsible for 'myself' – that is, for everything imputable to that which bears my name. This imputability presupposes freedom, to be sure – a non-present freedom; but also that what bears my name remains the 'same', not only from one moment to the next, from one state of that which bears my name to another, but even beyond life or presence in general – for example, beyond the self-presence of what bears the name. (Derrida 1997b, 250–1)

Not only does 'the proper name rigorously presuppose . . . a concept of subjectivity', but this concept of subjectivity, in turn, presupposes a metaphysical ethics and vice versa. Precisely because one not only *answers for* one's actions, thoughts and so on, in one's own name, but in one's own name, one *answers before* the universality of the law ('a court, a jury, an agency authorized to represent the other legitimately, in the institutional form of a moral, juridical, political community') (Derrida 1997b, 252). This connection between ethics and subjectivity, in turn, presupposes and is based on an ethics and subject of presence.

Identity and subjectivity are unified into the presence conveyed by the proper name, but this unification is simply an attempt to reduce identity and the Other to the same, and is therefore, Derrida argues, a 'fable' despite producing an 'affect of presence' (Derrida and Nancy 1991, 100). It is a fable because reduction is impossible. Derrida elaborates on this in *Politics of Friendship* when he argues that reduction is an impossibility assured by the third modality of response: 'to respond to', which encapsulates the anachronistic (disjoined; 'other') time of justice. In other words, unlike the previous two, the third modality, 'to respond to', is more originary and unconditional because it does not answer *for* or *before* the Other, and thus simply for oneself. Rather, the prepositions in 'to respond to' mark the indirect object of a verb, in this case the 'Other', and thereby brings to more prominent awareness the spectrality of the moral and ethical relation between subject and Other. The destination of subject 'towards' the Other (conveyed in and by the 'to' of 'respond *to*') is not the subject in control of its 'response to' the Other, so much as a response to a call, not to the call of reason, but a response to the response of the Other (in particular and in general). There is, then, a continual loop from/to or for/with (*fort/da*) the subject and Other's responses. This is why, for Derrida, 'one does not answer for oneself in one's own name, one is responsible only before the question, the request, the interpellation, the "insistence" of the other' (Derrida 1997a, 251). Consequently, this is why, as was discussed in detail in the previous chapter, the relation to the Other is dissymmetrical, and 'this dissymmetrical anteriority also marks temporalization as the structure of responsibility' (Derrida 1997a, 252).

To elaborate further, this response to the request of the Other is not simply or *only* a response to the Other 'known' person or situation in the here and now, the present. This being the case, the response to the call of the other is not one that is or can be produced by justice as law (ethical systems), which gather into unity in and through the present by rules and codes that constitute, in turn, calculated, prescriptive and deductive (reasoned) responses. This would simply be prescribed action. Rather, as Derrida confirms, and to return now to *Specters of Marx*, response to a call of the other is a justice that 'entails a commitment to "the life of a living-being"', and to the other 'beyond "present life or its actual being-there"'. In other words, '*justice*, must carry beyond *present* life, life as *my* life or *our* life. *In general*. For it will be the same thing for the "my life" or "our life" tomorrow; that is, for the life of others, as it was yesterday for other others: *beyond therefore the living present in general*' (Derrida 1994, xx). What does Derrida mean by the 'must' here, especially as he deconstructs the 'must', the 'ought', produced in and through rule-governed categorical imperatives based on the autonomy of reason, as well as end-orientated prescriptivism? And what has this 'must' to do with the 'beyond' present life, the 'to come'?

In 'The Last of the Rogue States' (2004), when talking about democracy, Derrida makes an interesting connection between the 'to come' and the messianic promise. He argues that the '"to" of the "to come" wavers between imperative injunction (call or performative) and the patient *perhaps* of messianicity (nonperformative exposure to what comes, to what can always not come or has already come)' (Derrida 2004, 336). This wavering reveals that 'to respond to' the other beyond present life (the here and now) is not only 'to respond to' what is to come, but enables us to comprehend the double move encapsulated in Derrida's notion of response both 'to' the living-being in the present, and the other beyond being. For 'to respond to' *both* simultaneously further reveals that response does not, and cannot, necessarily reject justice as law, conveyed in and through utilitarian end-orientated calculation or deontological duty. Response is this and also more, as this double move reveals: on the one hand, 'to respond to' 'goes beyond what would be "rightfully" expected, beyond what "duty dictates"' (Caputo 1997b, 150). That is, one responds (urgently) without calculation to that which cannot respond back, to what 'cannot be awaited *as such,* or recognized in advance therefore, to the event as foreigner itself, to her or to him for whom one must leave an empty place, always, in memory of the hope – and this is the very place of spectrality' (Derrida 1994, 65). Leaving an empty place is what Derrida calls hospitality without reserve:[24] it is to welcome, justly, what may possibly arrive, without ever being sure of the actual or possible arrival of the other. Our response to the other 'to come' is a response to the unknown that may or may not 'appear' or happen. What appears, happens or comes, then, is not the anticipated and therefore calculated event of the Other, rather the other to come is an (im)possible spectre, always pointing to or revealing the spectrality that defines our responses 'to'. That is, our response to the other, and hence justice as such, is a spectral relation, precisely because response and justice are relations marked by différance, by a disjointed temporalization that not only exposes heteronomy structuring the subject, and hence the 'present', but the heteronomy of future life and death. An understanding of the non-teleological, non-linear temporalization of life and death perhaps helps to clarify Derrida's statement in the 'exordium', the opening pages of *Specters of Marx,* when he argues that a 'living being . . . has no sense and cannot be *just* unless it comes to terms with death. Mine as (well as) that of the other' (Derrida 1994, xviii). This means coming to terms with what it means to live with, maintain ourselves in the face of, and thus be just to, 'specters' and 'spirits': to what we inherit and pass on.

On the other hand, 'to respond to' the past and future (the 'to come'), to that beyond present life, is a result of an ethical injunction: the *must* of justice to carry beyond present life. This *must* in Derrida's passage cited above ('justice must carry beyond present life') is non-prescriptive, non-utilitarian, and non-instrumentally reasoned. Consequently, this *must* is dissociated from a humanistic ethics, but also from a notion of what it means to be human. This *must* for Derrida is not contingent upon its general usefulness (utility) for achieving cooperation among members of society, or simply a result of rules of justice arising from the associative laws of the imagination as Hume would have it: for Hume imagination creates regularity of our beliefs, understandings, morals and personal identities; that is, our morality and ethics is psychological rather than empirical or logical (and based on reason). But for Derrida, neither is this *must* founded on Reason alone. In other words, without rejecting the 'Kantian architectonic and critique', and without giving up on reason (Derrida 2004, 330), Derrida argues that this *must* is not entirely akin to Kant's regulative ideal. Derrida in fact opposes Kant's regulative ideal – which 'remains on the order of the *possible*, an ideal possible' –

all the figures I place under the title of the *im-possible*, of what must remain (in a nonnegative fashion) foreign to the order of my possibilities, to the order of the 'I can', of ipseity, of the theoretical, the descriptive, the constative, and the performative (inasmuch as this latter still implies a power for some 'I' guaranteed by conventions that neutralize the pure eventfulness of the event; the eventfulness of the to-come exceeds this sphere of the performative). (Derrida 2004, 329)

The promise, and thus justice, exceeds the sphere of the traditional notion of the performative outlined by speech-act theory. This traditional performative restricts the promise, and promise-keeping, not only to that which has value because of its general utility to society, but to that which waits, that which is 'kept in memory', 'handed down (*léguée*), inherited, claimed and taken up (*alléguée*)' (Derrida 2004, 330). In exceeding this sphere, and thereby exceeding all humanist ethical and moral determinations and conceptions of humanity, the promise (and justice) is a 'response to' the unknown other of the future/past 'to come'. That is, in exceeding the traditional domain or structure of the performative, the promise, goes beyond it, and in doing so, reveals the performative as that which is always already affected, and changed by, the subject's response to the 'to come'. The performative cannot be restricted (as much as Searle and Habermas, for instance, might think it is), to categorical frames or restricted to operating by certain rules and laws.

Given this, 'to respond to' that beyond present life, the subject performing a 'promise', for instance, is not 'guaranteed by conventions' of the performative, but rather, the subject also exceeds the sphere of the performative that, at the same time, also constitutes the subject. The performative is inherently spectral and so too is the subject. It is because of the excess that haunts the performative and hence the subject that the 'I' does not have to be autonomous (as Kant and humanists would argue) in order to be responsible, or 'to respond to', or to be just, or to keep a promise. For example, the promise made is not only to the Other/other outside oneself, but to the other in ourselves: to the unanticipated, unexpected 'I' of ourselves 'to come' (the unexpected influence of the Other(s) on our future thoughts, feelings, beliefs, and so on). This is not to suggest, however, that the subject, because structured by heteronomy, is not simultaneously recognizably the same. There is no heteronomy without autonomy and vice versa, and by extension, a promise to the other in ourselves is what takes us beyond while at the same time constituting the 'same'.

This promise, for Derrida, then, is not the promise constituted by a traditional ethical system and the performative act. Rather, the promise in its excess and its response to the beyond of present life, is what Derrida calls the emancipatory and messianic affirmation. Importantly, this messianic promise, which is conveyed by the *must* of justice to carry beyond present life, this spectral justice, should not remain, Derrida argues, spiritual or abstract, and therefore moves beyond 'the memory of a determinate historical revelation', and a 'determinate messiah-figure' (Derrida 1999c, 251). In this sense, as Christopher Norris notes, what Derrida indeed has in common with Kant is a 'mistrust of materialist philosophies that think to place themselves "beyond" metaphysics at a stroke by declaring for the ontological primacy of matter, over mind' (Norris 1987, 149). What we have here, in Derrida's messianic promise, is justice as a quasi-transcendental relation. Justice is the response to the other 'to come' in the here and now, in the present, which enables the production of 'new effective forms of action, practice and organization and so forth' (Derrida 1994, 89). To respond to the other 'to come' is not simply abstract or utopian, because justice occurs and is experienced in and through our embodied selves in the present. But to respond to the other 'to come' is not only materialist, because the 'to come' haunts (in and through the spectres of the past and future, and as the unknown other) the present; and the presence of the present, as we saw earlier, is always already structured by différance, by the past and future: by a non-linear temporalization. All of this suggests, as Derrida makes clear in the quote below, that the other 'to come'; the impossible; the abstract, is real as it becomes embodied in and through our 'responses to' the call of the Other/other. This then is precisely why Derrida opposes his notion of the impossible to Kant's regulative ideal, it is why justice is quasi-transcendental, because the impossible

is not the inaccessible, and it is not what I can indefinitely defer: it announces itself, sweeps down upon me, precedes me, and seizes me *here* and *now* in a nonvirtualizable way, in actuality and not potentiality. It comes upon me from on high, in the form of an injunction that does not simply wait on the horizon, that I do not see coming, that never leaves me in peace and never lets me put off until later. Such an urgency cannot be *idealized*, no more than the other as other can. This im-possible is thus not a (regulative) *idea* or *ideal*. It is what is most undeniably *real*. And sensible. Like the other. Like the irreducible and nonappropriable difference of the other. (Derrida 2004, 329)

The *must* is not an ethical injunction in the sense that it requires the subject to obey certain rules and calculations prescribed by ethical systems. Rather, the *must* is a messianic 'promise', and it is urgent, and therefore this *must* is other than mere calculation. It is an injunction that does not come from the outside: from a law court, the rules of justice of an ethical system (deontology or utilitarian, and so on). It is not a command coming from outside and demanding that the subject perform particular actions to achieve moral outcomes. No, this injunction is the promise, and thus it happens in the moment, urgently, and beyond traditional decision-making. And this promise is the very structure of justice itself. The injunction to respond to the Other beyond present life is not within justice (which would suggest that it is something 'without' that has been internalized, incorporated, appropriated); rather it *is* justice itself. This injunction is constitutive of the promise and vice versa.

Ethics

Ernesto Laclau agrees with Derrida that the promise exists before any ethical injunction (the latter defined as a demand put forth by the law), but he finds unconvincing what he thinks is the link that can be made, in *Specters of Marx*, between 'the promise as a (post-)transcendental or (post-)ontological (non-)ground and the ethical and political contents of an emancipatory project' (Laclau 2007, 77). He argues that it does not follow that the former leads to the latter. This argument is reminiscent of the one Critchley makes about deconstruction, and undecidability, being unable to move from ethics to politics (Critchley 1999, 190).[25]

Building on this, Laclau further argues that while Derrida does not make this link explicit, the 'ambiguity' of *Specters of Marx* itself allows Derrida's defenders to make an 'illegitimate' leap in thinking: that is, from 'the impossibility of ultimate closure and presence' (precisely because presence and closure is marked and constituted by the heterogeneity of the Other and by undecidability) to a belief that 'some kind of ethical injunction to be responsible and to keep oneself open to the heterogeneity of the other necessarily follows'. However, while Laclau is in agreement with Derrida that the 'promise is an "existential" constitutive of all experience, it is always already there, before any injunction', there is no ethical imperative, insists Laclau, 'to "cultivate" that openness or even less to be necessarily committed to a democratic society' (Laclau 2007, 77). To make a deductive leap to an ethical imperative of being open to the heterogeneity of the Other is in danger of reinstating ethics as *a priori* (in the Kantian sense). Therefore, to make this leap is a false one according to Laclau who has argued, elsewhere, 'that ethical values are only "conversationally" grounded – that is (in my own terms) socially and discursively constructed. I do not see any reason to attribute to ethical values (or to a primacy experience of the alterity of the other) any foundational role' (Laclau in Mouffe 1996, 60).

This false leap is a consequence of the entanglement of Levinasian ethics with deconstruction made by some of Derrida's defenders, not necessarily by Derrida himself, because of course, as we have seen, Derrida does not make being open to the Other/other an ethical injunction if an ethical injunction is conceived as laws and rules of justice. But we should not jump to the opposite conclusion either. If Derrida questions the *a priori* grounds on which ethics is based in and through his deconstruction of the principle of Reason, this does not mean that Derrida takes a radical empirical (Humean) or materialist (Marxian) stance. And, as quoted in the previous section, what Derrida has in common with Kant, if not an *a priori* notion of ethics, is at least a 'mistrust of materialist philosophies that think to place themselves "beyond" metaphysics at a stroke by declaring for the ontological primacy of matter over mind' (Norris 1987, 149). Thus, when it comes to the promise, the promise comes before any injunction, and thus Laclau is right: this messianic promise does not offer a foundation from which an ethical injunction can be logically deduced. To produce an ethical injunction from this is to attempt to either fix (make present), or deny the impossibility of closure, undecidability, différance, the messianic promise, and so on. Therefore, as argued earlier, being open to the Other/other is not about an ethical injunction coming from the outside (from the laws of justice), as if the outside is not already constitutive of the inside, and vice versa. Rather, there is an undecidability structuring the decision 'to respond to' the unknown Other/other, whether or not we are aware or want to do this, or not. The 'choice', the 'decision', here is not a calculated one made by a humanist subject conceived of having autonomous agency, because we are always already responding to the Other/other. Does this mean, as Laclau argues, that the promise is nihilistic? We will return to this very shortly.

Meanwhile, there are two further and more pressing concerns for Laclau. First, he argues that the 'undecidability inherent in constitutive openness' can lend itself to ethical and political actions, beliefs and arguments that are in opposition to democracy:

[F]or instance, since there is ultimate undecidability and, as a result, no immanent tendency of the structure to closure and full presence, to sustain that closure has to be *artificially* brought about from the outside. In that way a case for totalitarianism can be presented starting from deconstructionist premises [sic]. Of course, the totalitarian argument would be as much as a *non sequiter* as the argument for democracy: either direction is equally possible given the situation of structural undecidability. (Laclau 2007, 77–8)

But isn't this precisely the risk Derrida has been labouring over when he argues in *Of Hospitality* and elsewhere that to open oneself to the Other, and thus to welcome and to say 'yes' to the Other, involves the risk of the Other bringing the worst, or of losing power and control by becoming hostage to the Other in which one is being hospitable? Or inversely the Other becomes hostage to the host? (Derrida 2000, 125). Opening to the unknown Other of course brings the possibility of the best or the worst; democracy or totalitarianism. So in response to Laclau, the more pressing question is what would it mean (ethically or politically) *not* to take the risk? An answer can be found in Derrida's *Of Hospitality* and also confirms why Derrida does not subscribe in full (although he does not reject) Kant's ethics of 'duty':

Kant founds pure subjective morality, the duty to speak the truth to the other as an absolute duty of respect for the other and respect for the social bond . . . But simultaneously, *on the other hand*, in laying out the basis of this right, and in recalling or analyzing its basis, he destroys, along with the right to lie, any right of keeping something to oneself, of dissimulating, of resisting the demand for truth, confessions, or public openness . . . by refusing the basis of any right to lie, even for humane reasons, and so any right to dissimulate and keep something to oneself, Kant delegitimates . . . any right to the internal hearth, to the home, to the pure self abstracted from public, political or state phenomenality. In the name of pure morality, from the point where it becomes law, he introduces the police everywhere. (Derrida 2000, 69)

To not take the risk then is to make ethics, the response to the Other (unknown or not), conditional. It is to attempt to strip ethics of the impossible (as if this were possible), and to reduce the Other and the subject within an instrumental reason that homogenizes behaviour and response. However, for Laclau, this leads to his second concern: that openness to the Other requires accepting 'the other as different *because* she is different [foreign], whatever the content of that heterogeneity would be. This does not sound like an ethical injunction but like ethical nihilism' (Laclau 2007, 78). If Derrida's messianic promise does not impose an ethical injunction, and if Laclau does not think an ethical injunction can follow from Derrida's notion of the messianic promise, how can there be ethical nihilism? It seems that the ethical injunction Laclau wants to ensure against nihilism is not the same as Derrida's defenders who think that the ethical injunction *is* being open to the unknown Other/other. Thus there is a tussle, not over whether or not the ethical injunction is *a priori* or Reason-based, but rather, what cultural social agendas and value judgements are going to dominate. But leaving this aside, the question becomes: if being open to the Other/other *is* an ethical injunction (albeit a violent one), why should openness to the Other/other assume ethical nihilism?

There are several responses one could take to Laclau at this point. One could argue that Derrida is not nihilistic, repeating the brief but necessary arguments made against both Rorty and Habermas in the Introduction. There it was argued that because différance makes undecidable the oppositions within language, Rorty believes Derrida's deconstruction leads to endless textual freeplay, which then leads Habermas to argue that Derrida's différance leads to language and meaning being indeterminate and nihilistic. However, as further argued in Chapter 2, while there is a play of differences within language, and thus ambiguity, ambiguity is what enables ethical possibilities to arise. These possibilities are not endless (Rorty) or indeterminate (Habermas), because even though the singularity of context(s) opens possibilities, context limits and constrains these possibilities. But possibility can never be purely empirical, because it is structured or haunted by impossibility, which allows for the other 'to come', for the past and future to come. This contamination is not the conjoining or the conjunction of two opposed terms, because impossibility is a spectral haunting that leaves within possibility 'a trace of its withdrawal' (Derrida 2002, 362). This contamination, this haunting, is quasi-transcendental, and each event, each possibility, is simultaneously normative (universal) and singular, and thus always already under erasure.

One could also argue in response to Laclau that opening oneself to the Other, whatever they may bring (the best or worst), assumes that the Other is so absolutely foreign (as if the border or limit between the subject and Other – inside and outside – that links the two, is impermeable) that the Other is not transformed, changed, or responds in kind to the other that is us. Or that the Other is not drawn into the normativity of social values and judgements (as if the other isn't inside the subject, or, more aptly, as if the other isn't that which is constitutive of the subject), or that being open to the other to come means passive acceptance. Laclau's response to the latter is that if we reformulate the argument to mean that 'openness to the other does not necessarily mean passive acceptance of her but rather active engagement which includes criticizing her, attacking her, even killing her, the whole argument starts to seem rather vacuous: what else do people do all the time without any need for an ethical injunction?' (Laclau 2007, 78) But as we have seen, for Derrida, being open to the Other may be risky, it may lead to totalitarianism and violence; but so too can following the law. Derrida is by no means advocating that we deliberately break the law. Instead what he is questioning is not whether or not we need 'ethics' or ethical injunctions, we do, so much as the basis on which these are formulated, and the foundation upon which we are constituted, and/or negotiate, 'Sameness': that is, whose ideologies, social and cultural values and standards, what norms are instituted, passed on and inherited, and how does this inheritance affect ethical practice in the present, in the here and now? And it is in questioning ethics as the principle of Reason that Derrida reveals the imbrications of ethics and politics, but also the alterity (the impossibility, undecidability, différance, and so on) that 'contaminates' or haunts our ethical responses.

It is this second concern that finally leads Laclau to argue the following: because the grounding of presence of the decision does not refer back to a foundational principle, but instead is reinscribed 'within the terrain of the undecidables (iteration, re-mark, difference, etcetera) that make its emergence possible', then this poses the problem of how to 'conceive of emancipation within this framework' (Laclau 2007, 79). Yet it all depends on how one defines emancipation. For Laclau there are several contradictory and conflicting dimensions of the notion of emancipation (Laclau 2007, 1). These dimensions do not conform to a logically unified whole or theoretical structure and thus make it hard to define; nevertheless, by juxtaposing them with each other can open up 'new liberating discourses, which are no longer hindered by the antinomies and blind alleys to which the classical notion of emancipation has led' (Laclau 2007, 2). In making this argument, Laclau is very close to both Derrida and Badiou, but surprisingly unconvinced by Derrida's 'terrain of undecidables' as being able to lead to emancipation. Let us unpack this seeming contradiction and address Laclau through Badiou's notion of ethics and emancipation.

For Badiou, ethics (rules and laws of justice) is a nihilistic and circular system that is deeply conservative precisely because it is the means by which to accept the status quo and thus blocks, 'in the name of Evil and of human rights, the way towards the positive prescription of possibilities' (Badiou 2002, 31). In other words, prescriptions, the rules of law, what Derrida calls 'justice as law', is about the 'status of the *Same*' (Hallward in Badiou 2002, xv). Because there is always already difference, and '[d]ifferences being simply *what there is*, the question of what "ought to be" must concern only what is valid for all, at a level of legitimacy that is indifferent to differences. Differences *are*; the Same is what may *come to be* through the disciplined adherence to a universal truth' (Hallward in Badiou 2002, xv). Ethics as the perpetuation of the status quo, or consensus (in the Habermasian sense) inevitably blocks emancipation. 'For what every emancipatory project does, what every emergence of hitherto unknown possibilities does, is to put an end to consensus . . . Ethics is thus part of what prohibits any idea, any coherent project of thought, settling instead for an overlaying unthought' (Badiou 2002, 32–3). For Badiou, emancipation is about liberating discourses and possibilities of thought and otherwise.

Given this, and to alleviate Laclau's concerns, I would suggest that it is precisely because of what Laclau calls Derrida's 'terrain of undecidables': impossibility, the messianic promise, différance, justice without law, and so on, that enables the possibility of 'emancipation' in all its varying forms, and in particular in the way Badiou defines the term, and despite Badiov's various critiques of Derrida's Levinisian heritage. And yet we also need to qualify this by reminding ourselves that while Derrida's, 'terrain of the undecidables' open up possibilities and new discourses, and can thus be conceived as emancipatory in non-classical ways, Derrida's *Specters of Marx* and his notion of 'inheritance' and 'hauntology' suggests that emancipation is only possible because of ethical, political and social restrictions, prohibitions, restraints; only possible because of what Badiou labels 'unthought'.

But inheritance here suggests something more. It suggests that we are always in negotiation with social contexts (past, present and future), and that these contexts are always 'under erasure'. Thus the ambiguity that Laclau rightly perceives in *Specters of Marx* (perhaps in most of Derrida's texts) is a result of putting the status quo in politics, ethics and philosophical thinking under erasure. We could go so far as to argue that the 'terrain of the undecidables' (différance, the trace, impossibility, hauntology, messianic promise, khora, and so on) convey the double movement of 'under erasure'. It is because of this double movement that the messianic promise, or justice without law, is never simply 'abstract and spiritual' and existential to the point of being solipsistic and nihilistic, and this is because justice and the promise is also grounded by its negotiation with socio-cultural value judgements (by justice as law): it takes place; is embodied in the subject's contextual position in the here and now. At the same time, the promise responds to the call from the other beyond, thus denying the ontological 'primacy of matter over mind', and thus the opposition this institutes (Norris 1987, 149). It is in this way that justice is quasi-transcendental, because it is always already under erasure. And the following final paragraphs unpack this notion of justice as quasi-transcendental in the context of a concluding summary of the argument of this chapter.

Justice as the messianic promise puts justice as law (ethics) under erasure. In doing so, the messianic promise (which is the positive response of the other beyond) reveals the spectrality that constitutes the promise (because the response is a response to the past and future to come), which means that so too does this promise haunt 'justice as law', revealing, in turn, that justice as law (ethics) is always already haunted by several spectres and spirits: of inheritances from the past and future 'to come'. Thus, ethics, on the one hand, is haunted by the spectral form of the promise in its call – response – to, and by the call of, the other. On the other hand, ethics is haunted by more than one law, one rule, and so on (which thus destabilizes its metaphysical foundations, precisely in and through the juxtapositions of these various hauntings). Given this, ethics (justice as law) structurally carries within itself its own erasure.

Furthermore, justice without law is not beyond justice as law. It is not solely spiritual or abstract in that it transcends the present (becomes a transcendental signified) and thus the embodied and contextual experience of the subject in the here and now. To put it another way, 'under erasure' in this context means that the promise does not annul justice as law, because justice as law (in)forms the here and now (the present). Rather, the promise puts the here and now under erasure: not forgetting, not deleting the present altogether; not deleting ethical institutions and laws but *transforming* them in and through the non-traditional injunction of the 'must' of justice to respond to the beyond.

Given this, not only are the metaphysical foundations or origins of ethics transformed, but so too are singularities. That is, both the context in which the subject is situated (as well as the subject itself), is put under erasure as it is transformed by the subjects singular response to the beyond; and so too is the singularity of the future/past (that is, the beyond) put under erasure by the context of the subjects ethical response, which is informed by the generic ethical same (justice as law). In other words, for Derrida, to be able to pass on, to inherit, to be haunted, means that what is inherited has to be recognizable, has to conform to a genre, to a genus, and thus dare I say, to the common, the Same, the universal. Of course, this is the paradox of under erasure: to be singular, the subject has to be both outside and beyond the common, or the Same, or the universal, and yet common enough to be understood as singular (Derrida 2006, 1, 8–9). In the next chapter, and in relation to an analysis of Todd Haynes' film *Far From Heaven*, and specifically the ethical relations between two of the characters, Cathy and Cybil, this notion of singularity and universality is taken further and developed by arguing that 'ethics under erasure' involves a continuous negotiation between universal (and unifying) ethical norms and particular situations requiring singular ethical responses and decisions, in our everyday practices.

Chapter 4

Ethical Experience: A Cinematic Example

'There is no responsibility without a dissident and inventive rupture with respect to tradition, authority, orthodoxy, rule, or doctrine.'
—*Derrida*, The Gift of Death, 27

Between Theory and Practice, an iteration

The phrase 'ethics under erasure' attempts to capture the profound paradox and complexity of the tension and relationship between the ethically singular and the general. In the Introduction to this book this paradoxical relationship was revealed in and through Derrida's deconstruction of responsibility, where irresponsibility was demonstrated to be constitutive of responsibility; and where 'absolute responsibility' involves acknowledging and belonging to, while simultaneously transgressing, ethical duty (metaphysical ethics). In Chapter 3, the paradoxical relation between the ethically singular and general was conveyed in and through 'hauntology': ethics is haunted by that which it inherits (other ethical principles or systems, laws and rules), and by the call of the Other/other. In this way, metaphysical ethics structurally carries within itself its own erasure.

To reveal the relevance of 'ethics under erasure' for our everyday experiences and lives, this chapter extends those theoretical discussions to a practical reading of a single cinematic text (Todd Haynes' *Far From Heaven*), with the aim of revealing a further contamination not only between the ethically singular and general (ethical duty), but between ethical duty and singularity, *and* social and moral norms. Recalling the discussion in Chapter 3, the difference between metaphysical ethics (prescriptive systems, rules and laws) and norms can be defined as such: ethics are those 'rules' of conduct instituted by legal and institutional (and religious) authorities. Furthermore, rules of conduct involve general principles that are considered universal across time and place (ethics): do not kill another person, do not steal, and so on. In turn, these principles constitute normative social behaviours and moral values in culture, which become instituted in and through custom and social practices. Although not all social norms and values necessarily comply with universal ethical principles. There is then constant negotiation between a metaphysical ethics (principles) and norms. As this chapter proceeds we will see that both of these are, in turn, put under erasure by singular ethical responses. In other words, there is a negotiation between not only the singular and the general, but also between one singularity and another, one general principle of duty (ethical theory) and another, so that our singular ethical responses to others entails negotiation with and within ethical systems (and hence social values and norms built on those systems) that carry universal status. It entails a negotiation with our ethical inheritance, and it is in this way that ethics under erasure extends, differently, through film analysis, Derrida's absolute responsibility.

While Todd Haynes' *Far From Heaven* (2003)[1] will be analysed with the aim of demonstrating a further contamination not only between the ethically singular and general (ethical duty), but between ethical duty and singularity *and* social norms and values, the questions that pose themselves at this point are: why film as the example (and not literature or art for instance)? And why *this* film in particular? In answer to the first question, as a cultural artefact, arguably more than literature, or art or any other narrative form, film is fundamentally multi-modal: the verbal (sound) is as important as the visual (changes in movement, colour, spacing, light, and so on). Indeed, film is a medium where meaning is typically constituted through a complex interplay between these modalities. Thus film movement creates identification so that the viewer too is moved along with the narrative and characters in 'real time'. This movement in real time means that a viewer doesn't simply analyse the experience but at the same time is affected by that experience in a way that viewers' thoughts and judgements are simultaneously challenged, undermined and confirmed in real time. This in turn enables viewers to imaginatively reflect on the past and present while also projecting further scenarios and reflections about the future. Therefore because the interplay between modalities creates 'affective responses' in the viewer, and coupled with cinematic devices which frame and contextualize those affective responses, film fiction and narrative constructs alternative or possible ontologies, raising philosophical questions about some of the most profound problems of human experience not only in the past, but for our culture and society today.

In answer to the second question, this particular film has been chosen for analysis for the following two reasons. First, by presenting us with a series of fictional ethical relations and (im)possibilities (such as inter-racial, class and homosexual relationships), *Far From Heaven* opens a space for critical reflection; for imaginatively rethinking such relations outside of the fictional, and for recognizing the simultaneous universality and singularity of any ethical moment. Second, the film enables this rethinking because it challenges (through its cinematic devices and narrative) the conventional understanding of political and ethical acts and the norms on which they are based: throughout the film, the relations between characters, their behaviours and the decisions they make are shown to be both ethically complex and ambiguous. In short, the film *iterates* previous theoretical discussion of ethics under erasure, in and through visual and narrative form, thus enabling identification with how ethics under erasure is lived or can be experienced in our contemporary everyday lives. While this ethical ambiguity characterizes all the relationships in the film, the focus of this chapter is on a single conversation. This conversation takes place towards the end of *Far From Heaven*, between Cathy Whitaker, the female lead (a white suburban housewife in 1950s America), and her black maid, Cybil. In the fourth section, entitled 'An Ethical Encounter: Cathy and Cybil', this conversation serves as an example of how ethics under erasure is manifested in an 'everyday' context. The fifth section entitled 'Erasing the Subject' re-examines this scene, this time concentrating on the consequences ethics under erasure has for the subject: ethics under erasure will allow us to rethink conventional theories of subjectivity.

Above it was mentioned that previous theoretical discussion of ethics under erasure is *iterated* in and through the film *Far From Heaven*. The word 'iterates' has been used here instead of 'application', so as to avoid putting theory into practice, which would only contribute to perpetuating the metaphysical theory/praxis opposition that also dichotomizes ethics and politics, and which is challenged in Chapter 1. This theory/practice opposition also implies that theory is not 'transformed' and changed by the context or practice (material or otherwise) in which it is discussed or placed, and vice versa. Similarly, iteration is used instead of 'representation', because to represent something conveys that there is some 'thing', world, object, person, and so on, that can be captured and depicted directly, and behind this conception of representation is a belief that there is one, true and permanent and essential meaning of the thing/ object/world. It implies there is an essential nature to objects in the world, and as a result there is one reality unchanging through time and space; eternal and independently of us: reality, in other words, exists without input from human beings. In contradistinction to this view, and following

Derrida here, iteration is used because it is not simply repeatability, which entails a traditional concept of representation. Rather, iteration reveals that 'there have never been anything but supplements, substitutive significations which could only come forth in a chain of differential references' and therefore 'the absolute present, Nature, . . . have always already escaped, have never existed' (Derrida 1976, 159).

The iteration that is produced in and through the discussion of ethics under erasure, in the context of film analysis, transforms theoretical discussion in the following ways: if film and everyday life and experience (texts) are open to interpretation, and that interpretation is constituted by how the viewer is constructed by their social contexts, then what the film iterates are the ethics and social values read into the film by viewers, while the film, in turn, iterates the ethics and norms embodied in everyday life. Moreover, this viewer/audience construction is conveyed in the second section, 'Contingent Norms: Todd Haynes' Homage', by demonstrating how *Far From Heaven* (2003) in its homage to the film *All That Heaven Allows* (1956), recreates the ideologies of the 1950s in order to prompt a contemporary viewer/audience to reflect upon current social norms and the ideologies that underpin them. Asking the viewer to compare, and reflect upon, norms and ideologies from the 1950s and the twenty-first century, the film not only renders visible its construction as text, and thus the constructedness of the viewer's positioning, but in doing so challenges more broadly the socially dominant attitudes in contemporary society regarding race, class, gender and sexuality. At the same time, the film's cinematic devices also perform 'under erasure'. We will return to this issue at the conclusion of this chapter. Meanwhile, the self-reflective reading position created by the cinematic devices of the film, and the comparison, in the following section, of the film's genre to the melodrama genre of the 1950s to which *Far From Heaven* pays homage, suggests that 'construction' of point of view, or perspective, actually informs all ethical and social normative behaviour and responses across different eras.

Contingent Norms: Todd Haynes' Homage to Douglas Sirk

Mary Beth Haravolich argues that Douglas Sirk's famous 1950s melodramas are subversive of 1950s consumerist society and gendered norms (Haravolich 1990, 58). Others, such as Barbara Klinger, disagree, arguing that 'we cannot consider the family melodrama of the 1950s as necessarily subversive to the repressive regimes of the decade. Rather . . . such films often helped realize the heightened sexual depictions and affluent ideologies that marked the culture' (Klinger 1994, 68). The ending to Sirk's film *All That Heaven Allows* (1956) is conventionally happy: despite a degree of social and emotional conflict, Cary (Jane Wyman) resumes her affair with Ron Kirby (Rock Hudson), her gardener. In some respects, it is true that this resolution sustains norms of gender and social positioning that reflect the ideologies of the affluent in the 1950s, just as Klinger suggests. Leaving aside the various arguments about audience participation in the construction of meaning and the affirmation of dominant ideologies,[2] it is nonetheless clear that sustaining these ideologies, and norms, does not result simply from overt 'authorial intention'. Furthermore, as Haravolich argues, melodrama as a genre typically generates ideological contradiction through character and narrative conflict. Melodrama, she argues,

> works ideologies through narrative and character in multiple ways. Characters are defined and motivated by the contradictory pressures of ideologies. Narrative conflict stems from the desires of characters being at odds with their social and sexual identities. Melodrama uses realist narrative space to both validate the presence of the social world and to identify the ideologies that motivate character and conflict. (Haravolich 1990, 61)

This tension is evident in *All That Heaven Allows* since Cary, while continually moulded by patriarchal norms, simultaneously refuses to conform to the social norms and expectations governing her role as widowed mother. Ironically, and paradoxically, not following the norm leads to the conventional happy ending expected by the studio, Universal Pictures. Sirk admits as much in his famous interview with Jon Halliday: 'I became a kind of house director for Universal. Conditions were not perfect . . . But . . . I restructured to some extent some of the rather impossible scripts of the films I had to direct. Of course, I had to go by the rules, avoid experiments, stick to family fare, have "happy endings", and so on' (Halliday 1997, 97). To a significant extent, Sirk was merely part of the wider economic, cultural, and social process that was filmmaking at the time.[3] However, the interview with Halliday suggests Sirk did not simply bow to the conventions of melodrama as genre, though we cannot conclude from this that he used the genre to deliberately subvert ideology. Yet if we follow Haravolich's claim here, we could in all probability assume this to be the case. In many respects, though, Sirk's 'intentions' are of no consequence because, as Haravolich implies in the quote above, the genre of melodrama is itself contradictory. That is, in order to create suffering and sorrow (the genre

was referred to in the 1950s as 'women's weepies') the genre produces conflict and tension which works implicitly, if not overtly, to identify, and thus
subvert, dominant ideologies of class, sexuality and affluence.

Sirk may or may not have used the genre as a method of subversion.
There can be little doubt that director Todd Haynes deliberately recreates,
and hence exposes, the social norms and ideologies of the 1950s in his film.
Far From Heaven is homage to *All That Heaven Allows,* and to Sirk's melodramas generally. Importantly, this homage is not ironic: *Far From Heaven* does
not take an ironic stance on the past, commenting smugly on how far attitudes have improved as ideologies and norms have changed in the twenty-
first century. Instead, the homage works to produce a certain 'distance'
through juxtaposition between the characters within the film (1950s, the
past) and the viewers of the film (twenty-first century, the present). This
distance creates emotional affects, but not entirely through identification
with the characters. Instead, the film is too emotionally poignant to be
ironic, because distance works to produce in the viewer an emotional affect
of sad contemplation and 'reflection' over the general state of human
affairs in the 1950s as well as in the twenty-first century. Moreover, distance
is also created by repeating, or more aptly iterating, Sirk's cinematic devices
of framing, objective point of view, the long shot, long take and saturated
colour. These cinematic devices will be discussed more fully during the
course of this chapter.

This homage to the genre itself, and to Sirk's use of cinematic devices,
runs contrary to the current trend (since the 1980s) of 'intensified continuity' in film-making. As David Bordwell defines it, rather than reflecting
a desire for fragmentation or incoherence 'the new style amounts to an
intensification of established techniques' (Bordwell 2002, 2), referred to
as 'intensification of classical continuity'. Thus, '[i]ntensified continuity
is traditional [classical] continuity amped up, raised to a higher pitch of
emphasis. It is the dominant style of American mass audience films today'
(Bordwell 2002, 2). For Bordwell, intensified continuity is characterized,
first, by 'rapid editing': modern films have used more shots and more
frequent cuts since the 1980s. The average contemporary film contains
1500 shots or more. Before the 1960s the average cut of most Hollywood
feature films was between 300 and 700 shots, with each shot around 8 to
11 seconds in length (Bordwell 2002, 2). Another feature is 'bipolar
extremes of lens length': action sequences use medium-long shots,
whereas there is a trend towards medium-close to close-up shots focusing
on one character at a time in scenes involving dialogue. Modern films,
argues Bordwell, also rely on 'desaturated and monochromatic color

schemes' (Bordwell 2002, 9). Intensified continuity has not only been the dominant mode in Hollywood mass-market feature films since the 1980s, but appears in Western independent films as well, because the filmic devices of intensified continuity are 'friendly to small budgets' (Bordwell 2002, 11). Indeed, in one of Todd Haynes earlier films, *Safe* (1995), he plays with the style of intensified continuity to an exaggerated degree (Bordwell 2002, 17).

However, in *Far From Heaven* Haynes frequently forgoes close-ups in favour of long shots, using long takes and less rapid transitions between shots to slow the tempo. His palette is characterized by a saturated rather than desaturated or monochromatic colour scheme. Going against the norm of contemporary cinema, then, Haynes faithfully reproduces Sirk's cinematic devices and camerawork, even though his film does not reconstruct the 'happy ending' typical of Sirk's melodrama. Haynes points out that in Sirk's films there are very few close-ups, and 'the characters rarely own the frame' (Haynes 2003, DVD). In his own film, Haynes imitates Sirk's use of objective narration. He eschews point-of-view shots, and positions the camera slightly to the side of the characters: as a result, orientation is spatial, not psychological, the over-the-shoulder shot-reverse-shot sequences do not construct subjective point of view, and the characters are not portrayed in close-up taking over the frame. Rather, the typical configuration is for both characters in a dialogue to be positioned within the same frame.

Haynes argues that, in regards to Sirk's films, the 'moviegoer's intense emotion doesn't come from identification' with the characters primarily, but from 'montage and music' and from the cinematic devices as a whole (Haynes 2003, DVD). By imitating Sirk's cinematic technique, Haynes creates a similarly intense emotional experience for the viewer. But we could go further, and suggest that the contrast between Haynes' homage to Sirk's cinematic devices and intensified continuity is not only deliberate on Haynes' part, but works to create a distance, between the 1950s and the twenty-first century norms and values construing gender, race, class and sexuality. This distance, then, exposes the unstable boundary between the ethical norms and values of the two eras. In this way the cinematic devises reveal our ethical, socio-cultural and filmic inheritances.

For example, the appropriation of 1950s saturated colour schemes not only serves a symbolic function in the film but, in being contrasted with the modern trend of desaturation characteristic of intensified continuity, and in combination with objective point of view, emphasizes the temporal distance between the past (the 1950s) and the present. Haravolich argues that colour in Sirk's films 'distracts from the realism of the film'

(Haravolich 1990, 58). Her argument is that '[c]olor can contribute to the "visibility" of ideologies through realist *misè-en-scene*, yet color can also subvert the "invisible" realism of narrative space' (Haravolich 1990, 57). Given that Haynes imitates Sirk's cinematic devices, including colour, then what Haravolich proposes here is certainly happening in *Far From Heaven*. Indeed, the technique is more pronounced here, because the use of saturated colour contrasts overtly with the modern desaturated colours favoured by most modern film-makers. Thus, in conjunction with the framing devices, the quaintness of the saturated colour in *Far From Heaven* in fact undermines realist narrative space, pointing not only to the construction of this 1950s world in the film, but also to the contingency of 1950s social and ethical norms. Thus, through the film's undermining of current cinematic norms (intensified continuity), and through its use of 1950s cinematic devices of saturated colour and objective point of view, what is made explicit is not only changing cinematic norms but the changing, and thus contingent, nature of 'ethical' norms.

Using saturated colour (along with objective point of view), then, the film positions the viewer of the twenty-first century to reflect on the 1950s social and ethical norms around gender, class and race precisely because of the striking similarities and contrasts of cinematic technique. That is, the techniques invite the viewer to compare the social norms of 1950s society in the film to those governing twenty-first century Western society and culture outside the film. *Far From Heaven* encourages a 'self-reflective' or self-conscious comparison between the norms and ideologies of two eras separated by half a century, asking how they differ, or, how the same norms and ideologies might be manifest in the present era in different ways. This contrast/comparison effect, between the different norms on gender, class, race and sexuality, prompts speculation on their contingency: if these norms were absolutely universal (existing in the same way across time and space), there would be no difference in the modern viewer's response either to 1950s norms or their cinematic iteration.

Looking backwards (to the 1950s) and forwards (from the 1950s to the present) at the same time (both reflectively and through the movement created by cinematic effects), *Far From Heaven* demonstrates and embodies the unstable boundary between the social and ethical norms of the past and the present, thus encouraging viewers to contrast the behaviour of characters in the 1950s (with whom they may or may not identify) with the norms of ethical behaviour governing their own lives in the twenty-first century. Let us stop at this point to suggest that this movement back and forth (achieved through cinematic devices) is the cinematic equivalent of putting under erasure. In his homage to Sirk, Todd Haynes doesn't simply recreate but exposes the ways in which both cinematic devices and ethical and socio-cultural norms are inherited and transformed. That is, in iterating the gender, class and race norms and values of the 1950s, Haynes demonstrates (through cinematic devices as we will see in the following paragraph) the ways in which they *haunt* our current everyday ethical experiences and socio-cultural norms.

An example of how this oscillating movement, and hence 'reflection', is achieved, is through the zoom used in long shots in the film. In the opening scene, imitating Sirk's opening in *All That Heaven Allows*, Haynes' elevated long shot of the town Hartford from above the tree line slowly zooms in through the trees to give viewers their first introduction to Cathy as she gets into her car in the central business district of Hartford. The camera then follows her car, in long shot, back to her home in the suburbs. The effect of these long shots is to make viewers aware that they are being drawn into the past, and thus into a world different from their own.[4] This cinematic device of an elevated zoom in and out through trees occurs repeatedly in the film. It works, on the one hand, to push (zoom) the viewer into the intimate, private world of Cathy and Frank. On the other hand, the film's frequent zoom-outs pull the viewer 'out' and away from the characters, often quite suddenly, so that the viewer is positioned objectively, looking down omnisciently, and from the twenty-first century, through the trees onto that 1950s world. This drawing away (zooming out) limits the viewer's full identification with that world and its characters, reminding them that this world is the past. It creates, in other words, a 'reflective' distance between the past and the present world of the contemporary viewer. This self-reflection and omniscient point of view is typical of 'classic realism'. 'Classic realism', argues Catherine Belsey, 'tend[s] to align the position of the reader [film viewer] with that of the omniscient narrator who is looking back on a series of past events' (Belsey 1980, 77). For Belsey, this classic realist position in fact 'assumes' that the viewer is a humanist subject (Belsey 1980, 73).[5]

While there are classic realist tendencies in this film, the zooming techniques used, coupled with objective point of view, framing, and saturated colour, in fact works against classic realism more generally by destabilizing viewers' full identification with the characters and their 1950s values, in order to draw attention both to the constructedness of this objective narrative voice, and exaggerating the space between 'then' and 'now'. These effects in turn put into question viewers' unconscious assumptions about identity and subjectivity. Thus the film deconstructs itself.

Using cinematic devices from the 1950s as homage to Sirk, Haynes ignores the current cinematic norms of intensified continuity. As a result, the film not only highlights the changes in cinematic techniques that have taken place during that fifty-year period, but takes advantage of the contrast to lay bare the 'quaintness' of 1950s social life, its ethical norms and ideologies. In doing so, *Far From Heaven* sets up a contrast with twenty-first century norms on gender, class, race and sexuality. Through the homage to Sirk, then, Haynes' film simultaneously constitutes and dismantles the universality of 1950s and twenty-first century norms by revealing their contextuality and their contingency. While norms and ideologies are made self-reflectively evident through this contrast, and through the cinematic devices themselves, it is in combination with the narrative, and the characters, that the contextuality and contingency of these norms are made poignant. The contingency of these norms exposes not only an unstable boundary between the norms and ideologies of the past and present, but between the characters in the film and the film's viewers. The film therefore complicates, and destabilizes, not only the characters' but also viewers' identities and subjectivity. Through this oscillation between past and present cinematic and ethical norms, *Far From Heaven* constitutes, and then manipulates, the potentially shifting position of the viewer (Cook 1999, 234). In doing so, the film not only reaffirms contingent identity positions, but simultaneously puts them into play, thus questioning them.

An earlier point in this discussion introduced Haravolich's argument that melodrama produces character conflict and tension. We can now develop this by arguing that *Far From Heaven* – through tension and conflict and through the continuous oscillation between the past and the present – produces aporia and paradox, in its representation of humanist subjectivity and ethical norms. It is a paradox that is simultaneously manifested in and by the film's structure: narrative/plot, cinematic devices (zooming, objective point of view, and so on) and *mise-en-scène*. This is why the film cannot simply be categorized as a 'classic realist' text: the classic realist cinematic devices (for example the zooming that produces viewer omniscience) work simultaneously to construct *and* to subvert traditional subject positions and ethical norms. In this oscillating movement between past and present, construction and subversion, the film, as argued in the conclusion to this chapter, performs the deconstructive process of 'ethics under erasure'. Meanwhile, it is to an actual discussion of ethics under erasure – through an analysis of Cathy and Cybil's relationship – that we will now turn.

From Absolute Responsibility to Ethical Singularity, a *Différance*

As homage to Sirk's melodramas, *Far From Heaven* encapsulates the melodramatic tensions of doomed love. The film comments on the social and ethical norms of the 1950s (and the twenty-first century) not only through cinematic devices, but also through the motif of the impossible love between Cathy and Raymond. In the climactic scene, Cathy and Raymond finally reveal their love for each other, though this revelation also entails the realization of the impossibility of that love because of the taboos surrounding mixed race and class relations. Moreover, this climax is a result of a series of chain reactions initiated by the infidelity of Cathy's husband Frank, which itself involves issues of taboo and love. For Todd Haynes, the aim of the film was

> to create a plot that had no villain but instead a tightly woven web of interdependencies in which one person's tiniest step outside that world would create a chain reaction of struggle and loss. I ultimately wanted to tell a story that would make you cry because the world itself is unfair, a place where people suffered by no fault of their own. (Haynes 2003, DVD)

The characters are bound, and formed, in and through the normative web in which they are situated, and Haynes suggests that the suffering of his characters is brought about by the 'social rules and restraints that keep them from realizing their desires' (Haynes in Taubin 2002, 2). Using Cathy and Cybil as my example, what follows is an argument that it is only because of these rules and norms that a *singular ethical* response to the Other is possible in the first place.

Borrowing Derrida's notion of 'singularity' to describe the subject's ethical response to the Other, singularity means that 'something', some 'event', is unrepeatable, unique, heterogeneous, idiosyncratic, and is 'irreducible to some general form', or cannot 'be saturated with universality' (Caputo 1997b, 176). Therefore, following Derrida's notion of singularity, the term *singular ethical* is employed to convey that the ethical response to the Other is always singular and not only universal and normative. But this is not to say that the singular ethical response (enacted always, everywhere, by everyone, in everyday practice) is the only possible ethical response to the Other. This is because the singular ethical response is not a rule (such as an ethical principle) that can be applied to every situation in the same way. If it were, the singularity of the ethical response would cease to be singular. Rather, ethical responses entail singularity in much the same way that undecidability 'traces' through the decision. This means that, because every response is situated and expressed within particular, ever changing contexts (emotional, physical, generational, racial, and so on), every response is singular.

At the same time, however, this singular ethical response *does not* deny or reject ethics (generality), or norms and values that carry universal status. This is because the singular ethical response is situated, expressed and framed within certain contexts. Given this, a singular ethical response to the Other takes place in relation to ethics and norms, which is why there is never one singular ethical response that can be applied across time and place to all situations. Instead, there is an oscillation and *negotiation*, and thus a contamination, between ethical principles (metaphysical ethics) and the norms and values (that carry universal status), and the singular ethical responses towards the Other. (Moreover, because of this oscillation, universality and singularity are never absolute, or fixed as a dichotomy). In a nutshell, ethics under erasure extends Derrida's 'irresponsibilization' and absolute responsibility to take account of this negotiation between singular ethical responses, metaphysical ethics, and social norms and values. Negotiation then is always already instituted by the différance between generality and singularity.

As a reminder, the phrase *ethics under erasure* extends Derrida's discussion of his term 'under erasure' in *Of Grammatology*. In this text, he uses the example of language, specifically his unconventional thoughts on the 'sign', to define under erasure. As discussed in previous chapters, Derrida's notion of the sign as différance developed in response to his reading of Saussure on the arbitrariness of signs, and Husserl's theory of meaning. In *Of Grammatology* Derrida argues that because the sign (signifier/signified) is a differential relation, in that the sign is constantly differing and deferring (différance), it is already and always 'under erasure'. This is so because Derrida's différance is multivalent in its meanings: it signifies both 'to defer' and 'to differ'. Consequently, the sign, through this differing/deferring movement, is a differential relation that produces and effaces the 'presence' of the sign (or the sign as a transcendental signified). Through a differing/deferring movement, différance becomes 'grammatology'. For Derrida, grammatology is that which questions metaphysical propositions. In other words, différance is not a rejection of metaphysical propositions, because the 'movement' of différance simultaneously conceals and 'erases' itself: différance simultaneously reveals or produces, and conceals or effaces, the full presence of the concept, subject, entity.

It is this simultaneous effacement and production of presence (of meta-physical concepts) that Derrida also calls 'erasure' or 'under erasure' (*sous rature*). Derrida argues that ' "[s]ignifier of the signifier" describes . . . the movement of language: in its origin, to be sure, but one can already suspect that an origin whose structure can be expressed as "signifier of the signifier" conceals and *erases* itself in its own production' (Derrida 1976, 7; italics mine). Thus, the signified is made possible by the play of signifiers, so that the signified does not escape the 'play of signifying references': therefore, all metaphysical concepts erase themselves, or are put under erasure. However, if the signified or metaphysical concepts are put under erasure by their inherent differing/deferring (non)structure, this does not mean that the signified is deleted altogether or 'rubbed out'. Rather, Derrida uses the term for any sign which stands for or signifies a metaphysical concept while simultaneously demonstrating its inadequacy. Or as Spivak explains in her 'Introduction' to *Of Grammatology*, 'under erasure' means 'to write a word, cross it out, and then to print both word and deletion. (Since the word is inaccurate, it is crossed out. Since it is necessary, it remains legible)' (Spivak in Derrida 1976, xiv). Therefore, the concept (and by analogy the subject or an entity) cannot be entirely deleted or rubbed out, but stays the same while simultaneously becoming different (what Derrida calls 'iteration' and 'heterology'). As Derrida argues, the sign *is* différance and thus is '*sameness* which is not *identical*' (Derrida 1973, 129).

Bringing together Derrida's term 'under erasure' with ethics, makes it possible to reconceive the play of ethical relations in everyday life. As analo-gous to this differing/deferring movement of différance for this reason eth-ics can only be thought 'under erasure'. Using Cathy and Cybil's relationship as an example will help us explore this alternative approach to the ethical. As outlined above, ethics under erasure can be defined as an oscillation, and thus a continual negotiability, between universal (and unifying) ethical norms and the particular situations requiring *singular ethical* responses. The universality of ethical norms as transcendental signified is 'inaccurate' (in Derrida's sense), because the everyday situations in which subjects find themselves require responses that do not necessarily, or only, follow rules and laws. At the same time, these singular ethical responses do not reject ethical or social norms either, for they cannot. Rather, singular ethical responses constantly negotiate, through this oscillation, with ethical and social norms and values that carry universal status. As Ernesto Laclau has argued in relation to Derrida's term 'undecidability', there is a continuous oscillation between 'the universality of the rule' and 'the singularity of the decision' (Laclau in Mouffe 1996, 58). This is why ethics under erasure, as a differing/deferring movement, is quasi-transcendental. Furthermore, it is the quasi-transcendental status of ethics under erasure that opens up the potential for the multiple ethical possibilities as discussed in Chapter 2. So how does 'ethics under erasure' relate exactly to Cathy and Cybil's relationship in *Far From Heaven*? To address this question, let us begin with a brief synopsis of the film plot.

An Ethical Encounter: Cathy and Cybil

Cathy and her husband Frank live in a small town, Hartford, Connecticut, in 1957, where Frank is a successful sales executive for the company Magnatech. They are affluent, have two kids, own a large home with all the latest appliances, and have a black gardener (Raymond) and a black maid (Cybil). They are 'Mr and Mrs Magnatech': prominent members of Hartford society who often grace the society pages of the local newspaper. To their friends and acquaintances they appear the perfect couple, not only because of their financial and social success, and their seeming domestic happiness, but most importantly because they do not transgress the very narrow social/ moral norms and ethical values of their middle-class white community. In fact, they encapsulate ideal American (and hence Western) family, patriarchal and affluent ideologies, and the opening scenes of the film narrative visually represents the social/moral norms of the 1950s consumerist and patriarchal society around which Cathy and Frank's lives revolve and on which their identities are founded. However, Frank is the first to step outside the social and moral norms of their 1950s world by becoming involved in an extramarital affair with another man. Frank's infidelity is a transgression of the social and moral norms that underlie these gendered sexual and familial values. (In the homophobic world of middle-class America in the 1950s, the scandal of infidelity is compounded by homosexuality.) This, in turn, is the catalyst for Cathy's own transgression of class and race, a transgression that finds expression through her friendship with, and eventual love for, Raymond, her black gardener.

The consequence is a predictable social scandal, and Cathy, as 'Mrs Magnatech', is pushed from her social pedestal and loses her social standing. Raymond, and his young daughter Sarah, are forced to leave Hartford due to the violence his friendship with Cathy provokes from both the white and black communities. Frank's release from this claustrophobic world comes when he finally leaves Cathy for a young man with whom he has fallen in love. Frank has the potential to find, if not happiness in love, at least a satisfaction in exploring a previously repressed sexuality. However, for Cathy, who unquestioningly and naively conformed to, and is shaped by, the moral and social norms of her world, the fall from grace leaves everything she believed in shattered. Unlike Frank, or even Raymond, who both disappear from this world, as a single mother Cathy is left to function in it alone. Thus, despite the heart-wrenching, typically melodramatic climax between Cathy and Raymond that Haynes describes as the saddest moment of the film (Haynes 2003, DVD), it is the conversation between Cathy and Cybil, which occurs in the same scene but just after the climax, that is arguably the most deeply moving. In the midst of Cathy's isolation, and loneliness, her response towards Cybil is ethically and socially significant.

This conversation occurs after Cathy has said goodbye to Raymond, and been divorced from Frank. The dialogue between Cathy and Cybil is restrained. That is, it seems that in this dialogue Haynes has created an emotional distance and restraint between the characters Cathy and Cybil, and between the characters and the viewers, in order to achieve 'a greater emotional reservoir of feeling' (Haynes 2003, DVD). This distance is achieved through the objective point of view shots, which then work in conjunction with the restrained gestures and dialogue between Cathy and Cybil. As we have already seen, unlike subjective point of view where the person speaking in a dialogue is focused on in close-up ('intensified continuity'), Haynes utilizes objective point of view by presenting both Cathy and Cybil (when they are speaking) in long shot, accentuating the physical distance between them. Moreover, there are none of the direct eyeline matches that are characteristic of subjective point of view in modern cinema. Instead, there are over-the-shoulder shot-reverse-shots where the camera is slightly off to the side, enacting spatial, but not psychological, perspective. As a result, the 'intense reservoir of feeling' is achieved, not necessarily by identification with the point of view of an individual character, but by the poignancy and sadness of the characters' situations, and by the context, which the cinematic devices render more visible. Through 'restraint' in dialogue and gesture, and through the distance achieved by objective point of view, Haynes is able to achieve a profound intensity of feeling. The scene not only evokes the loneliness of Cathy's situation on the one hand, but also her growing social awareness and loss of naiveté on the other.

The conversation between Cathy and Cybil is important, and as it will be the focus of the discussion of the singular ethical encounter that takes place between them in the rest of this chapter, it is worth quoting in full. Coming down the stairs of her home, Cathy notices Cybil polishing the dining room table and calls out:

> Cathy: Oh Cybil, you don't need to do that!
> Cybil: It's Friday [*without looking up from polishing*].
> Cathy: I know it's Friday, but there's so much to be done now I can hardly expect you to be polishing the tables.
> [*At this point Cathy is viewed from an over-the-shoulder shot so that she is framed in a long shot which highlights the distance between the hallway, where Cathy is standing, and the dining room, where Cybil is polishing*].
> Cybil: No reason not to keep things up, no reason at all [*said matter-of-factly, this time briefly looking at Cathy while still polishing*].
> Cathy: I know [*hesitatingly*].
> Cybil: Don't forget the grocery list.
> Cathy: Thank you. I don't know how on earth I'd manage . . . [*abruptly stops speaking*].
> [*There is a reverse over-the-shoulder shot framing Cathy in a long shot, while Cybil stops polishing and looks at her. Cybil is framed in close-up with her back to the camera. Both are in the frame, Cathy smiles and walks into the next room to put on her coat.*]
> Cathy: I shouldn't be long, Cybil [*she says as she comes back into the hallway with her coat on, and starts walking out the front door*].
> Cybil: Alright Mrs Whitaker.
> [*Again Cathy is in long shot, Cybil in close-up, both in the frame, both smiling at each other as Cathy walks out the front door*].

In previous scenes, the conversations between Cathy and Cybil have exposed Cathy's profound ignorance of Cybil as a person. One of these earlier scenes, in particular, highlights this: Cathy asks Cybil which church group she could donate clothes to, and learns in the process that Cybil is involved with a number of church choirs. This scene demonstrates, as Haynes puts it, 'how little Cathy knows Cybil, or anything about her. Cathy doesn't ask Cybil about her life, and neither do we as an audience' (Haynes 2003, DVD). Their conversations revolve around an exchange of domestic, not personal, information, and it is only by accident, *through* a domestic conversation, that Cathy learns something about Cybil. Cathy's lack of interest in her maid's personal life reveals Cathy's blind perpetuation of the boundary between herself and Cybil as, respectively, white middle- and black working-class women. Thus, because of her lack of awareness that comes from a sheltered and affluent life, Cathy inadvertently maintains the class and race boundaries and hierarchies, despite her desire to change prevailing negative attitudes towards blacks, evident in her 'involvement' in the NAACP, a support group for Negroes.[6]

In this dialogue between Cathy and Cybil, Cathy stops short of confiding her personal feelings, and changes the conversation back to a simple exchange of domestic information: 'Thank you. I don't know how on earth I'd manage [*abruptly stops talking*]. I shouldn't be long Cybil'. It may, at first, seem as if Cathy, in ignorance once again, is simply complying with the social norms governing race and class. And yet the hesitations, the silences (that say a lot in any conversation), and the looks and smiles that pass between them, as well as the context in which the conversation takes place, reveals a new awareness Cathy has developed since losing Frank, Raymond and her social standing. It is this new awareness of the social consequences that result from racial, class, gender and sexual transgressions that enable Cathy to respond to Cybil, this time, in this dialogue, not in ignorance but in a unique or *singular ethical* way. What is taking place here is 'ethics under erasure'.

By abruptly withdrawing from a potentially personal and confessional exchange with Cybil, when she says: 'Thank you. I don't know how I'd manage . . .', Cathy conforms to the rules and norms of her society by maintaining the universally recognized boundaries governing race and class. Paradoxically, however, Cathy's response, the very fact that she refuses to pursue the possibility opened up for a personal dimension in the conversation, is an enactment of responsibility toward Cybil. After her experience with Raymond, Cathy now appears to recognize the untenable situation she would create for Cybil if she attempted to initiate a more intimate friendship with her, and so puts Cybil's situation before her own need for friendship and support. This unselfish response is not a result of Cybil's minimal conversational response to Cathy's statements about polishing the tables. Earlier, Cybil had already tentatively offered support for Cathy by telling her that the little girl, who Cathy had heard was hurt by white boys throwing stones at her, was actually Raymond's daughter Sarah. Cybil approaches Cathy, confessing: 'There's something I've been wanting to tell you ma'am for some time, something you surely want to know, even if it's not my place.' Cathy responds angrily to the news: 'How in God's name could you have not told me Cybil: it was weeks ago.' And Cathy proceeds to rush out through the door to see Raymond. 'Please don't be angry with me, I didn't want to make things worse,' pleads Cybil. Cybil then offers to go with Cathy, but Cathy refuses and goes off alone, shutting Cybil out of her emotional life.

In this earlier conversation, Cybil reveals a marked awareness of her 'place', that is, her role, for Cathy, as maid and nothing more. At the same time, she expresses her willingness to support Cathy on a personal level. As a member of a subordinated minority, Cybil is more aware than Cathy of the racial and class divide and her place in it. As a result, her willingness to help Cathy demonstrates a courageous self-sacrifice. Thus Cybil's generosity towards Cathy is, in this instance, singularly ethical. In their later conversation Cybil is not so forthcoming in the conversation: she does not, for example, encourage Cathy to finish her sentence. Perhaps this can be seen as a consequence of Cathy shutting her out of her emotional life previously, reinforcing the boundaries of race and class. Following Cathy's lead, then, Cybil's reticence, her silence, is an expression of the hierarchic differences, in race and class, between them, where Cathy, as employer and white middle-class woman, is the one with power. Again, this is evident in the earlier scene, when Cathy reveals that she did not know Cybil was involved with a number of church choirs. Cybil does not offer this information, because it would be inappropriate for her to do so in her role as employee, and a breach of the conventions governing normal race and power relations.

Arguably, then, Cybil's reticence is unlikely to have influenced Cathy's decision to withdraw from a more personal conversation. Given Cybil's subordinated position, there is little likelihood, even if she wanted to, that Cybil could stop Cathy confiding in her. Any initiation of friendship that comes with the giving of personal information must come from Cathy. In this oppressively hierarchic race and class structure, Cybil is positioned as a subordinate, and Cathy seems finally to be aware of the implications of this. This is why the restraint exercised in this conversation is so profoundly affecting. Cathy has nothing to lose from a friendship with Cybil, and given that she is now utterly without friends or support as a single mother, it would be understandable, even forgivable, if Cathy reached out and befriended her. After all, it is the only meaningful adult relationship Cathy has left. But as Cathy now knows, Cybil has much to lose. Cathy's retreat from a more personal engagement with Cybil is a singular ethical response, because it is precisely by conforming to the norms, the rules, that Cathy is able to protect Cybil, and herself, from the consequences of the racial and class transgressions she and Raymond experienced by becoming friends. In this singular ethical response, the hierarchy of subordinate/superior which comes from class and race discrimination and division, is reversed. Cathy's singular ethical response leaves her utterly alone and thus vulnerable, and it is in her vulnerability that Cathy becomes subordinate to Cybil.

The significance of this 'inversion' of the hierarchy between subordinate/superior becomes even clearer if we return to the earlier discussion, in Chapter 1, of Derrida's radicalization of Levinas' thinking on the 'dissymmetrical' face-to-face relation. Derrida argues that the hierarchical dissymmetry between the same and Other that Levinas proposes (which Derrida does not deny or reject), is only possible because of 'symmetry'. This is because, for Derrida, the same is also Other for the Other (Derrida 1995a, 125). That is, the same and the Other, or the face-to-face (as Levinas terms it) is not only dissymmetrical (where the same is obligated, or responsible, to the Other), but also symmetrical (where the Other, as another Other, or ego, is obligated to the same).

Given this argument, it could be proposed, on the one hand, that an analogous dissymmetrical calling into question of the same occurs when Cybil (the Other) demands (not verbally, or consciously) obligation, or responsibility, from Cathy (the same) in the very moment that Cathy becomes aware of, and less naive about, the consequences of confiding in her. Thus, there is a non-equal, or dissymmetrical, relation unfolding dynamically between Cathy and Cybil, such that Cathy, in her singular ethical response to Cybil, becomes vulnerable and subordinate to her. Furthermore, the high/low oppositional compositions evident in the shots in this scene are iconic for the dissymmetrical ethical relation that holds between the two characters. Haynes acknowledges that throughout the film he maximizes the high/low oppositional shots by creating a house (the set) with lots of stairs, and split-levels. That way, the high/low camera angle effect, particularly in over-the-shoulder shot-reverse-shot sequences, appears 'natural', not staged (Haynes 2003, DVD).

Haynes only briefly mentions, and does not elaborate on, the effect of this high/low angle in representing visually the social and moral norms governing gender, class and race by which all the characters are situated. Nevertheless, the claim that high/low oppositional shots deliberately highlight the social norms and reaffirm gender, race, and class hierarchies and ideologies, is supported by an analysis of several important scenes in the film. For example, earlier in the film, on the patio of her home, in her first meeting with Raymond, Cathy places her hand on his shoulder to convey her sympathy for the death of his father, the Whitakers' previous gardener. However, she is standing on a step higher than Raymond so that she actually looks slightly down on him. Thus, at a moment where a gesture of emotional empathy from one character to another might suggest some degree of equality between them, the vertical angle works to covertly affirm the hierarchies of race and class that govern their social positioning, and to

emphasize Cathy's superiority. This is, perhaps, why Mrs Leycoch (a jour-
nalist) who is in Cathy's home interviewing her for the 'Women's Gazette',
and witnesses this scene, writes positively in the newspaper a couple of days
later that Cathy is 'nice to blacks'. Such an unusual kindness is newsworthy!
What saves Cathy from scandal here, unlike when she is seen 'out' with
Raymond in his truck later in the film, is that the high/low angle not only
portrays her as an employer, but suggests that her niceness to blacks is
harmlessly and ignorantly patronizing. Another example is the Magnatech
'57 cocktail party held at Cathy and Frank's home. Cathy, at one point, is
positioned on the lower level of her split-level lounge room while she talks
with a male guest who stands on the upper level. The effect is to reinforce
the gender hierarchy through the high/low over-the-shoulder shot-reverse-
shots in which Cathy has to look upwards at her male guest.

These examples of high/low angles, which are used to represent, symboli-
cally, the typical race and gender norms of 1950s society, contrast dramati-
cally with the camera angles used in the conversation between Cathy and
Cybil. Here it is Cybil who, unusually, appears on the higher angle while
Cathy is positioned on the lower angle during the over-the-shoulder (objective) shot-reverse-shot sequence of their conversation. (The high/low angle
is achieved by the split-level between the hall and the dining room. From
the hall, where Cathy is standing, stairs *lead up* to the dining room, the
higher level, where Cybil is polishing the table). In this scene, the inversion
of this high/low angle points to an inversion of the race and class norms,
thus conveying Cathy's vulnerability to Cybil, and to the viewer, as she
becomes 'aware' that her relationship with Cybil is the only one of consequence she has left. More significant, though, Cathy's vulnerability, depicted
by her vertical positioning, is also a reflection of her singular ethical response
towards Cybil: Cathy's responsibility reveals, and *is*, vulnerability.

On the other hand, the initial reversal of the opposition subordinate/
superior – where Cathy becomes subordinate, in her responsibility, to Cybil
– is not fixed, because the reversal (the new opposition) is then undermined in a way that reflects Derrida's notion of 'symmetry'. Thus, given
Derrida's argument that the same is also Other to the Other, then Cybil (as
Other) is also responsible to Cathy (the same). In earlier scenes, her support for Cathy has revealed a courageous willingness to break with racial
norms. However, in this scene, by complying, through her silence, with the
race and class norms her position requires, Cybil is perhaps protecting
Cathy. Her silence, then, is also a singular ethical response.

In its negotiability and oscillation between universal ethics and singular
responses to singular situations, ethics under erasure is already, in itself,

multiple, various, and hence always singular and never homogeneous. For example, ethics under erasure is performed in the unspoken negotiability governing Cathy's and Cybil's singular ethical responses to each other. At the same time, ethics under erasure is performed in and through both Cathy and Cybil's negotiation and oscillation between ethical principles (universal ethics), the moral norms and values (that carry universal status; the law), and the singular ethical responses they enact within the singular situation in which they find themselves. This oscillating negotiation is a contamination of the boundary between one singular ethical response and another, and between the universality of ethical norms and singular ethical responses. Yet, this oscillation does not simply contaminate the boundaries, but is precisely that which allows for the possibility that they will be maintained.

Both Cathy's and Cybil's singular ethical responses are negotiated in and through the universal laws, ethical principles, moral norms and values, and the politics of their society. And it is in this negotiation that we can also experience the contamination between ethics and politics. As Derrida argues, '[e]thical problems are already taken up in the so-called space of the political' (Derrida 2002, 302). That is, it is complying, or referring, to the ethical norms and values, and the politics of their society, that makes the singularity of both Cathy and Cybil's ethical responses possible. And it is what opens up an ethical difference and alterity in their relations with each other.

Initially, Cathy's singular response is *not* ethical in the sense that it does not follow the norms of her society. Cathy's response in fact breaks with norms. But in breaking with norms, her response is uniquely and singularly ethical, above and beyond norms. It is a response, therefore, that is not a blind following of rules and laws, but contains, as Derrida argues, a moment of incalculability or undecidability. And undecidability is what allows for otherness. As Derrida argues in *Adieu*, 'Levinas would probably not say it in this way, but could it not be argued that . . . decision and responsibility are always *of the other?*' (Derrida 1999a, 23). Second, Cathy's singular ethical response is singular because she breaks with social and ethical norms, and the law, *precisely by following and conforming* to ethical norms and the law, and this reveals that something 'other' (alterity), some singularity contaminates the law, and ethical norms, in the same way that the other (alterity) always inhabits the decision. It is the contamination, the continuous movement between singularity and universal laws and norms, that is 'ethics under erasure'. Therefore, it is only within a universal status of norms that a singular ethical response is made possible. By complying with these 'universal' norms surrounding gender, race and class, Cathy protects Cybil and their relationship from the consequences of transgressing the norms (even though her response is also a transgression). Cathy (and Cybil) performs 'ethics under erasure'.

While the singular ethical response is made possible by social norms, and ethics, the singularity of Cathy's response, in conjunction with the film's cinematic devices, also draws attention to the contingency and contextuality of the supposed transcendentality of social norms and ideologies. Thus, in its continuous oscillation, in its differing/deferring (non)structure, ethics under erasure undermines the unifying and universal position of social norms, and ethics. This is because these norms are mediated by events requiring singular ethical responses (possibilities) which simultaneously reshape and reconstitute the very norms, and ethics, on which they are founded. In other words, through erasure norms are reinvented. Thus, it is within possibility (the empirical structure of norms) that something other (the impossible; alterity) is opened. This section has focused on the way social norms are put under erasure. The next section, however, will argue, again using the example of the conversation between Cathy and Cybil, that if ethics is constantly under erasure then the notion of the ethical humanist subject is simultaneously undermined. The erasure of subjectivity is manifest in the simultaneous affirmation and contamination of the boundary between subject and Other evident in Cathy and Cybil's relationship.

Erasing the Subject

Is Cathy's singular ethical response transcendental? And what does this singular ethical response mean for identity, and subjectivity? For Derrida, singularity is that which comes about through an obligation and response to the Other. However, singularity does not mean that the same (ego) has an essence, or autonomy, in the humanist sense. It 'is not the individuality of a thing that would be identical to itself' (Derrida and Nancy 1991, 100). In fact, for Derrida, 'the discourse on the subject, even if it locates difference, inadequation, the dehiscence within autoaffection, etc., continues to link subjectivity with man' (Derrida and Nancy 1991, 105). We can understand more fully what Derrida means when he says that subjectivity has been, and continues to be, linked with 'man', by turning to a brief description of how the humanist subject developed from the notion of the 'philosophy of the subject'.

For the 'philosophy of the subject' the term 'subject' conveys the 'thinking thing', what René Descartes posits as the *ego cogito*. This thinking thing is separate from the person or body in which the thinking thing arises, which is why this account claims that there is a separation of the body and soul, or person and 'subject', respectively. Thus, the humanist version of the philosophy of the subject, Vincent Descombes suggests, has developed from the argument that 'one thinking thing' cannot be distinguished 'from another thinking thing' unless those thinking things have identities. In this approach, the 'subject' has been conflated, or assimilated, with 'an individual susceptible of being designated, identified, distinguished, etc.' (Descombes 1991, 128). In other words, subjectivity has been linked to and conflated with 'man', so that subjectivity has become synonymous with identity. It is this conflation of subjectivity with man, which has come to be known as the 'humanist subject' that, Derrida insists, is 'a fable'. What Derrida means by this is that there is no subject as origin, existing outside (con)text. Rather, there is only an '"effect" of "subjectivity"' (Derrida and Nancy 1991, 105), which Derrida defines or characterizes as 'presence to self'. 'Presence to self' is a phrase Derrida uses to convey the temporal characteristics of the humanist subject: 'identity to self, positionality, property, ego, consciousness, will, intentionality, freedom, humanity, etc.', not to mention objectivity, rationality and self-reflection.

This repetitious 'effect of subjectivity' is strongly tied to ethical, legal and political foundations that contribute to the construction of cultural norms and values. Derrida argues that 'these foundations were and remain essentially sealed within a philosophy of the subject' (Derrida and Nancy 1991, 104). Descombes confirms Derrida's argument by defining the position on ethics taken by the philosophy of the subject:

> As *ethics of the subject*, the 'philosophy of the subject' assigns to the concept of the subject the function of rendering possible an ethical and political thinking. We cannot pose ethical questions (*What is good or bad? Is it honorable or shameful?* etc.) if we cannot be guided by the ideal of free subjectivity . . . If we no longer had the possibility or the right to consider ourselves, even if only partially, as subjects, we could no longer pose ethical questions. (Descombes 1991, 121–2)

It is the ability for moral and ethical self-determination, characterized by free decision-making based on rationality, that defines the ethical humanist subject. For Derrida, then, the humanist subject is perceived as able to make decisions and pose ethical questions because 'the subject is . . . a principle of calculability . . . in the question of legal and human rights . . . and in morality' (Derrida and Nancy 1991, 108).

However, as argued in Chapter 2, if the subject's ethical decision is actually determined and constituted by the dichotomous structure of 'ethical questions' themselves, such as, what is good or bad, right or wrong, and so on, then the dichotomous structure of ethical norms draws ethical decisions into either/or responses. And this makes problematic the subject's autonomy in determining ethical questions. In other words, because ethical questions are constituted by prescriptive rules and laws, then ethical decisions do not require self-determination, objectivity or rationality. Rather, as Derrida claims, these rules and norms are in danger of instituting an unquestioning, blind following and obedience which, in turn, leaves no space for the alterity within the Other, or the same. Derrida argues:

> If there is responsibility, if there is an ethical and free decision, responsibility and decision must, at a given moment, be discontinuous with the normative or the 'normal', not in their misrecognition of norms, not in their ignorance of a knowledge about norms – rather they must take a leap and welcome a sort of discontinuity, a heterogeneity in relation to the normative as such. (Derrida 2002, 200)

Without rejecting norms, or the 'effects of subjectivity', Derrida's notion of responsibility and decision is more than blind obedience. Nor, as we have discussed in relation to *The Gift of Death*, is responsibility absolutely calculable. Calculation and decision, argues Derrida, have to pass through 'the incalculable or the undecidable' (Derrida and Nancy 1991, 108). For this reason Derrida proposes that, 'perhaps one should attribute the value of the decision to something other than a free and calculating subject' (Derrida 2002, 312). Further, Derrida argues that this 'something other' should be thought of as 'the finite experience of non-identity to self, as the underivable interpellation inasmuch as it comes from the other, from the trace of the other, with all the paradoxes or the aporia of being-before-the-law, etc.' (Derrida and Nancy 1991, 103–4). If subjectivity is constituted by the Other/ other and is not autonomous (that is, is *not* self-governing or independent of Others), then this non-humanist account of the 'subject' (a word that can only be used 'under erasure') suggests that the boundary between subject and Other is not stable, which in turn has implications for how ethics is enacted in the everyday world. Given this account, what can be proposed, through further analysis of Cathy and Cybil's relationship, is that ethics under erasure works to simultaneously maintain and contaminate that boundary. If the limit between subject and Other can be contaminated, or is informed by what Derrida calls a 'haunting', then this is because there is a limit between the subject and Other that can be contaminated, and made unstable. Without this limit (or division) there would be no contamination between subject and Other.

The complication for this limit, and this contamination, on the one hand, is that the 'Other' (and the way the Other's alterity affects the subject) is never absolutely or totally outside the subject but also inside the subject simultaneously. On the other hand, it also means that the subject is not only inside itself ('present' to self), but by the way it is informed and affected by the Other it is, at the same time, outside itself. The question which arises at this point is how does the limit (as separation, or division, between subject and Other) come into place? And how is it contaminated? To answer this we can once again turn to the conversation between Cathy and Cybil analysed in the previous section. But before discussing the manifestation of the contaminated boundary between Cathy and Cybil, let us start by showing that the separation, the limit, between subject and Other is maintained by Cathy's and Cybil's compliance with the ethical norms and laws of their society, and by the 'effects of subjectivity' as outlined by Derrida.

To enact a singular ethical response towards Cybil, Cathy conforms to, and repeats the social norms and values surrounding, and perpetuating, the ideologies of race, class and gender, in her society. Moreover, in this compliance, Cathy falls back on her domestic role, and thus her identity as a white, middle-class mother, to create a boundary, a separation, or limit between herself and Cybil. This boundary does not just occur in this scene between Cathy and Cybil. From the very beginning of the film it is obvious that Cathy's identity is constituted and informed by the norms and values of her society, era or generation. Thus, if 'identity' typically refers to the characteristics of a person; and 'characteristics' are produced by culture, society and family, then Cathy's identity is defined as much by the way she uses language, as by her behaviour. The two go hand in hand.

For instance, the conversation with her children, David and Janice, early in the film reveals that her identity is formed in and through the social ideal of the nuclear family, and, more specifically, around the role of 'mothering'. This is confirmed by her language of nurturing and caring. As Cathy drives her car into the driveway of their home, David, who is riding his bike in the street, cries out: 'Mother, mother, can I sleep over Hutchens' tonight? Mrs Hutchens gave permission!' Cathy responds: 'Not tonight dear, your father and I are going out and I need you to look after your sister . . . Now move out of the way so mother can park.' It is not only the quaintness of her language and her measured tone of voice that makes Cathy's response interesting here. It is also the way in which Cathy refers to herself in the third person, as 'mother'. Using the third person, Cathy reflects and repeats the hierarchy surrounding the nuclear family, because the third person works to confine, and reinforce, the children's roles ('Mother, mother' says David), as well as her own, in a hierarchy where the father is 'head' ('Your father and I'). If the nuclear family is a microcosm of social hierarchy and roles, this is because the 'nuclear family' (as portrayed in the 1950s by the film) mimics the patriarchal structure of the society on which Cathy's identity is constructed. Indeed, her gendered role as mother and housewife is commented on by the film when, later in the narrative, Cathy is being interviewed by Mrs Leycoch. In a quick camera cut to and from Cathy, we see the 'Mr and Mrs Magnatech' advertisement hanging on Cathy's lounge-room wall. In this advertisement, Frank is portrayed standing while Cathy is sitting on the floor at his feet. Thus, the visual semiotic of the advertisement constructs a vertical hierarchy where the higher position (Frank/man) is privileged over the lower (Cathy/woman) (Kress 1996, 39). The gendered and patriarchal language is driven home by the visual cues in the film, such as the reference to the Magnatech advertisement on the wall in the lounge-room, and also by the high/low camera angles that have already been discussed.

The use of the third person, then, implicitly refers to, and makes use of, this family hierarchy, lending support and authority to the demands and requests Cathy makes of her children (to help with the shopping, to take a bath, and so on). And in defining and reaffirming these rules through the third person, a distance is established between the roles and, thus, between the members of this hierarchy. Because of, and through, third person language, the objectification of Cathy's role as mother to her children also works to constitute, and is constitutive of, a self-reflection about the roles they each perform within the family. However, the subjectivity, or the 'effects of subjectivity', of those performing the roles is also constituted by first person language, the 'I'. The first and second person go hand in hand with third person language, because, as Belsey argues, 'consciousness of self is possible only through contrast, differentiation: "I" cannot be conceived without the conception "non-you", "you"' (Belsey 1980, 59). That is, the ideological humanist positioning of the subject, which functions through first person language, cannot be differentiated from the ideological positioning of the 'you', the Other, which functions through second and third person language. Thus, 'the subject', that which is 'self-identical or even conscious of self-identity, self-conscious', argues Derrida, 'is inscribed in the language . . . is a "function" of the language' (Derrida 1973, 145).

Ironically, Cathy's role as mother (nurturer and carer) uses distance and objectification created by second and third person language, to convey family unity and thus protect her family from the potential risk of rising tension. This tension is evident in a scene (there are several) that occurs after Cathy has discovered Frank's homosexual affair, and after Frank agrees to see a psychiatrist to beat his 'problem' and perform the role of husband and father which he believes is what he should and must do. Cathy, in her role as mother and housewife, follows the rules and norms of family life to unify her family by using conventional domestic discourse: 'Would you like another lamb chop dear?' she asks Frank. At this point, Frank is clearly uncomfortable with his heterosexual role as father and husband, but he attempts to fit into established norms by falling in with his role through polite domestic discourse. Thus he responds smilingly to Cathy's question with 'Oh, I'm fine.' But there is a menacing tension not only between Cathy and Frank here, but also in Frank's desire to be 'normal' and his uncertainty about that 'normality'. So when Cathy insists 'Are you sure? I have plenty in the oven,' Frank replies emphatically, with a touch of stress and anger, but through smiling gritted teeth: 'No! Thank you, I'm fine.' The attempt to cover over this tension in front of the children by falling into overly polite language ironically highlights this stress. For example, when David asks his father if he would come to baseball on Saturday, prompting Frank to look down uncomfortably at his plate (because this is the day Cathy and Frank have their therapy appointment), Cathy, in a gesture typical of her gendered role as mother and wife, speaks for him, thus minimizing any discomfort Frank might feel: 'We'll see, David.' She then pulls the family back into a seeming, but false, unity through her use of domestic language when she asks, with a smile: 'Janice, could you please pass the butter!'

In some ways Cybil is part of the family, but only in the sense that she is employed to make it function smoothly. So, although she may be pivotal in this sense, as already discussed, Cybil is marginalized by her race and class from ever becoming intimate with Cathy. Again, the topics of Cathy's conversation with Cybil revolve around domestic chores. Thus, in the scene after the romantic/love climax between Cathy and Raymond, when Cathy starts then abruptly terminates a personal conversation with Cybil, Cathy is able to fall back into this domestic discourse as a way of maintaining Cybil's role as maid, and her own role as mother and employer. By doing this, Cathy maintains the boundary between subject (Cathy/Cybil) and Other (Cybil/Cathy). What is evident in their domestic discourse is not only a boundary (or separation) between subject and Other, but a boundary which demonstrates and enacts the 'effect of subjectivity' (objectivity, self-reflection, distance). And yet, as we will see, it is because this boundary can be contaminated, enabling the possibility of singular ethical responses, that

Cathy's identity reveals an alterity within subjectivity itself. We will return to this later; meanwhile, suffice to say that the 'effect of subjectivity', perpetuated by the language the characters use, is further enforced by the physical boundary or distance between characters set up by the framing techniques of the film.

Techniques used in the film to frame characters convey polite society's lack of intimacy and its basis in the norms governing race, class, gender and family. While Haynes utilizes the long shot throughout the film, he also makes sure, following Sirk, that the characters, or actors, never fill or 'own the frame' (Haynes 2003, DVD). Characters are frequently pushed to the extreme edges of the frame (even in close-up shots) so that in some scenes only half of the character's body is in the frame. For example, in the scene in which Mrs Leycoch has Cathy photographed for the 'Woman's Gazette', we see Cathy posed for a photograph by the fireplace. In long-shot Cathy is placed at the edge of the frame standing by the fireplace while the photographer and Mrs Leycoch appear at the other side of, and only partly in, the frame. The subject of the frame is actually the space between the characters. This spatial distance, constructed by the framing, is a metonymy for the distance between characters set up by social relations, conventions and norms. It also suggests that the characters are contained and defined by social norms and circumstances. In other words, the space of the home, the *mise-en-scène*, symbolizes not only the claustrophobic nature of these 1950s norms and values, generally, but also the emotional distance between some of the characters, such as Cathy and Frank. For instance, the night Cathy discovers Frank's infidelity, their home, the *mise-en-scène*, fills the space between them as they are each pushed in opposite directions to the edges of the frame, thus enhancing their loneliness and their emotional distance from each other.

The aim of the discussion so far has been to point out that in the film there is a boundary, a separation between the subject and Other which is constituted and maintained through the distancing and objectifying effects of second and third person language, and supported by the framing device. This distancing, and the use of language, constructs Cathy's (and indeed, all the characters') identity. It also illustrates what Derrida calls the 'effects of subjectivity', or the humanist subject. Thus, while this distancing between subject and Other is used in the film to convey the lack of intimacy of polite society, it also works to represent iconically the perpetuation of the humanist subject. The materiality of the world (the *mise-en-scène* in the film), and the language we use, are appropriated in some ways for the construction and constitution of, what Derrida calls, 'identity to self', 'positionality', 'ego', and so on (Derrida and Nancy 1991, 103). Thus the film dismantles identity by revealing the social norms in which it is based, while at the same time, through cinematic devices, perpetuating the conflation of identity with 'subjectivity'. For example, the framing creates a distance between the characters, and this perpetuates objectivity, not only between the characters, but between the film and its viewers.

Yet how does the separation based on the 'effects of subjectivity' (that is, distance, objectification, and so on) fit with what was argued, in Chapter 1, and earlier in this chapter, to be Derrida's radicalization of Levinas' notion of separation and exteriority? To briefly summarize what has been argued so far: the separation of the subject and Other is maintained by social norms, and by the 'effects of subjectivity', evident in the film. Consequently, the repetitious effect of subjectivity produces a separation, a boundary that is homogenized and made normative. This homogenization of separation, in turn, perpetuates class, race and gender discrimination that could be argued to be unethical. However, this raises the question of ethical decision: who is to say that what I, or society, have proposed as unethical is in fact unethical? When ethics is based on the empirical and thus contingent structure of norms, there are always going to be counter-arguments regarding what may or may not be ethical or unethical.[7] Derrida argues, in contrast, that it is only within the empirical that the singular ethical response, one that is transcendental, is possible. This transcendentality, he argues, is a way 'to escape falling back into this naïve objectivism [empiricism]' (Derrida 1976, 61).

Traditionally, transcendentalism, as that which exists above, beyond and outside society, context and language, is what Derrida has constantly put into question through the sign (Saussure) and the 'Living Present' (Husserl).[8] Why is the transcendentalism of Saussure and Husserl different to the transcendentality used to undermine empiricism? Derrida refers to a transcendentality that is not 'beyond' or 'outside' society or context, but which is the trace, or arche-trace, within empiricism: 'to wrench the concept of the trace from the classical scheme, which would derive it from a presence or from an originary nontrace and which would make of it an empirical mark, one must indeed speak of an originary trace or arche-trace' (Derrida 1976, 61). In other words, by referring to a transcendentality that runs through empiricism (a quasi-transcendentality), Derrida is able to move away from the circular consequence of the empirical structure of norms but without rejecting them altogether, and we have seen how this works in Chapter 2 in the discussion of impossibility that traces through possibility.

Derrida argues that transcendentality is possible due to the empiricism of norms, and vice versa. The contamination between empiricism and transcendentality helps explain the difference between separation based on 'effects of subjectivity', and Derrida's radicalization of Levinas' notion of separation as described in Chapter 2. This outline of quasi-transcendentality as a 'trace' will perhaps also explain how the subject/Other separation is contaminated. It may also answer the question that opened this section: is Cathy's singular ethical response transcendental? If we take our cue from Derrida's arguments on the trace of transcendentality within the empirical, what is significant is that the singular ethical response works as a transcendentality (in its singularity) that traces through the empiricism of ethics and moral norms. Ethics under erasure, as a negotiation, as an oscillation, between norms, and ethics, and singular ethical responses, is quasi-transcendental. It is this quasi-transcendentality of ethics under erasure that explains the paradox of Cathy's behaviour in her conversation with Cybil. She is both compliant and complicit with norms (and thus she enacts the 'effects of subjectivity'). Yet at the same time her singular ethical response contaminates the boundary between the subject (Cathy) and Other (Cybil).

This quasi-transcendentality of ethics under erasure works between Cathy and Cybil in the following way: as discussed earlier, Cathy enacts the 'effects of subjectivity', thus creating a distance, a boundary or separation, between herself and Cybil, by falling back into an identity politics (white middle-class mother), and by using domestic language. Moreover, the boundary, the limit, she maintains in and through her identity, is based on the autonomy of the humanist subject. Yet, Cathy's singular ethical response to Cybil is *not* autonomous in the humanist sense. If there is any autonomy, it is a result of the subject (Cathy) being obligated to the Other (Cybil) and others (Cathy's society). The humanist notion of autonomy posits that the individual is entirely separated, and thus totally independent: free of, and from, others in the decisions the subject makes and the behaviours s/he enacts. However, ethics under erasure means that the subject is inevitably in continual negotiation between universal norms and ethical duty/laws, and singular situations that always require, and are always haunted by, the possibility of singular ethical response. If this is the case, then any autonomy, and any differentiation or separation between the subject and the Other, can only occur, paradoxically, in the moment when the subject is obligated to the Other, and thus contaminated with otherness. This notion of 'autonomy' follows Derrida's articulation of 'hospitality' and 'interruption' in *Adieu*. In his reading of Levinas, Derrida argues that the subject's 'singularity' arises only in its being hostage to, or in its responsibility for, the Other. That is, 'the subjectivity of the subject' (Derrida 1999a, 54) exists only in the subject's subordination, through responsibility, to the Other.

Derrida goes on to argue that in the subject's responsibility to the Other, the subject also interrupts itself: '[t]his interruption of the self by the self, if such a thing is possible, can or must be taken up by thought: this is ethical discourse – and it is also, as the limit of thematization, hospitality. Is not hospitality an interruption of the self?' (Derrida 1999a, 51) In other words, 'interrupting oneself' means 'the interruption of the self by the self as other' (Derrida 1999a, 52). In a similar way, the quasi-transcendental, or differing/deferring movement that is ethics under erasure, is a form of interruption to the humanist ethical subject. Thus, autonomy is not universal and fixed and it is not self-governing. Rather, autonomy occurs in conjunction with others. Furthermore, because our relations with others always require the possibility of singular ethical responses, this means that autonomy in this new sense is contextual. So autonomy is made possible by others (and is contextual). As a result, it is traced through with alterity, thus making the subject's autonomy unique and singular. Thus, the 'effects of subjectivity', with its humanist account of autonomy, is put under erasure precisely by the transcendentality of Cathy's ethical singular response: a transcendentalism that haunts social and moral norms (empiricism). If identity as it is lived every day in the world is tied to, and is a result of, the effect of subjectivity (objectivity, intentionality, positionality, will, ego, and so on), and if Cathy's singular ethical response puts subjectivity, and its humanist notion of autonomy, into question, then her identity is simultaneously the same and not the same. That is, ethics under erasure, on a personal and social level, enables and opens the way for an experience that is other.

On the personal level first, Cathy's new found social and personal awareness, born of suffering and loss, changes her and her relationship to Cybil. As director Todd Haynes comments, the conversation between Cathy and Cybil 'is the first indication of Cathy's awareness of its [her relationship with Cybil] importance . . . there's something hopeful because obviously she's learned something in the process: she becomes a *seeing* human being' (Haynes 2003, DVD). We can understand more fully Haynes' notion of 'a seeing human being' by briefly relating Robert Bernasconi's discussion of (in)visibility in his article, 'The invisibility of racial minorities' (2001), to the relationship between Cathy and Cybil.

In his article, Bernasconi discusses 'anti-Black racism among Whites in contemporary America' (Bernasconi 2001, 285), particularly focusing on the way the Black minority is made invisible by the dominant White group.

For Bernasconi, 'the invisibility of racial minorities arises from a refusal on the part of the majority to see them or, more precisely, to listen to them' (Bernasconi 2001, 284). Moreover, 'we Whites have trouble seeing past the stereotype as if it formed a layer of invisibility. It is a case of seeing without seeing' (Bernasconi 2001, 288). Following Bernasconi, Cathy's not 'seeing' Cybil as anything other than her black maid, evidenced early in the film by Cathy's lack of personal knowledge of Cybil, is a form of rendering Cybil 'invisible in the public realm, in the sense of being powerless, mute, and deprived of human rights' (Bernasconi 2001, 286). Cathy's new awareness, her perception of her own previous lack of awareness and occlusion of Cybil, enables Cathy to respond to the Other (Cybil) in a singular ethical way.

While the issues of race and class have not been the primary focus of this chapter, the contamination of the subject/Other boundary is inevitably also a contamination of the race and class boundaries between Cathy and Cybil. This is because in the moment of the singular ethical response Cathy and Cybil transcend the empiricism of their actual lived, material positions and social identities in the world, and therefore also the socially constructed boundary of race and class. However, this transcendence, through singular ethical response, is only possible because singularity is in constant oscillation and negotiation with the social and moral norms, and thus with the materiality of both Cathy and Cybil's situation, in the world. This oscillation/negotiation characterizes 'ethics under erasure'. What ethics under erasure reveals is that at the same time Cathy and Cybil transcend the race and class boundary, their singular ethical responses do not efface their material identities, or the political tension and conflict of race and class relations. Rather, it is precisely this tension, this conflict, which provides the locus for both Cathy's and Cybil's singular ethical responses. Ethics under erasure, then, does not efface, rub out, or delete Cybil's race or her class. It does not, to put it in Bernasconi's terms, render invisible Cybil's race and class by making her visible as a universal 'human being'. It does not efface, 'the attachment to social identity that is often found on the part of the oppressed' (Bernasconi 2001, 290). But also, ethics under erasure does not efface Cathy's social identity (as white middle-class mother). This is because while it has so far been argued that the hierarchy of subordinate/superior is reversed in the singular ethical response Cathy makes towards Cybil so that a non-equal, dissymmetrical relation unfolds dynamically between them (where Cathy becomes subordinate to Cybil), it is precisely by falling back on her role as employer that Cathy's identity and position as superior is nevertheless maintained.

What is maintained, as Linda Martin Alcoff argues, is a 'white dominant racial structure' (Alcoff 2001, 281). By becoming aware or conscious of both her and Cybil's racial place in the world and what this means for their 'relationship', Cathy (and Cybil) knowingly maintain the race, class and identity boundary between them. Thus, the objective point of view cinematically constructed in this scene works to not only highlight the loneliness of Cathy's situation, as discussed earlier, but also the distance between them. That is, the physical distance between Cathy and Cybil, produced by objective point of view (where they are both pushed to the edges of the film frame), is a metonymy for the racial and class distance ethically, politically and socially constructed between Cathy and Cybil.

Furthermore, Cathy's knowledge or reflexivity of the white dominant racial structure that constitutes her 'personal' experience of, and 'relationship' with, Cybil, is marked by the mirror in this scene. Just as Cathy is about to walk out the front door she turns to the mirror in the hall to adjust her purple headscarf. Arguably, what the mirror metaphorically reflects is Cathy's 'racialized' awareness. That is, the mirror is a useful metaphor for the way in which Cathy's new found awareness of racial issues is constituted within and by the white dominant racial structure. As Alcoff argues, the 'structure of contemporary perception' is the reason why 'racializing attributions are nearly impossible to discern and why they are resistant to alteration' (Alcoff 2001, 276), because they make up 'a part of what appears to me as the natural setting of all my thoughts. The perceptual practices involved in racializations are then tacit, almost hidden from view, and thus almost immune from critical reflection' (Alcoff 2001, 275). Applying Alcoff's insight to Cathy, the mirror then is arguably a useful metaphor for the way in which Cathy's new found awareness of race issues is constituted within and by the white dominant racial structure.

While Cathy maintains the white dominant racial structure and thus 'mirrors' it back to herself and Cybil, Cybil too knowingly maintains the race, class and identity boundary between them. In doing so, Cybil also (re) inscribes, albeit differently, the white racial structure of their society under which Cybil operates, and under which both Cathy and Cybil's identities and relations are founded. It is in and through this maintenance that Cybil is able to protect her own interests and life, as well as Cathy's (even though this, perhaps, constitutes Cybil as the 'mammy figure').

Both Cathy and Cybil not only knowingly maintain white dominant racial structures and thus white 'ethical' and 'political' schemas or norms that, ironically, perpetuate this structure, but both understand and know each other's complicity. It is a double complicity that personally, if not socially, connects them in a relationship that has already been marked by a singular ethical encounter: an encounter that changes them and their understanding of each other. Thus, despite their complicity of the norms that maintain white dominant racial structures, it is only in negotiation with those norms surrounding race and class, on the one hand, and on the other, with the very visibility of Cybil's social identity, that Cathy is able to respond to the Other (Cybil) in a singular ethical way.

Cathy's singular ethical response reveals not only an experience of her responsibility and her ethical obligation to the Other (Cybil), but also the otherness (the alterity) of the same, of Cathy. Cathy's singular ethical response in itself *is* other. In enacting ethics under erasure Cathy exposes the alterity that is herself, an alterity that is truly singular. Thus, ethics under erasure, which produces the simultaneous maintenance and contamination that is the limit, in turn produces alterity inside and outside the subject. As Derrida argues, '[t]he relation to self . . . can only be *differance*, that is to say alterity, or trace' (Derrida and Nancy 1991, 100).

Second, on a cultural and social level, ethics under erasure not only opens a particular ethical encounter, but also opens the future to otherness: to the hauntings of otherness in our everyday encounters. As Derrida poignantly argues, '[t]he future can only be anticipated in the form of an absolute danger. It is that which breaks absolutely with constituted normality' (Derrida 1976, 5). That is, alterity or otherness is a danger because it is unknowable, that which cannot be anticipated, and is therefore not the norm. Thus, ethics under erasure opens a hope for an existence that is other to the dominant norms of society, not as a 'utopia', something outside of society or norms, but from within, and by, the dominant norms. It opens a promise for the future, and various possibilities of being within society. After all, if norms were universal and transcendental, across time and place, there would be no opening, no possibility for political change or hope. Cathy's singular ethical response to Cybil, based on her new awareness of the 'Other' (as race and class positioned), is a manifestation of social and political change and reinvention, because her quasi-transgression of race and class norms and boundaries breaks with 1950s' ideology in the film. In other words, Cathy and Cybil's maintenance of white dominant racial and ethical structures are not absolutely repeated. Rather, to use Derrida's term, they are 'iterated', and this iteration enables, as Alcoff puts it, 'the potential to disrupt the current racializing processes' (Alcoff 2001, 281), a political disruption that takes place in the singular ethical encounter between Cathy and Cybil.

If Cathy's ethical identity has been constituted by the norms and values of her society, and if these norms are contingent, then ethics under erasure reveals not only the contingency of the construction of humanist subjectivity, but also the alterity, the différance, or heterology that makes the subject as presence possible. Given this, Cathy's singular ethical response to Cybil, her enactment of ethics under erasure, reconfigures and provides an opening to a subject that is also 'other'. Thus, ethics under erasure allows subjectivity to be, not rejected, but rethought, yet only within the bounds of subjectivity as we know it. In other words, like ethics under erasure (which is the contamination, and oscillation, between norms, and ethics/laws, and ethically singular situations and responses), the Other is made possible by the 'effects of subjectivity'. Inversely, it is because of the 'otherness' that, like a trace, moves through the humanist subject that Derrida is able to argue that the subject, paradoxically, is 'a fable'. Thus, Cathy can manifest the 'otherness' of the ethically singular response precisely by enacting the distance, objectivity, intentionality, and so on – or what Derrida calls the 'effects of subjectivity' – that come from her identity (Derrida and Nancy 1991, 100). Her identity politics (white middle-class), constructed by social norms and laws, is then contingent and contextual.

Conclusion

The idea that subjectivity and norms and ethics (that is, ethical systems based on metaphysical presumptions) are contextual and contingent is not new.[9] However, this chapter has attempted to follow Derrida by suggesting that empirical and contingent subjectivity and norms are traced through with an alterity which deconstructs their pure empirical status. That is, this quasi-transcendentality not only questions the fixed and universal status of those norms, but in doing so also reveals that they, and subjectivity, are constantly (re)negotiated and made different, in and through singular ethical responses. What this chapter hopes to have demonstrated, then, is that 'ethics under erasure' can help us account for how we engage with and produce humanist subjectivity and the norms and ethics we experience in everyday life. This in turn reveals the relevance of Derrida's work for (re)thinking ethics as they apply to, and are enacted in, our everyday experiences.

Using Cathy and Cybil's relationship as the example, this chapter has argued that the cinematic devices create an objectifying distance between the subject (Cathy/Cybil) and the Other (Cybil/Cathy), and thus affirm and perpetuate humanist subjectivity. However, at the same time, these cinematic devices also subvert subjectivity and the ethics on and by which it is formulated and constructed. Both subjectivity and political, social and moral norms are put 'under erasure', meaning that they are retained while demonstrating their inadequacy. Ethics under erasure can help us recognize how a singular ethical response is made possible in and through Western society's norms and ethics. Inversely, because of the transcendentality of the singular ethical response that haunts these norms and ethics, they contain alterity, and thus difference. Norms are therefore neither absolutely universal nor unchanging.

Furthermore, this chapter has focused on the relationship between Cathy and Cybil *within* the film to argue that ethics under erasure occurs *outside* the film in *all* relations in everyday life. However, it is not only in our relations on an everyday level that ethics under erasure is manifest, because these everyday relations are also culturally iterated in and through film, art and literature, and so on. *Far From Heaven* is an example of how this works, because, as argued at the outset, Todd Haynes deliberately recreates the social norms and ideologies of the 1950s in his film in order to comment, socially and politically, on the norms and values of the 1950s *and* the twenty-first century.

While Haynes subverts norms through cinematic devices, these same devices reconfirm and perpetuate norms and values, and humanist subjectivity. We can only speculate on the extent to which Haynes was aware of this as he made the film. More important is the fact that the film can be interpreted as enacting ethics under erasure in two ways. First, as argued at an earlier point in the chapter, the way Haynes uses the zoom makes viewers aware of the congruencies and differences between ethical norms and values of the past and the present, making it possible for the film to subvert these norms. This subversion, in turn, relies on the device of 'zooming' to create in the viewer a self-reflective reading position. Second, once the viewer has adopted a self-reflectivity about past and present ethical norms, the film is able to demonstrate that reflection on present norms is made possible by re-enacting past norms, thereby highlighting how all norms across all eras are not only the same but simultaneously different, and thus contingent. And of course, the way in which the film reflects these norms is also contingent and ideological.

Cathy, as we have seen, enacts a singular ethical response by reinforcing the effects of subjectivity, falling back onto identity politics and ethical norms. In the same way, through its cinematic devices, the film also *operates* to subvert the norms of the past and present while simultaneously relying on the effects of subjectivity to do so. This operation works as a deconstructive double movement, an erasure, which we can liken to Derrida's differing/deferring movement which enables an opening to alterity. Because of this movement, inherent within the structure of the film itself, *Far From Heaven* performs ethics under erasure. As a result, ethics and subjectivity are both constituted and subverted at the same time. However, all metaphysical concepts, all texts, contain the potential for their own deconstruction, not just melodramatic texts, as Haravolich rather reductively argues. That is, all texts structurally harbour the seed of their own subversion and thus erase themselves 'in [their] own production' (Derrida 1976, 7).

Accepting this, in conclusion, ethics under erasure is not only manifest in all our relationships, but precisely because it is manifest in these everyday contexts, it inevitably, whether we are aware of it or not, permeates all our relationships and cultural artefacts (film, art, literature, for instance). It is important to note, however, that this is not to claim that 'ethics under erasure' is the one true reality or meaning that can be accurately and universally (re)presented as such. Rather, like deconstruction, because ethics under erasure is already multiple, various, singular, heterogeneous, never homogenous, it cannot be consistently applied to all situations across time and space. In its heterogeneity and its ambiguity, ethics under erasure is that which ensures that our everyday normative relations and situations are inflected, and traced with a singularity which is not the 'same', but always and already different. In other words, it is only in and through the maintenance of the lived material and bodily consequences and implication of social norms that singular ethical responses are articulated and enacted, leading to a difference that does not simply efface or delete norms but renders them potentially transformable. In this way, it is by complying, or referring, to the norms and values of their society that makes the singularity of both Cathy's and Cybil's ethical responses 'possible'.

Notes

Introduction

[1] Both the Cambridge and Heidegger Affairs are reproduced and published in *Points...Interviews 1974–1994* (Derrida 1995d).

[2] Those scholars famous for criticizing Derrida's work as nihilistic, indeterminate and unethical include: Hans Bertens (1995), John Ellis (1989), Jürgen Habermas (1987), Gillian Rose (1984), John Searle (1977), Barry Smith (1992), Gregory Bruce Smith (1996), etc.

[3] See also N. Anderson (2006).

[4] In the original French version, the quote reads: 'Une telle différance nous donnerait déjà, encore, à penser une écriture sans présence et sans absence, sans histoire, sans cause, sans archie, sans télos, dérangeant absolument toute dialectique, toute théologie, toute téléologie, toute ontologie' (Derrida 1972, 78). See the bibliography for full publishing details of this French edition of *Margins of Philosophy*.

[5] Derrida's 'under erasure' is a palaeonymy. Palaeonymies and neologisms are common throughout his work in order to convey the play of undecidability in language and meaning. Thus, in traditional usage, under erasure is a phrase that means something is obliterated altogether, but as we will see, Derrida uses this old phrase to convey how something is both obliterated and retained simultaneously.

[6] Throughout this book the 'other' refers to alterity; to otherness. While the 'Other' refers to another person, the You, or some form of presence (whether abstract or not), such as God or an Idea or material event, and so on. See endnote 6 in Chapter 1. Both senses of Other/other contaminate each other, but at times it becomes necessary to convey this by 'Other/other'.

[7] Derrida incredulously comments in a footnote in *Limited Inc*:

> The most massive and most recent example of the confusion that consists in attributing confusions to me in places where quite simply I have not been read is furnished by Habermas, precisely concerning the debate with Searle. The second of the two chapters devoted to me ... *I am not cited a single time* ... not one of my texts is even indicated as a reference in a chapter of twenty-five pages that claims to be a long critique of my work. (Derrida 1997a, 156, n.9)

While the urgency of combining political and philosophical forces against the 'West's' war with Iraq (in 2002) led to a rapprochement between Derrida and Habermas (Habermas and Derrida 2003), this rapprochement does not occlude the real and significant differences between them.

[8] 'Speech act theory' was pioneered by the linguist-philosopher J. L. Austin. Austin classified the performative aspect of speech acts (as opposed to the constative) into locutionary acts, illocutionary acts and perlocutionary acts. Locutionary acts can be defined as the meaningful phonetic, grammatical forms produced. Illocutionary acts indicate what is actually 'performed' when uttering words or a sentence, such as promising, demanding, accusing, etc. The perlocutionary acts are those that directly affect their hearer(s): for instance, frightening or embarrassing someone, and so on. Felicitous speech acts are successful acts in that the speaker has the social or institutional authority to make the act effective. Infelicitous speech acts are utterances that are not effective: for example, in a locutionary act, when one makes a promise one does not intend to keep (illocutionary).

[9] In his book *The Tain of the Mirror* (1997), Gasché refers to archewriting, différance, trace, supplement, etc. as infrastructures of quasi-transcendentality (Gasché 1997, 149). They can be defined as (non)structures because archewriting, différance, trace etc., can be used interchangeably (as a relation of economy), while also being, at the same time, separate and singular. As Derrida remarks, 'the kind of bringing together proposed here has the structure of an interlacing, a weaving, or a web, which would allow the different threads and different lines of sense or force to separate again, as well as being ready to bind others together' (Derrida 1973, 132). Furthermore, Gasché interprets and defines Derrida's term quasi-transcendental 'by demarcating it from that to which it seems to correspond in Heidegger's philosophy, from what I should like to call *finite* or *immanent transcendentals*' (Gasché 1997, 316). Gasché also explains that 'the quasitranscendentals are situated at the margin of the distinction between the transcendental and the empirical' (Gasché 1997, 317). Similarly, Geoffrey Bennington in 'Derridabase', following and interpreting Derrida's word 'ultra-transcendental' in *Of Grammatology* (1976, 61), claims that: '"Quasi-transcendental" names what results from this displacement, by maintaining as legible the trace of a passage through the traditional opposition [empirical/transcendental]' (Bennington and Derrida 1993, 279). See Joshua Kates 2005 (in Bibliography), for a detailed discussion of the history of the development of this term and its use by Bennington, Gasché and Rorty.

[10] For Derrida, a decision comes about not because of blind obedience to a programme, set of laws, or rules. Following ethical laws and norms is not a decision, precisely because it is an application of a law to a certain situation. A decision, rather, depends on a moment of 'undecidability', a moment which is not a direct manifestation of a formulated law or rule, but rather is a moment imbued both with impossibility and possibility or potentiality. In other words, it is in that moment of suspending the rules, laws and norms that any proper decision can occur.

[11] Closure will be defined and discussed in detail in Chapter 1.

[12] Let us note that ethics and morality are not necessarily equivalent (although they overlap and are thus often conflated). That is, if ethics is defined as a universal system that prescribes rules and laws for regulating behaviour, then morality is concerned with how to apply those rules and laws according to a community or person's sense of right and wrong, good and bad. Often, social norms develop from this general moral sense, which in turn influences and contributes to developing the principles and rules that *ought* to govern conduct or behaviour (ethics).

While there is a fine line between the two, there is a line nonetheless. Furthermore, if 'absolute responsibility' is not ethical in the metaphysical universal sense defined here, then it is not equivalent to morality or a personal morality either.

[13] The term 'aporia' is originally from Aristotle, who defines it as the inability or paradox of judgement, and the conundrum of time. That is, aporia implies an impossible passage or path that suspends judgement. Derrida in his book *Aporias*, however, goes beyond this traditional conception, suggesting that there is a plural logic to the term aporia, where 'the partitioning [*partage*] among multiple figures of aporia does not oppose figures to each other, but instead installs the haunting of the one in the other' (Derrida 1993a, 20). Derrida suggests that thinking the multiple figures of aporia is part of a deconstructive process, if not deconstruction itself. In his book, he reminds us that in his article 'Psyche: Inventions de l'autre' he has shown that 'deconstruction is explicitly defined as a certain aporetic experience of the impossible' (Derrida 1993a, 15).

[14] J. Hillis Miller enters into a chapter-length dialogue and discussion of Derrida's *The Gift of Death* in his book *For Derrida* (2009). The chapter is entitled 'Derrida's Ethics of Irresponsibilization'. In this chapter, J. Hillis Miller gives a more thorough and detailed exposition of *The Gift of Death* as a whole than what can be done in the space of this Introduction. See also Derek Attridge's chapter on ethics and *The Gift of Death*, entitled 'The Art of the Impossible?' (2007).

[15] In fact, choice, if based on the autonomy of the humanist subject, is to some extent an illusion.

[16] The word 'iteration' is used here (rather than application, for instance) so as to avoid putting theory into practice, which contributes to perpetuating the metaphysical theory/praxis opposition that also dichotomizes ethics and politics, which is challenged in Chapter 1.

[17] We could probably ask the same question of Derrida's *The Gift of Death*, where the story of Abraham and Isaac is the focus, rather than the story of Lot, or indeed any other biblical story that offers similar ethical aporias.

[18] And yet Nietzsche claims that the Dionysian 'developed alongside' and is 'married' to the Apollonian (Nietzsche 1956, 34). In other words, the senses and Becoming (the Dionysian) developed in correlation with reason and Being (the Apollonian) (Valadier 1995, 248). Instead of reading Dionysian rapture as that which decentres subjectivity and abandons reason, as Habermas does (Habermas 1987, 91–2; Valadier 1995, 248), we can read Nietzsche's Dionysus and Apollo as two sides of the same coin, and, thus, intimately connected.

Chapter 1

[1] For Simon Critchley's renegotiated position regarding the political in Derrida's work, see his 'Remarks on Derrida and Habermas' (2000). Even in the Preface to the second edition of *The Ethics of Deconstruction*, Critchley states that 'based on a reading of Derrida's work since 1992, I am more positive about the political possibilities of deconstruction' (Critchley 1999, xii). Examples of excellent books and edited book collections that deal with deconstruction and politics, include:

Bennington's 'Derrida and Politics' (2000 and 2001); McQuillan (ed.), *The Politics of Deconstruction* (2007); Cheah and Geurlac (eds), *Derrida and the Time of the Political* (2009). The titles of these books belie the fact that the term 'politics' is complicated by the authors' revelations that there is no easy way to unravel a discussion of politics from ethics, especially given that deconstruction is such that makes (im)possible such oppositions.

² In this historicizing depiction there develops an opposition between the first wave, and its emphasis on the literary applicability of deconstruction, and the second wave, which focuses on the philosophical aspect of Derrida's work. It is an opposition that, in many respects inadvertently, perpetuates the philosophy/literature distinction that Derrida deconstructs.

³ Presence is never absolute precisely because within the sign (word, concept, body, object, etc.) there is a play of protension and retention. (Derrida 1973, 66). In other words, within the sign there is an expectation and memory of a living past, a non-present presence (for example the author of a book, or the history of a meaning or cultural context of a word or concept, etc.). It is this protension and retention as a movement of spacing and temporalization, of differing and deferring (that Derrida also calls différance), as well as iterability (repetition as différance, or '*sameness* which is not *identical*') that constitutes the 'living present' (Derrida 1973, 129). Différance, which is at work in both graphic and non-graphic expressions, is therefore common to both speech and writing. Derrida adopts the palaeonymy 'archewriting' to convey the way in which absence, iterability, différance, and so on, functions within graphic writing as well as speech. (For more on archewriting, see Bennington 1993; Simon Morgan Wortham 2010.)

⁴ See, for example, Dooley (2001), Grebowicz (2005), Hägglund (2004, 2008), Plant (2003).

⁵ In this sense, Critchley is faithful to Levinas' distinction between his ethics as first philosophy and an ethics of ontology (metaphysics), a distinction Derrida complicates.

⁶ **Definition of the Other/other:** In 'Violence and Metaphysics' Derrida follows Alfonso Lingis' translation of Other/other in Levinas' *Totality and Infinity*. For consistency, I will also follow Lingis and Derrida's translation throughout this book. Thus, the 'other' refers to alterity, to otherness, and the 'Other' refers to another person, the You, or some form of presence (whether abstract or not), such as God or an idea, or material event, and so on. In his engagement with Levinas in 'Violence and Metaphysics', Derrida also refers to the other as the 'infinite other' or 'Infinite other', and to the Other as 'finite Other'. The term Other is further complicated by the fact that it encapsulates, or is haunted by, the other (alterity). That is, as Derrida argues, the Other is not just an ego, or another Other, but also other.

Definition of the 'same': The notion of the 'same' is used extensively in both Levinas' *Totality and Infinity* and Derrida's 'Violence and Metaphysics'. Levinas (1996) defines 'the same' as identification: 'the same is essentially identification within the diverse, or history, or system' (40). This identification is not the identity given to the individual from without, rather it is identification of one self from within (interiority): 'The identity of the individual does not consist in being like to itself, and in letting itself be identified *from the outside* by the finger that points to it; it consists in being the *same* – in being oneself, in identifying oneself from within' (289). The 'same', then, in order to be the same, that is, in order to be a totality (or as Derrida would say, 'presence'), suspends, possesses, or absorbs and engulfs the Other/other (alterity), precisely in and through identification. So identification becomes a form of reduction: 'The possibility of possessing, that is, of suspending the very alterity of what is only at first other, and other relative to me, is the *way* of the same' (38). Thus, while Derrida points out 'the same' 'does not mean identical, or one, or equal' (Derrida 1995a, 141), Levinas (1996) argues that there is a connection or logical passage 'from the like [identity, ego] to the same' (289), which is why the term 'same' incorporates, or makes reference to, the sameness of the individual person. The same, then, is the ontological position of Western metaphysics.Throughout this chapter (and book) I will be referring to the 'same' as defined by Levinas and Derrida here.

7 This notion of 'responsibility' can be likened to Derrida's notion of 'invention' (discussed in Chapter 2), which Bennington reveals is an appropriation by Derrida (in 'Force of Law') of Kant's concept of 'duty' to his notion of 'justice' (Bennington 2000, 204 n.10). See also Kant's *Foundations of the Metaphysics of Morals* (1959), where Kant argues: '(By analogy), then, the universal imperative of duty can be expressed as follows: Act as though the maxim of your action were by your will to become a universal law of nature' (39). Similarities and differences between Derrida and Kant have also been explored by John Caputo (1997a), Irene Harvey (1989) and Alison Ross (2001). See also Derrida's *The Truth in Painting*.

8 Derrida also argues that 'when I refer to the "closure" (*clôture*) of metaphysics, I insist that it is not a question of considering metaphysics as a circle with a limit or simple boundary. The notion of the limit and boundary (*bord*) of metaphysics is itself highly problematic. My reflections on this problematic have always attempted to show that the limit or end of metaphysics is not linear or circular in any indivisible sense. And as soon as we acknowledge that the limit-boundary of metaphysics is divisible, the logical rapport between inside and outside is no longer simple. Accordingly, we cannot really say that we are "locked into" or "condemned to" metaphysics, for we are, strictly speaking, neither inside nor outside. In brief, the whole rapport between the inside and the outside of metaphysics is inseparable from the question of the finitude and reserve of metaphysics as language' (Derrida 1995g, 162).

9 The Cérisy colloquium took place in 1980, long before Derrida's *Specters of Marx* was published in French in 1993 (English translation, 1994). My aim is not to make a comparison between what Lacoue-Labarthe has to say and Derrida's argument in *Specters of Marx*. Rather, the discussion of *le politique* and *la politique* is necessary for understanding Critchley's position on politics. As we will see, this is in turn the basis on which he constructs the opposition between ethics and politics in Derrida's work.

10 See Nancy Fraser's article for a thorough discussion of this debate (in Bibliography). See also Philippe Lacoue-Labarthe and Jean-Luc Nancy, et al., *Le retrait du politique* (Galilée, Paris, 1983).

11 See Critchley's argument in Chantal Mouffe (ed.), *Deconstruction and Pragmatism* (1996). Rorty, like Critchley, thinks that Derrida's work is not politically useful,

which is why he distinguishes Derrida's work into earlier (bad), later (good). The later work is good, for Rorty, precisely because it is 'private irony'.

[12] While Derrida defends Husserl here, he also questions Husserl's arguments in *Speech and Phenomena*. This questioning of Husserl is most evident in Derrida's deconstruction of expressive and indicative language.

[13] 'Dissymetrical' is Derrida's term used in response to Levinas' 'assymetry' in *Totality and Infinity* (1996, 215–16).

[14] Robert Bernasconi provides an excellent summary of the three accounts of the 'third party' that can be found in Levinas' work:

> The third party is the site of the passage to the political in Levinas's thought. Justice begins with 'the third man' in the sense of the third party (AE 191; OB 150). However, there are two other 'thirds' in Levinas. Alongside the notion of the third party (*le tiers*), there is the notion of the third person (*la triosième personne*), the neutral observer whose standpoint corresponds to that of universal reason, and there is also the difficult notion of 'illeity' (*illéité*), which derives from the third person singular pronoun 'il' (Bernasconi 1999, 76).

[15] This reading of Derrida's is confirmed by Levinas himself in *Totality and Infinity*. Levinas argues that the 'essence of discourse is ethical. In stating this thesis, idealism is refused' because '[i]dealism completely carried out reduces all ethics to politics' (Levinas 1996, 216).

[16] Critchley is aware of this 'dialogue', as the editor's introduction which he wrote with Bernasconi for *Re-Reading Levinas* (1991) clearly shows. This was published the year before Critchley's *The Ethics of Deconstruction* (1992).

[17] The most 'Hegelian of modern novelists' is Derrida's reference to James Joyce.

Chapter 2

[1] While Derrida remains generally elusive regarding any congruence between himself and Nietzsche, he does discuss, and refer to Nietzsche explicitly, in *Spurs: Nietzsche's Styles*, in Chapter 2 of *Politics of Friendship*, and in an interview with Richard Beardsworth, entitled 'Nietzsche and the Machine' in *Negotiations*.

[2] In *The Will to Power* (1968), Nietzsche also says, 'insofar as the word "knowledge" has any meaning, the world is knowable, but it is otherwise, it has no meaning behind it, but countless meanings – "Perspectivism"' (p. 267).

[3] I am aware of course that this makes problematic my own attempt at the interpretation of Nietzsche's writings.

[4] In an interview with Jean-Luc Nancy entitled '"Eating Well" or the Calculation of the Subject', Derrida acknowledges that the reason for rarely speaking of the subject, or of 'subjectivity', is because 'the discourse on the subject, even if it locates difference, inadequation, the dehiscence within autoaffection, etc., continues to link subjectivity with man' (Derrida and Nancy 1991, 105). As he goes on to argue several pages later, the attributes that traditionally associate the term 'subject' with the concept 'man' are ordered 'around being present (*etant-present*), presence to self – which implies therefore a certain interpretation of temporality: identity to self, positionality, property, personality, ego, consciousness, will, intentionality,

freedom, humanity, etc. It is necessary to question this authority of the being-present' (Derrida and Nancy 1991, 109).

[5] In *Spurs*, Derrida links the idea of woman – as having no 'essence' ('endless and unfathomable, she engulfs and distorts all vestige of essentiality, of identity, of property' (51)) – with 'style' and 'truth'. Derrida argues:

> It is impossible to dissociate the question of art, style and truth from the question of woman. Nevertheless the question << what is woman? >> is itself suspended by the simple formulation of their common problematic. One can no longer seek her, no more than one could search for woman's femininity or female sexuality. And she is certainly not to be found in any of the familiar modes of concept or knowledge (71).

Derrida relates the 'question of woman' to Nietzsche in the following way: 'Nietzsche's writing ... even if we do not venture so far as to call it the feminine itself, is indeed the feminine << operation >> ... Woman, inasmuch as truth, is scepticism and veiling dissimulation' (57). While I do not have the space to analyse this idea of woman in relation to style, it is nevertheless an important motif throughout *Spurs*, and has implications for the way ethics can be rethought. For accounts on Derrida, Nietzsche and woman, or sexual difference, see Rosalyn Diprose's article, 'Nietzsche, Ethics and Sexual Difference' (1995), and Gayatri Spivak's article, 'Love Me, Love My Ombre, Elle' (1984).

[6] Derrida has talked about this constraint in *Limited Inc*, p. 64.

[7] By text I mean, not simply or only, books or literature of any sort (defined by marks on a page), but anything that can be analysed or that produces or makes meaning.

[8] The entire poem (set out in two columns in French and English) is quoted in *Psyche* (2007b, 8), and runs as follows:

FABLE

With this word with commences then this text
Of which the first line states the truth,
But this silvering under the one and the other
Can it be tolerated?
Dear reader already you judge
There as to our difficulties ...

(AFTER seven years of misfortune she broke her mirror).

[9] If the 'impossible' can never be fully represented, or presented, then I would suggest that Derrida's argument that the impossible can only be thought through the possible, is analogous to the idea of 'analogical appresentation' which was discussed in Chapter 1. That is, the possible allows the other (the impossible) to be experienced, but not totally or absolutely, for then the other would cease to be other. This, perhaps, makes it clearer why Derrida says that the other (as the impossible) can never come!

[10] The other influence in this radicalization has been Husserl.

[11] Also, in the same way that différance, undecidability, trace, pharmakon, etc., cannot simply be substituted for one another because they operate within, and by, specific contexts, so too ethics under erasure cannot simply be substituted as, or for, the condition of (im)possibility that runs through justice and law, or 'irresponsibilization' that runs through responsibility (in *The Gift of Death*).

Chapter 3

[1] See Derrida's 'Marx and Sons' in *Ghostly Demarcations*, ed. Michael Sprinker (1999). Derrida's essay is a defence against critiques of, and clarification of his ideas and position in, his book *Specters of Marx*.

[2] As the condition of inheritance is a mode of haunting, it evokes a form of (in) visibility associated with spectres/ghosts, which Derrida, in turn, argues is 'indissociable' from the trace (Derrida 1999c, 268, n. 73).

[3] The difference between spirit and spectre for traditional philosophy is that the 'spirit' is that which never appears; it is that which is forever invisible. While the spectre is that which *appears* without appearing in the living flesh (ghost-like): 'The ghost is the phenomenon of the spirit' argues Derrida (Derrida 1994, 135). But to argue this Derrida is deconstructing the opposition between spirit and spectre by revealing, as Ernesto Laclau puts it, how the spectre is that which is 'undecidable between the two extremes of body and spirit, these extremes themselves become contaminated by that undecidability' (Laclau 2007, 68). Thus for Derrida there is no pure spirit, in other words,

> [f]or there is no ghost, there is never any becoming-specter of the spirit [thought; idea] without at least an appearance of flesh, in a space of invisible visibility, like the dis-appearing of an apparition. For there to be ghost, there must be a return to the body, but to a body that is more abstract than ever ... Once ideas or thoughts (*Gedanke*) are detached from their substratum, one engenders some ghost by *giving them a body*. Not by returning to the living body from which ideas and thoughts have been torn loose, but by incarnating the latter in *another artifactual body, a prosthetic body*, a ghost of spirit, one might say a ghost of the ghost ... (Derrida 1994, 126).

Therefore, the supposed invisibility of spirit is only known through being made visible. Spirit, then, is never purely invisible, in fact, 'the very constitution of spirit requires the visibility of the invisible' (Laclau 2007, 69).

[4] This is an ironic manoeuvre given that Marx*ism*, as Derrida argues, produced and continues to produce multiple spectres.

[5] It is on the basis of this religious inheritance that Derrida invokes the quasi-transcendental notion of 'messianicity without messianism' to further complicate this genealogy, and which will be discussed further on in the chapter.

[6] In his interweaving of inheritances, Will Maley (2000) argues that Derrida also plays with the exorcism of ghosts: 'the question of co-authorship, central to the study of Marx and Engels, seems conspicuous by its absence in *Specters of Marx*. This omission is glaring in so far as Engels is one of the most awesome specters of Marx' (384).

[7] In an article entitled 'Reconciling Derrida: "Specters of Marx" and Deconstructive Politics', in *Ghostly Demarcations*(1999), Aijaz Ahmad has accused Derrida of attempting to be Marx's only rightful heir.

[8] Later in *Specters of Marx* Derrida writes: '*To be*, this word in which we earlier saw the word of the spirit, means, for the same reason, to inherit. All the questions on the subject of being or of what is to be (or not to be) are questions of inheritance' (Derrida 1994, 54).

[9] To live justly in the Derridean sense is, I suggest later in the chapter, an ethics *without* ethics. Therefore to shift the question to an ethical one does not entail

living only according to prescriptive rules and laws and without negotiation with the particular.

[10] See Chapter 2 for details of how Derrida plays with his proper name.

[11] These are the two books where Derrida initially introduces the notion of 'under erasure' using the chiasm. Under erasure, however, is used throughout Derrida's oeuvre. For example, in later work such as *Resistances of Psychoanalysis* (1998) Derrida again discusses the chiasm, this time to put consciousness/the subject under erasure.

[12] This is why the object 'played' with is thought to contain particular meaning in the traditional concept of 'play'. A ball is for throwing: it is given, and thus contains a meaning, which excludes other meanings. The meanings associated with an object in some ways construct the notion of play. You play with a ball this way not that way, etc.

[13] The disjointedness of time is enacted or performed in *Specters of Marx* especially when Derrida speaks for and against the spectres he inherits: a form of putting under erasure, and transforming the tradition he himself has inherited.

[14] In *Resistances to Psychoanalysis* Derrida says: '*iterability* ... is for this reason the becoming-objective of the object or the becoming-subjective of the subject, thus the becoming-analyzable in general. But (double bind), it is also what perturbs any analysis because it perturbs, by resisting, the binary and hierarchized oppositions that authorize any principle of distinction in the common discourse as well as in philosophical or theoretical discourse' (Derrida 1998, 31).

[15] In *Marx and Sons* Derrida is deconstructing, among others, Spivak's critique and 'interpretation' of his notion of spectrality and hauntology as 'metaphysical' and 'abstract' concepts with therefore no political effectiveness. See my discussion of Simon Critchley's similar critique of Derrida in Chapter 1.

[16] Ironically, to conclude that ethics appeals to rationality is a form of deductive reasoning. This of course raises the question of what it means to 'think' and whether or not we can think otherwise, that is, apart from metaphysical thought. Arguably, one of the problems with this mode of thought is that it privileges a comparatively narrow understanding of what it means to 'think', and thus what it means to think 'man'. 'Thinking' requires deductive reasoning, and thus what is accorded value is the deductive and logical reasoning associated with producing argumentative evidence, such as objectivity, differentiation, and the use of counter-examples to refute generalizations to build upon and move from one universal truth to another, and in this way, as Derrida throughout his oeuvre suggests, perpetuates the phallogocentrism of humanistic thought. For Derrida, this mode of thinking is an establishment of relations based on a metaphysical complicity of a common element or notion of man (Derrida 1986, 112).

[17] However, for some ethical theories this avoidance of reasoning by subjects is precisely the aim of ethical 'rational' prescriptions. For instance, as the utilitarian J. J. Smart argues, '[t]he utilitarian position is here put forward as a criterion of rational choice. It is true that we may choose to habituate ourselves to behave in accordance with certain rules, such as to keep promises, in the belief that behaving in accordance with these rules is generally optimific, and in the knowledge that we most often just do not have time to work out individual pros and cons. When we act in such a habitual fashion we do not of course deliberate or make a choice' (Smart and Williams 1996, 42).

[18] Debate within utilitarianism about the definition of consequences is rife, and this debate has led to various forms of utilitarianism: from rule-, act-, hedonistic-, non-hedonistic-, negative- utilitarianism. See Smart and Williams (1996).

[19] The Hypothetical Imperative is the means by which one achieves an end.

[20] We have seen the problem with this according to Adorno in the Introduction to this book.

[21] For Marx, this authorization of discourses that serve technopolitical powers produces the inability to be able to see the way in which society operates or functions (what Marx calls 'false consciousness'); it is the inability to see material reality for what it is: the social creation of inequality through economic (and technological) modes of production which determine class. See, for example, his *Economic and Philosophic Manuscripts of 1844* (1982).

[22] Once again, for Marx, this notion of ethical autonomy produced as a result of the independence of reason from all social and political influence (aesthetic, ethical and religious) is a form of false consciousness, precisely because consciousness is determined by the material reality of social existence (Marx 1982, 83, 91–3).

[23] I also want to suggest that affects are not a-contextual or 'free-floating' in the Rortyian sense, but are contextually formed: by genre, by socio-cultural contexts, by what Derrida calls in *The Truth in Painting*, 'framing'. This contextuality guides subjects' conceptual and affective responses. For instance, watching the heroine of a drama-genre film being violently beaten does not, generally speaking, produce the affect of hilarity (unless it's a black comedy, in which the subject is guided by other conventions to laugh). And this affect, in turn, guides how to 'think' conceptually about particular texts, experiences or situations. In this sense, the material and social situation in which we find ourselves frames the ideological perspectives we have of the world generally, and thus the way in which we may philosophically reflect on the world, specifically.

[24] As discussed in Chapter 2 in relation to *Of Hospitality*, the unexpected outcome of the other 'to come' may indeed bring the worst. Likewise, as discussed earlier in this chapter in relation to disjointure, 'just response' to the unknown other entails a risk.

[25] Chapter 1, however, challenged Critchley's position, arguing that undecidability is not a refusal of the empirical, ontic, factical. Rather, undecidability is precisely what makes possible the decision, the empirical, in the first place. Moreover, since it does not deny the transcendental either, the empirical decision cannot become unified and homogenizing (or totalitarian).

Chapter 4

[1] *Far From Heaven* was released in cinemas in 2002, and released on DVD and video in 2003, by Universal Studios. Written and Directed by Todd Haynes. Executive Producers: Steven Soderbergh and George Clooney. Cast: Julianne Moore (Cathy), Dennis Quaid (Frank), Dennis Haysbert (Raymond), Viola Davis (Cybil).

[2] There are various theories and positions taken on the construction of meaning of a text, and whether or not this resides with the author or the reader (reader-response theory). Often they are formulated around what Belsey (1980) argues are the 'classic realist', structuralist and post-structuralist debates.

[3] This is not to say that Sirk was entirely a puppet for an ideological machine. Indeed, Sirk has said that, although he had to ensure Universal made money by sticking to Hollywood conventions, the studio did not interfere directly with his camerawork or post-production editing (Halliday 1997, 97). Still, it is not clear from this interview, as Haravolich wants to argue, if Sirk's creative license in the area of camerawork and cutting purposively, or inadvertently, contributed to identifying, and thus subverting, the normative ideologies articulated through character conflict in 1950s melodrama.

[4] From a twenty-first century perspective this 1950s world is different. However, from the perspective of a 1950s viewer of Sirk's films, we can only speculate if this zooming device might have had the effect of creating a sense of familiarity, and thus identification with that world. However, the zooming device in Sirk's films that Haynes imitates would not work to juxtapose the norms of two different eras, as it does for a twenty-first century viewer. Rather, it would work to construct identification between the 1950s viewer and the characters, and thus perpetuate the ideology of that era.

[5] Belsey defines the classic realist text as such:

> Classic realism, still the dominant popular mode in literature, film and television drama ... performs, I wish to suggest, the work of ideology, not only in its representation of a world of consistent subjects who are the origin of meaning, knowledge and action, but also in offering the reader, as the position from which the text is most readily intelligible, the position of subject as the origin both of understanding and of action in accordance with that understanding (1980, 67).

[6] The acronym stands for 'National Association for the Advancement of Colored People'.

[7] For example, for Richard Rorty ethics and morality is not about some ultimate truth underlying our actions, our behaviours, but is based instead on 'loyalty' to a particular community or group. The ground for such loyalties, Rorty insists, is based on the majority of the members of the groups' overlapping political and moral beliefs, desires and emotions, which are then reinforced by being contrasted with other groups (Rorty 1991a, 200). As we have seen, ethics under erasure problematizes this entirely contingent position.

[8] For discussions on Saussure and Husserl, see Derrida 1973 and 1982a.

[9] See Alasdair MacIntyre (1998) for an account of contingent norms. And also Richard Rorty (1991a) is an example of a belief in contingent subjectivity and values.

Bibliography

Adamson, Jane, Freadman, Richard and Parker, David (eds) (1991), *Renegotiating Ethics: In Literature, Philosophy, and Theory*. Cambridge: Cambridge University Press, pp. 1–17.

Adorno, Theodore (2001), *Metaphysics: Concepts and Problems*, Rolf Tiedemann (ed.), trans. Edmund Jephcott. Cambridge: Polity Press.

Ahmad, Aijaz (1999), 'Reconciling Derrida: "Specters of Marx" and Deconstructive Politics', in Michael Sprinker (ed.), *Ghostly Demarcations*. London and New York: Verso, pp. 88–109.

Alcoff, Linda Martin (2001), 'Toward a Phenomenology of Racial Embodiment', in Robert Bernasconi (ed.), *Race*. Oxford and Massachussetts: Blackwell Publishers, pp. 267–83.

Allison, David B. (ed.) (1995), *The New Nietzsche*. Cambridge, MA and London, England: The MIT Press.

Anderson, Nicole (2003), 'The Ethical Possibilities of the Subject as Play: in Nietzsche and Derrida'. *Journal of Nietzsche Studies* 26: 79–90.

—. (2006), 'Freeplay? Fairplay! Defending Derrida'. *Social Semiotics* 16(3): 407–20.

Aristotle (1998), *The Metaphysics*, trans. Hugh Lawson-Tancred. Penguin Books.

Attridge, Derek (2007), 'The Art of the Impossible?', in Martin McQuillan (ed.), *The Politics of Deconstruction: Jacques Derrida and the Other of Philosophy*. London and Ann Arbor, MI: Pluto Press, pp. 54–65.

Badiou, Alain (2002), *Ethics: An Essay on the Understanding of Evil*, trans. Peter Hallward. London and New York: Verso.

Balibar, Etienne (2009), 'Eschatology Versus Teleology: The Suspended Dialogue between Derrida and Althusser', in Pheng Cheah and Suzanne Guerlac (eds), *Derrida and the Time of the Political*. Durham and London: Duke University Press, pp. 57–73.

Barker, Stephen (2008), 'Strata/Sedimenta/Lamina: *In Ruin(s)*'. *Derrida Today* 1(1): 42–58.

Beardsworth, Richard (1996), *Derrida and the Political*. London and New York: Routledge.

—. (2007), 'The Irony of Deconstruction and the Example of Marx', in Martin McQuillan (ed.), *The Politics of Deconstruction: Jacques Derrida and the Other of Philosophy*. London and Ann Arbor, MI: Pluto Press, pp. 212–34.

Belsey, Catherine (1980), *Critical Practice*. London and New York: Methuen.

Benjamin, Andrew (ed.) (1988), *Post-structuralist Classics*. London and New York: Routledge.

—. (1989), 'Discussion and Comments', in Andreas Papadakis, Catherine Cooke and Andrew Benjamin (eds), *Deconstruction: Omnibus Volume*. New York: Rizzoli Press, p. 76.

—. (2008), 'Indefinite Play and "The Name of Man"'. *Derrida Today* 1(1): 1–18.

Bennington, Geoffrey (1988), 'Deconstruction and the Philosophers (The Very Idea)'. *The Oxford Literary Review* 10(1): 73–130.

—. (1994), *Legislations: The Politics of Deconstruction*. London and New York: Verso.

—. (2000), *Interrupting Derrida*. London and New York: Routledge Press.

—. (2001), 'Derrida and Politics', in Tom Cohen (ed.), *Jacques Derrida and the Humanities: A Critical Reader*. Cambridge: Cambridge University Press, pp. 193–212.

—. (2007), 'Demo', in Martin McQuillan (ed.), *The Politics of Deconstruction: Jacques Derrida and the Other of Philosophy*. London and Ann Arbor, MI: Pluto Press, pp. 17–42.

Bennington, Geoffrey and Derrida, Jacques (1993), *Jacques Derrida*. Chicago, IL: University of Chicago Press.

Berkowitz, Peter (1998), *Nietzsche: The Ethics of an Immoralist*. Cambridge, MA and London, England: Harvard University Press.

Bernasconi, Robert (1987), 'Deconstruction and the Possibility of Ethics', in John Sallis (ed.), *Deconstruction and Philosophy: The Texts of Jacques Derrida*. Chicago: University of Chicago Press, pp. 122–41.

—. (1988), 'The Trace of Levinas in Derrida', in David Wood and Robert Bernasconi (eds), *Derrida and Difference*. Evanston, IL: Northwestern University Press, pp. 13–29.

—. (1991), 'Skepticism in the Face of Philosophy', in Robert Bernasconi and Simon Critchley (eds), *Re-Reading Levinas*. Bloomington and Indianapolis: Indiana University Press, pp. 149–61.

—. (1999), 'The Third Party: Levinas on the Intersection of the Ethical'. *British Society for Phenomenology* 30(1): 76–87.

—. (2001), 'The invisibility of Racial Minorities in the Public Realm of Appearances', in Robert Bernasconi (ed.), *Race*. Oxford and Massachussetts: Blackwell Publishers, pp. 284–99.

Bernasconi, Robert and Critchley, Simon (1991), 'Editor's Introduction', in Robert Bernasconi and Simon Critchley (eds), *Re-Reading Levinas*. Bloomington and Indianapolis: Indiana University Press, pp. x–xviii.

Bernstein, Richard J. (1987), 'Serious Play: The Ethical-Political Horizon of Jacques Derrida'. *Journal of Speculative Philosophy* 1(2): 93–117.

—. (1992), *The New Constellation: The Ethical-Political Horizons of Modernity/Postmodernity*. Cambridge, MA: The MIT Press.

—. (1993), 'An Allegory of Modernity/Postmodernity: Habermas and Derrida', in Gary B. Madison (ed.), *Working Through Derrida*. Evanston, IL: Northwestern University Press, pp. 12–27.

Bertens, Hans (1995), *The Idea of the Postmodern: A History*. London and New York: Routledge.

Bordwell, David (2002), 'Intensified Continuity: Visual Style in Contemporary American Film'. *Film Quarterly* 55(3): 16.

Bordwell, David and Thompson, Kristin (2001), *Film Art: An Introduction*. New York: McGraw Hill.

Bouman, Majero (2007), 'Racism's Specters: Inheriting the Unthought Future (Racism's Last Word)'. *Mosaic* 40(2): 261–77.

Caputo, John D. (1987), *Radical Hermeneutics: Repetition, Deconstruction, and the Hermeneutic Project*. Bloomington and Indianapolis: Indiana University Press.

—. (1989), 'Disseminating Originary Ethics and the Ethics of Dissemination', in Arleen B. Dallery and Charles E. Scott (eds), *The Question of the Other: Essays in Contemporary Continental Philosophy*. Albany, NY: State University of New York Press, pp. 55–62.

—. (1993), 'On Not Circumventing the Quasi-Transcendental: The Case of Rorty and Derrida', in Gary B. Madison (ed.), *Working Through Derrida*. Evanston, IL: Northwestern University Press, pp. 147–69.

—. (1997a), *The Prayer and Tears of Jacques Derrida: Religion Without Religion*. Bloomington and Indianapolis: Indiana University Press.

—, (ed.) (1997b), *Deconstruction in a Nutshell: A Conversation with Jacques Derrida*. New York: Fordham University Press.

Carroll, Nöel and Jinhee Choi (2006), *The Philosophy of Film and Motion Pictures: An Anthology*. Malden, MA: Blackwell Publishers.

Cascardi, Anthony J. (1984), 'Skepticism and Deconstruction'. *Philosophy and Literature* 8(1): 1–14.

Cheah, Pheng and Guerlac, Suzanne (eds) (2009), *Derrida and the Time of the Political*. Durham and London: Duke University Press.

Clarke, Stanley G. and Simpson, E. (eds) (1989), *Anti-Theory in Ethics and Moral Conservatism*. Albany, NY: State University of New York Press.

Cohen, Tom (ed.) (2001) *Jacques Derrida and the Humanities: A Critical Reader*. Cambridge: Cambridge University Press.

Colebrook, Claire (2007), 'Graphematics, Politics and Irony', in Martin McQuillan (ed.), *The Politics of Deconstruction: Jacques Derrida and the Other of Philosophy*. London and Ann Arbor, MI: Pluto Press, pp. 192–211.

Cook, Pam (1999), 'No Fixed Address: The Women's Picture from *Outrage* to *Blue Steel*', in Steve Neale and Murray Smith (eds), *Contemporary Hollywood Cinema*. London and New York: Routlegde, pp. 229–46.

Cornell, Drucilla (1988), 'Post-Structuralism, The Ethical Relation, and the Law'. *Cardozo Law Review* 9(6): 1587–1624.

—. (1992), 'The Philosophy of the Limit: Systems Theory and Feminist Legal Reforms', in Drucilla Cornell, Michel Rosenfeld, and David Gray Carlson (eds), *Deconstruction and the Possibility of Justice*. New York and London: Routledge, pp. 68–91.

Cowie, Elizabeth (1999), 'Classical Hollywood Cinema and Classical Narrative', in Steve Neale and Murray Smith (eds), *Contemporary Hollywood Cinema*. London and New York: Routledge Press, pp. 178–90.

Critchley, Simon (1999), *The Ethics of Deconstruction*. Edinburgh: Edinburgh University Press.

—. (2000), 'Remarks on Derrida and Habermas'. *Constellations* 7(4): 455–65.

Culler, Jonathan (2007), *On Deconstruction: Theory and Criticism After Structuralism*. Ithaca, NY: Cornell University Press.

Deleuze, Gilles (1984), *Kant's Critical Philosophy*, trans. Hugh Tomlinson and Barbara Habberjam. Minneapolis, MN: University of Minnesota Press.

Derrida, Jacques (1972), *Marges: de la philosophie*. Paris: Les Éditions de Minuit.

—. (1973), *Speech and Phenomena: and Other Essays on Husserl's Theory of Signs*, trans. David B. Allison. Evanston, IL: Northwestern University Press.

—. (1976), *Of Grammatology*, trans. G. C. Spivak. Baltimore, MD: John Hopkins University Press.

—. (1978), 'The Retrait of Metaphor'. *Enclitic* 2(2): 4–33.

—. (1979), *Spurs: Nietzsche's Styles*, trans. Barbara Harlow, bilingual edition. Chicago, IL: University of Chicago Press.

—. (1981), *Dissemination*, trans. Barbara Johnson. Chicago, IL: University of Chicago Press.

—. (1982a), *Positions*, trans. Alan Bass. Chicago: University of Chicago Press.

—. (1982b), 'All Ears: Nietzsche's Otobiography'. *Yale French Studies* 63: 245–50.

—. (1983), 'The Principle of Reason: The University in the Eyes of Its Pupils'. *Diacritics* (Fall): 3–21.

—. (1986), *Margins of Philosophy*, trans. Alan Bass. Chicago, IL: University of Chicago Press.

—. (1987), *The Truth in Painting*, trans. Geoffrey Bennington and Ian McLeod. Chicago, IL: University of Chicago Press.

—. (1988a), *The Ear of the Other: Otobiography, Transference, Translation*, Christie McDonald (ed.), trans. Peggy Kamuf. Lincoln: University of Nebraska Press, Bison Books.

—. (1988b), 'Letter to a Japanese Friend', in David Wood and Robert Bernasconi (eds), trans. David Wood and Andrew Benjamin, *Derrida and Différance*. Evanston, IL: Northwestern University Press, pp. 3–6.

—. (1988c), 'The Deaths of Roland Barthes', in Hugh Silverman (ed.), trans. Pascale-Anne Brault and Michael Naas, *Philosophy and Non-Philosophy Since Merleau-Ponty*. New York: Routledge.

—. (1989a), *Edmund Husserl's Origin of Geometry: An Introduction*, trans. John P. Leavey, Jr. Lincoln and London: University of Nebraska Press.

—. (1989b), 'Right of Inspection'. *Art & Text* 32, 20–97.

—. (1990a), *Glas*, trans. John P. Leavey, Jr, and Richard Rand. Lincoln: University of Nebraska Press.

—. (1990b), 'Some Statements and Truisms About Neologisms, Newisms, Postisms, Parasitisms and other small seismisms', in David Carroll (ed.), *The States of 'Theory': History, Art, and Critical Discourse*. New York and Oxford: Columbia.

—. (1991), 'At This Very Moment in This Work Here I Am', in Robert Bernasconi and Simon Critchley (eds), *Re-Reading Levinas*. Bloomington and Indianapolis: Indiana University Press, pp. 11–48.

—. (1992a), 'Psyche: Inventions of the Other', in Derek Attridge (ed.), *Acts of Literature*. New York and London: Routledge Press, pp. 310–43.

—. (1992b), 'Force of Law: The "Mystical Foundation" of Authority', in Drucilla Cornell, Michel Rosenfeld, and David Gray Carlson (eds), *Deconstruction and the Possibility of Justice*. New York and London: Routledge, pp. 3–67.

—. (1992c), 'Signsponge', in Derek Attridge (ed.), *Acts of Literature*. New York and London: Routledge Press, pp. 344–69.

—. (1992d), 'Derrida in Oxford'. *Times Literary Supplement*, May 1.

—. (1992e), 'Passions: "An Oblique Offering"', in David Wood (ed.), *Derrida: A Critical Reader*. Oxford, UK and Cambridge, USA: Blackwell, pp. 5–35.

—. (1993a), *Aporias*, trans. Thomas Dutoit. Stanford, CA: Stanford University Press.

—. (1993b), 'Le Toucher: Touch/to touch him'. *Paragraph* 16(2): 122–57.

—. (1993c), *Memoirs of the Blind: The Self-Portrait and Other Ruins*, trans. Pascale-Anne Brault and Michael Naas. Chicago, IL: University of Chicago Press.

—. (1994), *Specters of Marx: The State of the Debt, the Work of Mourning, & the New International*, trans. Peggy Kamuf. New York and London: Routledge.

—. (1995a), *Writing and Difference*, trans. Alan Bass. London and New York: Routledge Press.

—. (1995b), *The Gift of Death*, trans. David Wills. Chicago, IL: University of Chicago Press.

—. (1995c), *On the Name*, trans. David Wood, John P. Leavey, Jr, Ian McLeod, and Thomas Dutoit. Stanford, CA: Stanford University Press.

—. (1995d), *Points ... Interviews, 1974–1994*, Elizabeth Weber (ed.), trans. Peggy Kamuf. Stanford, CA: Stanford University Press.

—. (1995e), 'The Question of Style', in David B. Allison (ed.), *The New Nietzsche*. Cambridge, MA: MIT Press, pp. 176–88.

—. (1995f), 'Interpreting Signatures (Nietzsche/Heidegger): Two Questions', in Peter R. Sedgewick (ed.), *Nietzsche: A Critical Reader*. Oxford, UK and Cambridge, USA: Blackwell, pp. 53–68.

—. (1995g), 'Deconstruction and the other', in R. Kearney (ed.), *States of Mind*. Manchester University Press, pp. 156–76.

—. (1996a), 'Remarks on Deconstruction and Pragmatism', in Chantal Mouffe (ed.), *Deconstruction and Pragmatism: Simon Critchley, Jacques Derrida, Ernesto Laclau & Richard Rorty*. London and New York: Routledge, pp. 77–88.

—. (1996b), *Archive Fever: A Freudian Impression*, trans. Eric Prenowitz. Chicago, IL and London: The University of Chicago Press.

—. (1997a), *Limited Inc*, Evanston, IL: Northwestern University Press.

—. (1997b), *Politics of Friendship*, trans. George Collins. London and New York: Verso Press.

—. (1997c), 'The Villanova Roundtable', in John D. Caputo (ed.), *Deconstruction in a Nutshell: A Conversation with Jacques Derrida*. New York: Fordham University Press.

—. (1998), *Resistances of Psychoanalysis*, trans. Peggy Kamuf, Pascale-Anne Brault, and Michael Naas. Stanford, CA: Stanford University Press.

—. (1999a), *Adieu: To Emmanuel Levinas*, Werner Hamacher and David E. Wellbery (eds), trans. Pascale-Anne Brault and Michael Naas. Stanford, CA: Stanford University Press.

—. (1999b), 'Hospitality, Justice and Responsibility: A Dialogue with Jacques Derrida', in Richard Kearney and Mark Dooley (eds), *Questioning Ethics: Contemporary Debates in Philosophy*. London and New York: Routledge Press, pp. 65–83.

—. (1999c), 'Marx & Sons', in Michael Sprinker (ed.), *Ghostly Demarcations: A Symposium on Jacques Derrida's Specters of Marx*. London and New York: Verso, pp. 213–69.

—. (2000), *Of Hospitality*, Miele Bal and Hent de Vries (eds), trans. Rachel Bowlby. Stanford, CA: Stanford University Press.

—. (2001), *The Work of Mourning*, Pascale-Anne Brault and Michael Naas (eds). Chicago, IL and London: The University of Chicago Press.

—. (2002), *Negotiations: Interventions and Interviews 1971–2001*, trans. Elizabeth Rottenberg. Stanford, CA: Stanford University Press.

—. (2004), 'The Last of the Rogue States: The "Democracy to Come", Opening in Two Turns'. *The South Atlantic Quarterly* 103(2/3): 323–41.

—. (2005a), *On Touching—Jean-Luc Nancy*, trans. Christine Irizarry. Stanford, CA: Stanford University Press.

—. (2005b), *Rogues: Two Essays on Reason.* Stanford, CA: Stanford University Press.

—. (2006), *Geneses, Genealogies, Genres and Genius: The Secrets of the Archive*, trans. Beverley Bie Brahic. Edinburgh: Edinburgh University Press.

—. (2007a), *Learning to Live Finally: The Last Interview*, trans. Pascale-Anne Brault and Michael Naas. NSW, Australia: Allen &Unwin.

—. (2007b), *Psyche: Inventions of the Other*, Vol. 1. Stanford, CA: Stanford University Press.

—. (2008), *The Animal That Therefore I Am*, Marie-Louise Mallet (ed.), trans. David Wills. New York: Fordham University Press.

Derrida, Jacques and Nancy, Jean-Luc (1991), '"Eating Well", or the Calculation of the Subject: An Interview with Jacques Derrida', in Eduardo Cadava, Peter Connor and Jean-Luc Nancy (eds), *Who Comes After the Subject?* New York and London: Routledge Press, pp. 96–119.

Derrida, Jacques and Norris, Christopher (1989), 'Jacques Derrida: In discussion with Christopher Norris', in Andreas Papadakis, Catherine Cooke and Andrew Benjamin (eds), *Deconstruction: Omnibus Volume.* New York: Rizzoli Press.

Descombes, Vincent (1991), 'Apropos of the "Critique of the Subject" and the Critique of this Critique', in Eduardo Cadava, Peter Connor and Jean-Luc Nancy (eds), *Who Comes After the Subject?* New York and London: Routledge Press, pp. 120–34.

Deutscher, Penelope (2006), *How to Read Derrida.* W.W. Norton & Co.

Dillon, Michael (2007), 'Force [of] Transformation', in Madeleine Fagan et al. (eds), *Derrida: Negotiating the Legacy*, Edinburgh: Edinburgh University Press, pp. 80–93.

Diprose, Rosalyn (1994), *The Bodies of Women: Ethics, Embodiment and Sexual Difference.* London and New York: Routledge Press.

—. (1995), 'Nietzsche, Ethics and Sexual Difference', in Peter R. Sedgwick (ed.), *Nietzsche: A Critical Reader.* Oxford, UK and Cambridge, USA: Blackwell, pp. 69–83.

Docherty, Thomas (2002), 'Douglas Sirk: Magnificent Obsession', *The Chronicle of Higher Education* 49(12): 16–19.

Dooley, Mark (2001), 'The civic religion of social hope: A response to Simon Critchley'. *Philosophy and Social Criticism* 27(5): 35–58.

Edmundson, Mark (1988), 'The Ethics of Deconstruction'. *Michigan Quarterly Review* 27, 622–43.

Ellis, John (1989), *Against Deconstruction.* Princeton, NJ: Princeton University Press.

Falcon, Richard (2003), 'Magnificent Obsession'. *Sight and Sound* 13(3): 12–15.

Fish, Stanley (1985), 'Pragmatism and Literary Theory I: Consequences'. *Critical Inquiry* 11: 433–58.

Fraser, Nancy (1984), 'The French Derrideans: Politicizing Deconstruction or Deconstructing Politics', *New German Critique* 33: 127–54.

Gasché, Rodolphe (1981), 'Unscrambling Positions: On Gerald Graff's Critique of Derrida'. *MLN* 96: 1015–34.

—. (1988), 'Postmodernism and Rationality'. *Journal of Philosophy* 85(10): 528–38.

—. (1994), *Inventions of Difference: On Jacques Derrida.* Cambridge, MA and London, England: Harvard University Press.

—. (1997), *The Tain of the Mirror: Derrida and the Philosophy of Reflection*. Cambridge, MA and London, England: Harvard University Press.

Gates, Henry Louis (1992), 'Statistical Stigmata', in Drucilla Cornell, Michel Rosenfeld, and David Gray Carlson (eds), *Deconstruction and the Possibility of Justice*. New York and Britain: Routledge, pp. 330–45.

Grebowicz, Margret (2005), '"Between Betrayal and Betrayal": Epistemology and Ethics in Derrida's Debt to Levinas', in Eric Nelson, Antje Kapust, Kent Still (eds), *Addressing Levinas*. Evanston, IL: Northwestern University Press.

Haar, Michael (1995), 'Nietzsche and Metaphysical Language', in David B. Allison (ed.), *TheNew Nietzsche*. Cambridge, MA and London, England: The MIT Press, pp. 5–36.

Habermas, Jürgen (1981), 'Modernity versus Postmodernity'. *New German Critique* 22: 3–14.

—. (1984), 'The French Path to Postmodernity: Bataille Between Eroticism and General Economics'. *New German Critique* 33: 79–102.

—. (1987), *The Philosophical Discourse of Modernity: Twelve Lectures*, trans. Frederick Lawrence. Cambridge: Polity Press.

—. (1993), 'Modernity – An Incomplete Project', in Hal Foster (ed.), *The Anti-Aesthetic: Essays on Postmodern Culture*. Seattle, Washington: Bay Press, pp. 3–15.

Habermas, Jürgen and Derrida, Jacques (2003), 'February 15, or What Binds Europeans Together: A Plea for a Common Foreign Policy, Beginning in the Core of Europe'. *Constellations: An International Journal of Critical and Democratic Theory* 10(3): 291–7.

Hägglund, Martin (2004), 'The Necessity of Discrimination: Disjoining Derrida and Levinas'. *Diacritics* 34(1): 40–71.

—. (2008), *Radical Atheism: Derrida and the Time of Life*. Stanford, California: Stanford University Press.

Halliday, Jon (1997), *Sirk on Sirk: Conversations with Jon Halliday*. London and Boston: Faber and Faber.

Hamacher, Werner (1999), 'Lingua Amissa: The Messianism of Commodity-Language and Derrida's *Specters of Marx*', in Michael Sprinker (ed.), *Ghostly Demarcations*. London and New York: Verso, pp. 168–212.

Haralovich, Mary Beth (1990), '*All That Heaven Allows*: Color, Narrative Space, and Melodrama', in Peter Lehman (ed.), *Close Viewings: An Anthology of New Film Criticism*. Tallahassee, FL: University Presses of Florida, pp. 57–72.

Harpham, Geoffry Galt (1999), *Shadows of Ethics: Criticism and the Just Society*. Durham and London: Duke University Press.

Harvey, Irene E. (1983), 'Derrida and the Concept of Metaphysics'. *Research in Phenomenology* 13: 113–48.

—. (1989), 'Derrida, Kant, and the performance of parergonality', in Hugh Silverman (ed.), *Derrida and Deconstruction*. New York and London: Routledge, pp. 56–75.

Haynes, Todd (1995), *Safe*. DVD recording. Sony pictures.

—. (2003), *Far From Heaven*.DVD recording. USA: Universal Studios.

Hegel, Georg W. F. (1977), *Phenomenology of Spirit*, trans. A.V. Miller. Oxford: Oxford University Press.

Heidegger, Martin (1958), *The Question of Being*, trans. Jean T. Wilde and William Kluback. New Haven: College and University Press.

—. (1993), *Basic Writings*, David Farrell Krell (ed.). London and New York: Routledge Press.

Hobson, Marion (1998), *Jacques Derrida: Opening Lines*. London and New York: Routledge Press.

Hodge, Joanna (2007), *Derrida on Time*. London and New York: Routledge.

Howells, Christina (1999), *Derrida: Deconstruction from Phenomenology to Ethics*, Cambridge: Polity Press.

Hoy, David Couzens (1996), 'Splitting the Difference: Habermas' Critique of Derrida', in Maurizio Passerin de Entrèves and Seyla Benhabib (eds), *Habermas and the Unfinished Project of Modernity*. Cambridge: Polity Press.

Hoy, Terry (1983), 'Derrida: Postmodernism and Political Theory'. *Philosophy and Literature* 15(3): 55–84.

James, Nick (2003), 'Interview: Todd Haynes'. *Sight and Sound* 13(3): 14–15.

Jameson, Fredric (1999), 'Marx's Purloined Letter', in Michael Sprinker (ed.) *Ghostly Demarcations*. London and New York: Verso, pp. 26–67.

Jay, Martin (1991), 'Habermas and Postmodernism', in Ingeborg Hoesterey (ed.), *Zeitgeist in Babel: The Postmodern Controversy*. Bloomington and Indianapolis: Indiana University Press, pp. 98–110.

Jayamanne, Laleen (2001), *Toward Cinema and its Double*. Bloomington and Indianapolis: Indiana University Press.

Kandell, Jonathan (2004), 'Jacques Derrida, Abstruse Theorist, Dies in Paris at 74'. *The New York Times*, October 10.

Kant, Immanuel (1934), *Critique of Pure Reason*, trans. J. M. D. Meiklejohn. J. M. Dent & Sons Ltd: London.

—. (1959), *Foundations of the Metaphysics of Morals*, trans. Lewis White Beck. New York: The Liberal Arts Press.

—. (1970), *On the Foundation of Morality*, trans. Brendan E. A. Liddell. Bloomington and London: Indiana University Press.

—. (2003), 'Lectures of Mr. Kant on the Metaphysics of Morals', in J. B. Schneewind (ed.), *Moral Philosophy from Montaigne to Kant*. Cambridge: Cambridge University Press, pp. 651–64.

Kates, Joshua (2005), *Essential History: Jacques Derrida and the Development of Deconstruction*. Evanston, IL: Northwestern University Press.

Kearney, Richard (1993), 'Derrida's Ethical Re-Turn', in Gary B. Madison (ed.), *Working through Derrida*. Evanston, IL: Northwestern University Press, pp. 28–50.

Klinger, Barbara (1994), *Melodrama and Meaning: History, Culture, and the Film of Douglas Sirk*. Bloomington and Indianapolis: Indiana University Press.

Kress, Gunter and van Leeuwen, Theo (1996), *Reading Images: The Grammar of Visual Design*. London and New York: Routledge.

Laclau, Ernesto (2007), *Emanicpation(s)*. London and New York: Verso.

Levinas, Emmanuel (1991), 'Wholly Otherwise', in Robert Bernasconi and Simon Critchley (eds), *Re-Reading Levinas*. Bloomington and Indianapolis: Indiana University Press, pp. 3–10.

—. (1994), *Outside the Subject*, trans. Michael B. Smith. Stanford, CA: Stanford University Press.

—. (1996), *Totality and Infinity*, trans. Alfonso Lingis. Pittsburgh: Duquesne University Press.

Levy, Ze'ev (1988), 'On Deconstruction – Can There Be Any Ultimate Meaning of Text?' *Philosophy and Social Criticism* 14(1): 1–23.

Lewis, Tom (1999), 'The Politics of "Hauntology" in Derrida's *Specters of Marx*', in Michael Sprinker (ed.), *Ghostly Demarcations*. London and New York: Verso, pp.134–67.

Llewellyn, John (1986), *Derrida on the Threshhold of Sense*. New York: St Martin's Press.

—. (2002), *Appositions of Jacques Derrida and Emmanuel Levinas*. Bloomington and Indianapolis: Indiana University Press.

Lowe, E. Jonathan (2002), *A Survey of Metaphysics*. Oxford: Oxford University Press.

Lucy, Niall (1997), *Postmodern Literary Theory: An Introduction*. Oxford: Blackwell Publishers.

—. (1999), *Debating Derrida*. Melbourne: Melbourne University Press.

Macherey, Pierre (1999), 'Marx Dematerialized, or the Spirit of Derrida', in Michael Sprinker (ed.), *Ghostly Demarcations*. London and New York: Verso, pp. 17–25.

MacIntyre, Alasdair (1998), *A Short History of Ethics*. London and New York: Routledge.

Madison, Gary B. (1992), 'Coping with Nietzsche's Legacy: Rorty, Derrida, Gadamer'. *Philosophy Today* 36(1): 3–19.

Magnus, Bernd and Higgins, Kathleen M. (eds) (1996), *The Cambridge Companion to Nietzsche*. Cambridge: Cambridge University Press.

Malabou, Catherine (2007), 'Again: "The Wounds of the Spirit Heal, and leave no scars behind"'. *Mosaic* 40(2): 27–37.

Maley, Will (2000), 'Specters of Engels', in Martin McQuillan (ed.), *Deconstruction: A Reader*. Edinburgh: Edinburgh University Press.

Mansfield, Nick (2010), *The God Who Deconstructs Himself: Sovereignty and Subjectivity Between Freud, Bataille, and Derrida*. New York: Fordham University Press.

Marx, Karl (1982), *Economic and Philosophic Manuscripts of 1844*. Moscow: Progress Publishers.

McQuillan, Martin (ed.) (2000), *Deconstruction: A Reader*. Edinburgh: Edinburgh University Press.

—. (ed.) (2007a), *The Politics of Deconstruction: Jacques Derrida and the Other of Philosophy*. London and Ann Arbor, MI: Pluto Press.

—. (2007b), 'Karl Marx and the Philosopher's Stone, or, On Theory and Practice', in Martin McQuillan (ed.), *The Politics of Deconstruction: Jacques Derrida and the Other of Philosophy*. London and Ann Arbor, MI: Pluto Press, pp. 235–53.

Megill, Alan (1985), *Prophets of Extremity: Nietzsche, Heidegger, Foucault, Derrida*. Berkeley, CA: University of California Press.

Miller, J. Hillis (1987), *The Ethics of Reading: Kant, de Man, Eliot, Trollope, James, and Benjamin*. New York: Columbia University Press.

—. (1989), 'Is There an Ethics of Reading?', in James Phelan (ed.), *Reading Narrative: Form, Ethics, Ideology*. Columbus, OH: Ohio State University Press, pp. 70–101.

—. (1992), 'Laying Down the Law in Literature: The Example of Kleist', in Drucilla Cornell, Michel Rosenfeld, and David Gray Carlson (eds), *Deconstruction and the Possibility of Justice*. New York and Britain: Routledge, pp. 305–29.

—. (2009), *For Derrida*. New York: Fordham University Press.

Mouffe, Chantal (ed.). (1996), *Deconstruction and Pragmatism*. London and New York: Routledge.

Mulvey, Laura (2003), 'Far From Heaven (motion picture review)'. *Sight and Sound* 13(3): 40–1.

Naas, Michael (2008), *Derrida From Now On*. New York: Fordham University Press.

Nietzsche, Friedrich (1956), *The Birth of Tragedy, and The Geneology of Morals*, trans. Francis Golfing. New York: Doubleday Anchor Books.

—. (1968), *The Will to Power*, Reginald John Hollingdale (ed.), trans. Walter Kaufman. New York: Vintage Books.

—. (1969), *Thus Spoke Zarathustra*, trans. R. J. Hollingdale. London: Penguin Books.

—. (1970), *The Portable Nietzsche*, Walter Kaufman (ed.). New York: Viking Press.

—. (1986), *Beyond Good and Evil*, trans. R. J. Hollingdale. London: Penguin Books.

—. (1992), *Ecce Homo*, trans. R. J. Hollingdale. London: Penguin Books.

—. (1994), *Human, All Too Human*, trans. Marion Faber and Stephen Lehmann. London: Penguin Books.

Norris, Christopher (1985), *The Contest of Faculties: Philosophy and Theory After Deconstruction*. London and New York: Methuen.

—. (1986), 'Deconstruction Against Itself: Derrida and Nietzsche'. *Diacritics* (Winter): 61–9.

—. (1987), *Derrida*. Cambridge, MA: Harvard University Press.

—. (1988), *Deconstruction and the Interests of Theory*. London: Pinter Publishers.

—. (1989a), 'Philosophy is Not Just a "Kind of Writing": Derrida and the Claim of Reason', in Reed Way Dasenbrock (ed.), *Redrawing the Lines*. Minneapolis, MN: University of Minnesota Press, pp. 189–203.

—. (1989b), 'Deconstruction, Postmodernism and Philosophy: Habermas on Derrida'. *Praxis International* 8: 426–46.

—. (1997), *Against Relativism: Philosophy of Science, Deconstruction and Critical Theory*. Oxford, UK and Cambridge, USA: Blackwell Publishers.

Norris, Christopher and Benjamin, Andrew (1988), *What is Deconstruction?* London: St. Martin's Press and New York: Academy Editions.

O'Neill, Onora (1994), 'Kantian ethics', Peter Singer (ed.), *A Companion to Ethics*. Cambridge, Massachusetts and Oxford, UK: Blackwell Publishers.

Papadakis, Andreas, Cook, Catherine and Benjamin, Andrew (eds) (1989), *Deconstruction: Omnibus Volume*. New York: Rizzoli Publications.

Parker, David (1998), 'Introduction: The Turn to Ethics in the 1990s', Jane Adamson, Richard Freadman and David Parker (eds), *Renegotiating Ethics: In Literature, Philosophy, and Theory*. Cambridge: Cambridge University Press, pp. 1–17.

Patton, Paul (1986), 'Ethics and Postmodernity', in Elizabeth Grosz (ed.), *Future Fall*. Sydney: Sydney University Press, pp. 128–45.

Plant, Bob (2003), 'Doing Justice to the Derrida-Levinas Connection: A Response to Mark Dooley'. *Philosophy and Social Criticism* 29(4): 427–50.

Plato (1973), *Phaedrus and the Seventh and Eighth Letters*, trans. Walter Hamilton. Harmondsworth: Penguin Books.

—. (1974), *The Republic*, trans. Desmond Lee. London and New York: Penguin Books.

Rancière, Jacques (2009), 'Should Democracy Come? Ethics and Politics in Derrida', in Pheng Cheah and Suzanne Guerlac (eds), *Derrida and the time of the political*. Durham and London: Duke University Press, pp. 274–88.

Rapaport, Herman (2003), *Later Derrida: Reading the Recent Work*. New York and London: Routledge.

Roderick, Rick (1987), 'Reading Derrida Politically (Contra Rorty)'. *Praxis International* 6(4): 442–9.

Rorty, Richard (1982), *Consequences of Pragmatism (Essays: 1972–1980)*. Minneapolis, MN: University of Minnesota Press.

—. (1984), 'Deconstruction and Circumvention'. *Critical Inquiry* 11: 1–23.

—. (1989a), *Contingency, Irony and Solidarity*. Cambridge: Cambridge University Press.

—. (1989b), 'Is Derrida a Transcendental Philosopher?' *The Yale Journal of Criticism* 2: 207–17.

—. (1991a), *Objectivity, Relativism and Truth: Philosophical Papers*, Vol. 1, Cambridge: Cambridge University Press.

—. (1991b), '"Two Meanings of Logocentrism": A Reply to Norris', in *Essays on Heidegger and others: Philosophical papers*, Vol. 2. Cambridge: Cambridge University Press, pp. 204–16.

—. (1999a), 'Habermas, Derrida and the Functions of Philosophy', in *Truth and Progress: Philosophical Papers*, Vol. 3, Cambridge: Cambridge University Press, pp. 307–26.

—. (1999b), 'Derrida and the Philosophic Tradition', in *Truth and Progress: Philosophical Papers*, Vol. 3, Cambridge: Cambridge University Press, pp. 327–50.

Rose, Gillian (1984), *Dialectic of Nihilism: Post-Structuralism and Law*. New York: Basil Blackwell.

Ross, Alison (2001), 'Errant Beauty: Derrida and Kant on "Aesthetic Presentation"', *International Studies in Philosophy* 33(2): 87–104.

Rotzer, Florian (ed.) (1995), *Conversations with French Philosophers*, trans. Gary E. Aylesworth. New Jersey: Humanities Press.

Royle, Nicholas (2000), 'The Phantom Review', in Martin McQuillan (ed.), *Deconstruction: A Reader*. Edinburgh: Edinburgh University Press, pp. 178–89.

Ryan, Michael (2000), 'Marx and Derrida', in Martin McQuillan (ed.), in *Deconstruction: A Reader*, Edinburgh: Edinburgh University Press, pp. 379–82.

Sallis, John (ed.) (1987), *Deconstruction and Philosophy: The Texts of Jacques Derrida*. Chicago, IL: University of Chicago Press.

Saussure, Ferdinand (1991a), 'The Object of Study', in David Lodge (ed.), *Modern Criticism and Theory: A Reader*. London: Longman, pp. 2–9.

—. (1991b), 'Nature of the Linguistic Sign', in David Lodge (ed.), *Modern Criticism and Theory: A Reader*. London: Longman, pp. 10–14.

Schrift, Alan D. (1996), 'Nietzsche's French Legacy', in Bernd Magnus and Kathleen M. Higgins (eds), *The Cambridge Companion to Nietzsche*. Cambridge: Cambridge University Press, pp. 323–55.

Searle, John R. (1977), 'Reiterating the Differences: A Reply to Derrida'. *Glyph* 1: 198–208.

Sedgwick, Peter R. (1995), *Nietzsche: A Critical Reader*. Oxford, UK and Cambridge, USA: Blackwell Publishers.

Shapiro, Gary (1984), 'Peirce and Derrida on First and Last Things'. *University of Dayton Review* 17(1): 33–8.

Silverman, Hugh J. (ed.) (1988), *Philosophy and Non-Philosophy Since Merleau-Ponty*. New York and London: Routledge.

—. (ed.) (1989), *Continental Philosophy II: Derrida and Deconstruction*. New York and London: Routledge.

Singer, Peter (ed.) (1994), *A Companion to Ethics*. Oxford: Basil Blackwell.

Smart, J. J. C. and Williams, Bernard (1996), *Utilitarianism: For and Against*. Cambridge: Cambridge University Press.

Smith, Barry (1992), 'Derrida Degree a Question of Honour'. *The Times*, May 9.

Smith, Gregory Bruce (1996), *Nietzsche, Heidegger and the Transition to Postmodernity*. Chicago, IL: University of Chicago Press.

Spivak, Gayatri Chakravorty (1984), 'Love Me, Love My Ombre, Elle'. *Diacritics* (Winter): 19–36.

Sprinker, Michael (ed.) (1999), *Ghostly Demarcations: A Symposium on Jacques Derrida's Specters of Marx*. London and New York: Verso.

Staten, Henry (1986), 'Rorty's Circumvention of Derrida'. *Critical Inquiry* 12 (Winter): 453–61.

Stephens, Chuck (1995), 'Gentlemen prefer Haynes'. *Film Comment* 31(4): 76–80.

Tannsjo, Torbjorn (2002), *Understanding Ethics: An Introduction to Moral Theory*, Edinburgh: Edinburgh University Press.

Taubin, Amy (2002), 'Behind the scenes of Todd Haynes's domestic weepie, *Far From Heaven*'. *Film Comment* 38(2): 2.

Thomassen, Lasse (2006), *The Derrida-Habermas Reader*. Edinburgh: Edinburgh University Press.

Trifonas, Peter Pericles (ed.) (2002), *Ethics, Institutions, and the Right to Philosophy: Jacques Derrida*. USA: Rowman and Littlefield Publishers.

Valadier, Paul (1995), 'Dionysus versus the Crucified', in David B. Allison (ed.), *The New Nietzsche*. Cambridge, MA and London, England: The MIT Press, pp. 247–61.

de Vries, Hent (2001), 'Derrida and Ethics: Hospitable Thought', in Tom Cohen (ed.), *Jacques Derrida and the Humanities: A Critical Reader*. Cambridge: Cambridge University Press, pp. 172–92.

Wartenberg Thomas (2011), 'Philosophy of Film', *The Stanford Encyclopedia of Philosophy* (Winter 2011 edition), Edward N. Zalta (ed.). <http://plato.stanford.edu/archives/win2011/entries/film/>

Weber, Samuel (1992), 'In the Name of the Law', in Drucilla Cornell, Michel Rosenfeld, and David Gray Carlson (eds), *Deconstruction and the Possibility of Justice*. New York and Britain: Routledge, pp. 232–57.

Wood, David (1987), 'Beyond Deconstruction'. *Philosophy* 87 (Supplement 21): 175–94.

—. (ed.) (1998), *Derrida: A Critical Reader*. Oxford, UK and Cambridge, USA: Blackwell Publishers.

—. (1999), 'The experience of the ethical', in R. Kearney and M. Dooley (eds), *Questioning Ethics: Contemporary Debates in Philosophy*. London: Routledge, pp. 105–19.

Wood, David and Bernasconi, Robert (eds) (1988), *Derrida and Différance*. Evanston, IL: Northwestern University Press.

Wortham, Simon Morgan (2010), *The Derrida Dictionary*. London and New York: Continuum.

Žižek, Slavoj (2008), *In Defense of Lost Causes*. London and New York: Verso.

Index